HAUNTED WAR TALES

HAUNTED WAR TALES

True Military Encounters with the Bizarre, Paranormal, and Unexplained

R. C. BRAMHALL

Essex, Connecticut

An imprint of Globe Pequot, the trade division of The Rowman & Littlefield Publishing Group, Inc.
4501 Forbes Blvd., Ste. 200
Lanham, MD 20706
www.rowman.com

Distributed by NATIONAL BOOK NETWORK

British Library Cataloguing in Publication Information available

Library of Congress Cataloging-in-Publication Data available
ISBN 978-1-4930-7576-8 (paperback)
ISBN 978-1-4930-7642-0 (e-book)

♾️™ The paper used in this publication meets the minimum requirements of American National Standard for Information Sciences—Permanence of Paper for Printed Library Materials, ANSI/ NISO Z39.48-1992.

Contents

Welcome to Weird War

IT SEEMS MANKIND HAS ALWAYS HELD A FASCINATION AND INTEREST for both unexplainable paranormal events and profound martial experiences, so the mash-up that occurs when these two subjects intersect can be absolutely irresistible for many of us. The addictive alchemy of surging adrenaline, stark terror, and thrilling excitement manifests in both types of events. In addition, people in general seem more likely to accept the credibility of an incident when military or law enforcement personnel are involved. The prevailing attitude is that with a job so serious and the consequences often so high (life and death or professionally), there's just not much room for next-level shenanigans and serious hoaxes.

The time- and history-spanning events that have been researched, investigated, and retold in this collection have the common theme of having been experienced by or occurred to members of the armed forces, whether American or international, during training or combat missions in the field or while stationed in garrison. Many of these tales have never been collected before, and the stories from the recent wars in Iraq and Afghanistan can now add to the extensive and historical canon of both bizarre and unexplainable military occurrences. These investigations cover a wide range of rarely explored subjects—from disturbing but real documented history and weird natural hazards to the controversial realms of unidentified cryptids, ghosts, and paranormal happenings—but I have left encounters with UFOs and aliens to the many other books covering those experiences.

From a very young age, I knew that before anything else I would experience in life, I wanted to be a soldier. I joined the U.S. Army while still a high school junior through the Delayed Entry Program and embarked a year later for Basic Combat Training (BCT) at Fort Dix, New Jersey, two months after my 18th birthday. I served four years active duty in intelligence, getting to experience a multitude of assignments and deployments with infantry and armor units at both division (G2) and battalion (S2) level. While attending college, I served an additional two years with a National Guard Special Forces Group in its Military Intelligence Detachment (MID). Working within the dark shadow world of "secret squirrel" deep-level, top secret code word clearances and need-to-know intelligence, there was no shortage of bizarre stories and rumors floating around at any given time. Disappointingly, I never experienced anything weird or paranormal myself *while in uniform*, but always kept a watchful eye and sensitive ear to the reports of fellow soldiers, sailors, and airmen who have.

However—at the risk of sounding contrived—I did experience something unexplainable on the East Cavalry Field at Gettysburg on August 23, 2021, en route to a writer's residency in northern Pennsylvania to start on this very book. Having had the past privilege of my mother and stepfather owning a home near Gettysburg for many years, I've spent more time than most roaming the battlefields and constantly learning new facts about the iconic events that occurred there. My travels had brought me there once again, and I planned to wake up early and tour a portion of the national park before getting on the road for the final leg of my trip. The hotel I was staying at was closest to the more remote, separated, and less-visited park grounds east of town and north of Hanover Road, which I held in the highest reverence. It was the battlefield where George Armstrong Custer's Michigan horsemen had clashed with J. E. B. Stuart's Virginian cavalry on July 3, 1863.

Horse cavalry has always been my favorite type of troops, and I've long been fascinated by the martial skills and larger-than-life personalities of both these generals. As I entered the park grounds on the narrow road and pulled off at the first line of Confederate artillery, I was delighted to realize that absolutely no one else was there. I had the entire space to myself. I knew the events of this engagement well, and the landscape literally remains unchanged from the day it happened, so it was easy to begin imagining what it would have been like to fight there. I drove along slowly, stopping and getting out at various vantage points and historical markers to take pictures and soak it all in. At the spot where Union defenders held off the Confederate advance across still-standing Rummel Farm, I parked and examined the towering memorial to the 1st New Jersey Cavalry.

I got back in my car and just sat there a few minutes, absorbing the beautiful summer morning and the waves of emotion I always experience at places of heroism and death. The engine was off and the transmission was in park on level ground. Suddenly, I felt myself and the car being bumped forward, enough to make me physically move back and forth in the seat and to believe that another car must have pulled in and slightly tapped me. Yet, when I turned around, there was nothing there. I had been sitting in the car for several minutes before it moved, and I am certain it was somehow pushed forward, bouncing back at the resistance of the parked gears. Slightly rattled, I kept my head on a swivel as I pulled out and drove on.

The next stop was the actual cornfield where the hard-fought charges and countercharges between the northern and southern horsemen had happened—a spectacle that Captain William Miller of the 3rd Pennsylvania said, "A more determined and vigorous charge . . . was never my fortune to witness."[1] It was easy to imagine Stuart's 6,000 troopers emerging from the distant woodline and accelerating in formation from walk to full gallop, sabers and carbines shining in the hot and unforgiving sun. This is where Custer had reacted by spurring his mount to the front of the 1st Michigan, and I suddenly felt compelled (as no one else was around) to shout out his famous battle cry, "Come on, you Wolverines!"[2] My booming voice resounded through the stalks of unpicked corn, and I half-expected something to happen. Captain Miller's vivid words fired my imagination: "The sound was like the falling of timber, so sudden and violent that many of the horses were turned end over end and crushed their riders beneath them. The clashing of sabers, the firing of pistols, the demands for surrender and the cries of the combatants now filled the air."[3] I took pictures of the massive memorial to the Michigan Cavalry Brigade, the 4,500-man force that Custer had led to victory, and moved on down the road.

The last area before exiting the battlefield road was where the Union horse artillery had been positioned, and I exited my vehicle for the last time to take more photos of the 12-pounders and historical markers. The very last photograph—out of 24 total taken at the battlefield that morning—was of a granite marker with a metal plaque honoring one of the federal artillery units that supported Custer: Battery M of the 2nd U.S. Artillery. I snapped the last picture and headed for the highway, having lingered far too long and now behind schedule for reaching Soaring Gardens Artist Retreat in Laceyville, Pennsylvania, by late afternoon.

It wasn't until later that evening, unpacked and settled in my room, that I had the time to review my Gettysburg pictures. Scrolling until I reached the last one, my eyes narrowed and my mind's wheels started turning as I looked at the strange vertical slash of weird and unexplainable lightning-like light that appeared across the image. My camera had never displayed anything like it before on any other picture I had ever taken, or on any since. Inspecting even closer, I could discern what almost seemed like a human face and form outlined by light shading across the metal plaque, seemingly holding something long and thin (like a rifle or cannon ramrod) over the right shoulder. Look at the photo yourself and determine your own impression (see Figure 1). I make no claims, but the car push and the strange last photograph makes me wonder if I really was completely alone out on the East Cavalry battlefield that August morning—while on my way to begin writing a book about paranormal military encounters.

Now, before we head out on this night patrol together, I want to assure the reader that I approached all of these extraordinary events with a skeptical and analytical eye, just like the Army Intelligence Corps taught me to do at Fort Huachuca, Arizona. Sometimes the non-fantastical truth can be discovered as being just as incredible as anything perceived to be paranormal or supernatural. Other times, through the course of diligent research, legends and conspiracies can be found to be debunked and baseless. That being said—be warned—because most of the reports documented in this collection are not easily explained and will remain a mystery to be pondered. The realm of these "weird wars" are often in uncharted enemy territory.

Figure 1

So, lock and load, soldier, you're on point, and the night ahead looks long and dark, a reconnaissance full of terrors and deaths both imagined and real for us all.

Chapter 1

MAM, FAM, or Monster?

.

Major General Mikhail Stephanovich Topilski of the Soviet Red Army surveyed the hostile terrain surrounding Vanj Range and couldn't help but smile. He had been pursuing and destroying his prey through the unforgiving Pamir Mountains for weeks and had finally cornered one of the last pockets of anti-Bolshevik resistance remaining. Although the Russian civil war had ended in 1922, the general was still cleaning up the more remote corners of the newly formed Soviet Union even now, three years later. Chased into a foreboding cave and surrounded by his Communist soldiers, the small force inside was likely preparing to make a final stand.

Suddenly, a bloodcurdling, demonic howl rose above the slashing winds, followed by several human screams and then three quick gunshots. General Topilski waved his men forward, and they cautiously approached the dark void with rifles raised. Bursting out of the blackness, a lone fighter suddenly emerged, immediately dropping his weapon and begging to be taken prisoner. The terrified man kept looking behind him, as if expecting something to follow him out of the earth. When forcibly questioned, he claimed he was the only survivor from the group, who had been ferociously attacked in the cavern by several beasts that were apparently already living there. He said, "Some hairy, man-like creatures, howling inarticulately, appeared in the cave through a crevice, which possibly leads upwards from the cave. There were several of them and they had sticks in their hands."[1] As the rest of his group were quickly being attacked and killed by the primitive-looking humanoids, the traumatized man reported, he had sprinted for the cave entrance under pursuit, turning and shooting one of the things three times.

The general and his men laughed at the outrageous tale. Topilski was ready to be finished with this business and finally return home. He immediately ordered his soldiers onward to root out the rest, causing their smiles to quickly fade with the realization of facing the suddenly frightful task. They nervously entered the hole in the mountain and faded into black. After several tense minutes, the excited men returned, unbelievably dragging the dead body of something none of the Russians had ever seen—or imagined—before.

General Topilski observed in stunned amazement, reporting in his own words: "At first glance I thought the body was that of an ape. It was covered with hair all over. But I knew there were no apes in the Pamirs. Also, the body itself looked very much like that of a man. We tried pulling the hair, to see if it was just a hide used for disguise, but found that it was the creature's own natural hair."[2]

The male corpse measured about 5.5 feet (1.7 meters) in length and was judged to be elderly, based on the presence of grayish hair in several areas. This hair was close-cropped and thick on the belly, but changed to thinner and longer strands of brown where it covered the muscular chest. The soldiers noted the complete absence of any underfur and that the buttocks had the least amount of hair. Their unit doctor guessed that this was caused by the creature sitting like a human being. The knees, feet, and palms were completely bare and covered in hard, calloused skin. The dead creature's hairless face was dark, with a slanting forehead framed by thick, matted strands of hair. Topilski described looking into its dark, open eyes and viewing humanlike teeth that were large and even, in a face with a massive protruding jaw and a flat nose that featured a deeply sunk bridge. He observed that the ears were a little more pointed than a human's, with longer lobes.

A sharpened stick made from very hard wood had also been discovered inside the cavern near the corpse. After ensuring nothing else alive remained inside the cave, the Red Army unit was relieved to have accomplished their mission. Not being able to carry the body of the mysterious creature with them, the soldiers buried it under a stone cairn before the mouth of the cavern, then tried to forget the nightmare fuel they had unexpectedly encountered that disturbing day.

* * *

When deployed internationally for combat operations, training in a specialty school or on a field exercise, or just standing overnight fire-watch guard in the barracks, military members are most often in a semi-paranoid state of heightened awareness—anticipating, listening, observing, and carefully reporting. Whether it's because of the fear of pissing off a drill sergeant, the humiliation of getting eliminated by Opposing Forces (OPFOR) in a training simulation, or the harsh reality of being "blowed up" by a roadside Improvised Explosive Device (IED), an armed forces member on duty must stay alert and prepared for just about anything.

During actual war operations and the relentless search for the enemy, our troops often find themselves in the most remote and inaccessible geographic locations in the combat theater, places that humans have rarely, if ever, occupied in significant numbers. It's amazing how many people are completely unaware of the amount of wild areas remaining throughout the world, holding the common misinformed opinion that every inch of the planet has been explored and there are no mysteries remaining. Nothing could be further from the truth. Our nation attempts to provide our armed forces with every piece of cutting-edge technology and all resources available for conducting surveillance and reconnaissance in these remote places: satellites in space, Unmanned Aerial Vehicles (UAVs) in the sky, and thermal imagers and night vision goggles in the operator's hands. Rarely does that much attention get focused on these areas of the world, and it would seem that sometimes as we're searching for the possible human enemy—a Military Age Male (MAM) or Fighting Age Male (FAM)—it's possible we might discover monsters and inhuman entities instead.

It will likely be no surprise to the reader that one of the most commonly observed cryptids by military personnel worldwide are giant, hair-covered, upright-walking beings, presumed to be relict hominins or an undiscovered species of great ape. The multitude of encounters involving American soldiers serving stateside with creatures known as Sasquatch or Bigfoot will be explored extensively later in this book. Basically an American icon, most people by now recognize the general appearance and characteristics of these purported mystery species. But what most people, and especially the typical recliner-chair skeptics, don't recognize is the legitimate history and science that supports the existence of these types of creatures.

My induction into the wonderful world of Sasquatch was quasi-military related. Back in 2010, I was working as an elementary schoolteacher in Texas and had recruited my fifth-grade students for a weekend clean-up project at a local park in preparation for the arrival of the Vietnam Traveling Memorial Wall, a three-quarter-scale replica of Washington, DC's Vietnam Veterans Memorial. As a veteran who has lost a close friend to war, I always stressed to my students the importance of honoring and remembering a soldier's sacrifice.

The father of one of my students was wearing a Texas Bigfoot Research Conservancy (TBRC) T-shirt, and I remember being amazed to discover that the creatures even had a presence in the Lone Star State. I had always believed the phenomenon was only attached to the Pacific Northwest. A short time and many questions later, I found myself attending the TBRC's 2010 Texas Bigfoot Conference in Tyler. The TBRC is now known as the North American Wood Ape Conservancy (NAWAC), a very active and respected scientific research organization that has accumulated mind-boggling amounts of data and field reports. Looking back, that year's conference had a legendary lineup of panelists, and I was able to meet and interact with some of the greatest names in Sasquatch science, including Dr. Jeffrey Meldrum (author and professor of anatomy and anthropology) and Bob Gimlin (of the most famous 1967 Patterson-Gimlin Bigfoot film).

The fascinating and fun topic has held my interest ever since and led to my own field investigations in an area of protected wilderness surrounding Navarro Mills Lake near Corsicana, Texas. The spot was close to my home at the time and had a history of several very convincing sighting reports that had been thoroughly investigated by the TBRC.[3] The lake is connected through a network of small waterways to a larger body of water named the Richland-Chambers Reservoir, and the whole area has a history of sightings involving a creature known as the Chambers Creek Monster.[4] Over the course of the year 2011, I routinely scouted the area looking for evidence and once found a possible (I make no claims) bedding area for an apparently large animal, with an oversized humanlike footprint impression in the tall grass nearby.

Around the same time, I had a bizarre experience while in the company of a good friend and excellent outdoorsman, Adam Thompson. We were enjoying a late-night fire on my property, a five-acre tract surrounded by miles of cattle fields and woods and, as the crow flies, only about 20 miles (32 km) north of the Navarro Mills Lake area I had been reconnoitering. The subject of Sasquatch lore had come up, and I was explaining the concept of wood-knocks to Adam. Wood-knocks (or tree-knocks) are a theorized form of communication or warning employed by these creatures that consists of deliberate and deeply powerful strikes of wood on wood, resulting in a loud and distance-traveling sound, often repeated three times. There are countless filed reports of these strange disturbances being heard in remote and uninhabited areas, often accompanied by increasing activity that eventually leads to actual physical Bigfoot encounters.

It is important to note that both of my dogs (which were large, capable, and country) were sitting near us instead of doing their usual running and roving through the woods. Immediately after having finished explaining this phenomenon, very near to us and very clearly, we all heard three deliberate and loud knocks, as if on cue. Adam and I looked at each other in disbelief, while my normally aggressive and protective dogs put their tails between their legs and "noped" the hell out of there, heading toward the house. After confirming with each other that we both had definitely heard it, and seeing nothing after a scan of the darkened mesquite tree woodline, these two grown and armed men decided it was time to go in too.

I offer no explanation, and we didn't go searching for the answer. Remembering it now, it strikes me how oddly we both reacted, with resignation and no desire to investigate, something out of character for both of us. It would seem most likely to have been a human being hidden in the woods, near enough to listen to our conversation, and perhaps attempting to initiate a prank. And brave enough to risk death, especially in the rural area I lived in at the time. There was one way in and out to my house, with a clear and straight approach, so the person would have had to walk in. I did have distant neighbors, but I knew all of them and couldn't imagine any of them creeping around in my woods after midnight. Most disturbing was that if it had been a person out there, I can guarantee my rottweiler and husky would have confronted them aggressively.

Apparently, there *are* things that go knock in the night.

WE WERE NOT ALONE

With so much recent discovery and better knowledge regarding the biology and evolutionary relationships of different living things, science is constantly revising classifications to develop more accurate evolutionary trees. As a result, modern humans and all of our (possibly) extinct ancestor species are now known as hominins rather than hominids, including the genera *Homo*, *Australopithecus*, *Paranthropus*, and others.[5] *Homo sapiens* are (believed to be) the only survivors of a once diverse group of human and humanlike apes that includes at least over 21 known and scientifically recognized species.[6] It's very complicated to attempt to figure out exactly how many distinct species of humans existed, as researchers keep unearthing new fossils of totally separate and previously unknown types. The number is rising and varies depending on where you look. The important fact to recognize is that all of these different versions did exist, and many coexisted at the same time. They weren't all our evolutionary ancestors—some were sister species, evolving in parallel.

Modern humans appear to have evolved in Africa from an ancient group of "ape people" called the australopiths.[7] Somewhere around 5 million years ago, our ancestor species is believed to have developed the ability to walk on two legs, but with a different gait and with skeletons that retained features to help them climb trees. Much later, at around 1.7 million years ago, early humans began to shed body hair as an evolutionary adaptation. This allowed sweating and consequently provided the ability to hunt during hot days, unlike most competing nocturnal predators.[8] The oldest unquestioned evidence of upright walking are 3.7-million-year-old bipedal hominin footprints discovered at Laetoli, Tanzania, in 1978, believed to be from an *Australopithecus afarensis* like the famous "Lucy."[9] Interestingly, a re-excavation of the site in 2019 revealed the existence of a second distinct group of five consecutive footprints—with a very Sasquatch-like large heel impression and big toe—conclusively proven to be from a different unknown hominin than the one that left the other trackway.[10] Perhaps it was made by *Homo habilis* ("handy" man), a species discovered in 1960 by researchers in Tanzania whose fossils seem to fall in the gap between the australopiths and humans. *Homo naledi* ("star" man) could be another candidate, as they display a small brain and strange mix of ancient and modern skeletal features. Discovered in 2013, unconfirmed evidence suggests *H. naledi* was still alive just a few hundred thousand years ago, supporting the idea of a very primitive hominin species surviving much longer on earth than expected.[11]

Homo erectus ("upright" man), discovered in 1891, is the earliest indisputable human species, possibly even using fire to cook their meat. *Homo heidelbergensis* is also believed to have possibly been a "parent" human species. *Homo rhodesiensis* was identified in 1921, *Homo floresiensis* (the "hobbit") in 2003, and the pygmy *Homo luzonensis* in 2019. Decades before Darwin's theory of natural selection, the famous *Homo neanderthalensis* (the Neanderthal) was the first ancient human to become known, in 1829. The Denisovan population was discovered through genetic sequencing in 2010, then the equally mysterious Red Deer Cave People in 2012.[12] As recently as 2021, an international research team verified that a well-preserved cranium belonged to a new species of later-Pleistocene human dubbed *Homo longi* ("dragon" man). Their analysis showed that this group shared the same last ancestor as *H. sapiens* and was closer to us than even Neanderthals. This third East Asian lineage represents a completely new type of human.[13]

Yet, by around 10,000 years ago, all of these other human species had burned out and are theorized to have gone extinct. And it was almost surely our fault.

Prehistoric World War Won

Humanity appears to have split somewhere around 550,000 years ago, with our ancestors staying and evolving in Africa, while other groups roamed into Europe and Asia and became the Neanderthals, Denisovans, and other species.[14] *Homo sapiens* ("wise" man) didn't leave the mother continent in significant numbers until around 100,000 years ago. It would take another 60,000 years before they were able to establish themselves throughout Europe and the rest of the world, where DNA evidence has proven they sometimes interbred with the regional varieties of archaic humans. One interesting theory explores the idea that why this all took so long was because Neanderthals waged a territorial war to resist our expansion for hundreds of thousands of years. Early *H. sapiens* fossils have been found in Israel and Greece, dated to around 200,000 years old.[15] These fossils seem to represent failed attempts by early humans to hold ground in the north, with their settlements likely being overrun and replaced by local Neanderthal tribes.

Imagine the damage their massive, muscular physique would have inflicted on early versions of us in close-quarter combat. Neanderthals' wide hips and short, stocky frames provided great power to their arms and legs for ambushing prey. Their huge eyes gave them a low-light vision advantage for attacking in the dark. It may not have been until our development of abstract thought and the invention of superior weapons that we were able to stand toe-to-toe and start to win ground against them.

Danny Vendramini's 2009 Neanderthal Predation (NP) theory suggests that our cousins weren't peaceful, humanlike omnivores, as so often depicted in popular culture.[16] Instead, they were savage, cannibalistic carnivores who were the most ruthless and efficient apex predators of the Stone Age. Using 3D scans of actual Neanderthal skulls and bones, Vendramini produced terrifying computer-generated images of much more primate-looking creatures, commenting, "These guys came from the frozen north—they had flat, apelike noses, large nocturnal eyes, were covered in thick hair and were six times stronger than the average human. They were not a pretty sight."[17] The Neanderthal's estimated daily need for 6,000 calories would have required 4.5 pounds (2 kg) of meat, and must have included the flesh of early humans, which they hunted and ate for thousands of years. Vendramini also theorized that Eurasian Neanderthals abducted, raped, and interbred with early humans in the Middle East.

In order to spread across the world, *H. sapiens* had to respond to this predation by adapting into more hyper-aggressive and predatory beings that fought back and eliminated any species that was a threat—finally using superior-range weapons, numerical superiority, and cooperative strategy to their advantage.[18] The other hominins were pushed farther away, retreating to the most inhospitable and remote places that modern humans could not and did not want to live in. Eventually we killed all the Neanderthals and other-looking hominins in our way, until they were all gone. Evolution by genocide.

This could logically explain why the majority of various "wildmen" sightings and encounters happen in the most uninhabited, harsh locations around the world—northern Canada and the Pacific Northwest of America, the Outback in Australia, the mountains of Sumatra, and the Himalaya, Altai, and Hindu Kush ranges of Asia. The last survivors of various early human species were forced to adapt and survive in these areas, existing far beyond what is accepted, and influencing the folklore and oral histories of every culture around the planet.

A subarctic archaeological site at Byzovaya, on a river bluff in the foothills of Russia's Ural Mountains, sitting at the same 65 degrees north latitude as Iceland, may have been one of the last-stand refuges of a hardy band of Neanderthals until about 31,000 years ago.[19] A 2011 study suggests that this group was the longest-lasting and farthest north ever known, having still existed 9,000 years after the species' previously presumed extinction date. The seclusion of the area, at a chilly location 100 miles (161 km) south of the Arctic Circle, may have protected the tribe for millennia. Previous evidence had placed the last known Neanderthal holdouts on the Iberian Peninsula—Spain, Portugal, and Gibraltar.[20]

Evidence may indicate that some may yet remain to fight their very last stand in the battles of Weird War.

WE ARE NOT ALONE

Throughout the mountains of central Asia, in what was once part of the Soviet Union, and centered in western Mongolia, consistent reports of a large, manlike bipedal creature between 5 and 6 feet tall (1.5–1.8 meters) and weighing up to 500 pounds (227 kg) have persisted for centuries.[21] Known as the Almas or Almasty (Chuchunaa in western Siberia), their black- or dark-gray-skinned faces have been described as being simi- lar to humans except for a heavily protruding brow ridge; a wide, flat, apelike nose; and large, deep-set eyes. Their massive jaws are portrayed as tapering to a receding chin, and the tops of their head are flat with a sloping forehead. The thick, well-developed muscles and skin of their stocky bodies can be seen through a layer of coarse reddish-brown or black hair that sprouts from head to toe, sparser around their faces. The females are reported to have large, long, and sometimes hairless breasts, and both genders have hairless hands and wide, long feet. Their teeth are large, with widely separated canines, and they are believed to survive on an omnivore's diet of just about anything. Likely nocturnal, as many encounters have occurred at dusk or overnight, Almas are said to possess extraordinarily fast and agile running, climbing, bounding, and possibly swimming skills, despite a bowlegged or stooped-over stance. Legends state they live in remote mountain caves stretching from the eastern coast of the Black Sea and the Russian Caucasus range north of Turkey and Iran, to the Hindu Kush and Pamir Mountains of Tajikistan (the location of General Topilski's cave) and northeastern Afghanistan, and over to the Altai of western Mongolia. You'll know one is around by their powerfully foul odor or distinctive and loud scream.

This cryptid differs greatly from the other supposed mystery spe- cies in the region. Both the world-famous Himalayan Yeti and the lesser-known Yeren of China's Hubei Province are much larger, hairier, and apelike, having more in common with neo-giants like North Amer- ica's Sasquatch species or Australia's Yowie than the subhuman Almas. Almas are considered to be distinctly "more human"—some possibly using simple tools, communicating through gestures and vocalizations, and even wearing simple fur clothing. Could the Almas actually represent a well-hidden relict population of *Homo erectus* or Neanderthals?

In the late 1960s, Soviet historian Dr. Boris Porshnev presented the "Porshnev theory," which identified relict Neanderthals as the explanation for Asian and Russian wildman sightings.[22] Dr. Myra Shackley, of Leicester University in England, is one of the few Western researchers who agreed. Visiting Mongolia in 1979, she pointed out that the entire region was rife with Neanderthal artifacts.[23] If any had survived, it would have been in the exact geographic locations the Almas were being reported in.

Armies and Almas

The Roman legions documented everything during their military campaigns. In their histories of the Gallic Wars (58–50 BCE), there is a very obscure mention of a tribe of giant, hairy men enlisted to help fight against the Gauls in Germany. They spoke their own primitive language and didn't enjoy their meat cooked. After achieving victory on the battlefield, they returned to their homeland in the east—the Ural Mountains.[24] It's amazing and entertaining to imagine that they could have been a surviving band of hybrid Neanderthals descended from the group discovered at Byzovaya.

After the Battle of Ankara in 1402 between the Ottomans and Mongols, a capable German nobleman named Johann Schiltberger was taken prisoner and kept by the conqueror Timur (aka Tamerlane) as a court runner. His far-reaching travels were unique for a European at the time, and after his return to Bavaria years later, he published an account of his journeys in 1427 called the "Reisebuch." He described an encounter with Almas: "On the same mountain there are savages, who are not like other people, and they live there. They are covered all over the body with hair, except the hands and face, and run about like other wild beasts in the mountain, and also eat leaves and grass, and anything they can find. The lord of the country sent to Edigi, a man and a woman from among these savages that had been taken in the mountain."[25]

Not long after General Topilski's encounter with a dead Almas in 1925, there was an incident during the Soviet-Japanese Border War. In 1937, a Russian reconnaissance unit in Mongolia fighting the Japanese spotted two unnatural silhouettes moving down a hill toward them in the dark and issued a challenge. With no response given, the Russians shot them. The rising sun revealed the man-size bodies to be "strange anthropoid apes" covered in long, red hair. Because of the ongoing and intense fighting, the corpses were unable to be preserved and recovered for further study.[26]

A unit of Mongolian soldiers on the border with China in 1940 opened fire on what they thought was a group of saboteurs. When they got close enough to examine the bodies, they reported realizing that the victims were not "people," but some kind of unknown species.[27] Around the same time frame, Chinese soldiers reportedly observed an Almas and would put food out so they could watch it eat.

During World War II, refugees, combatants, and prisoners of war all reported seeing the Almas. In his book *The Long Walk* (adapted into the 2010 film *The Way Back*), Slavomir Rawicz and six fellow prisoners escaped a Soviet labor camp in Yakutsk in 1941 and traversed thousands of miles by foot—out of Siberia, through China, the Gobi Desert, Tibet, and over the Himalayas to British India. A close encounter with two 7-foot-tall (2.1-meter) creatures covered in red hair, possibly Yetis, caused them to change their route and lose a man in a crevasse.[28]

Also in 1941, a Soviet medical service officer, Lieutenant Colonel Vazhgen S. Karapetyan, reported that partisan troops captured what likely was an Almas in the Caucasus Mountains near Buynaksk, who they thought may have been a Nazi spy.[29] It had been kept in a barn because when it was indoors it stank too badly and excreted copious amounts of sweat. After it was brought to him, the Russian officer quickly realized it was some type of wildman. The frightened captive was naked, covered in fine dark hair, and infested with lice. It seemed unintelligent, blinked often, and did not (or would not) speak. The "man" had no reaction when Karapetyan pulled hairs from his body. Having more serious issues to deal with, the officer ordered it to be executed and returned to treating human patients.

In 1958 the Russians established the Snowman Commission to investigate Almas, documenting over 500 sightings through recorded interviews; the Mongolian government did its own investigations in 1959. The Chinese government actually deployed a 100-member expedition in 1976, concentrating on the mountains of northwestern Hubei Province, for a yearlong attempt at capturing a Yeren or collecting evidence of their existence. Supposedly, when the opportunity actually presented itself, a Chinese soldier's encounter with one was so frightening that he shot himself in the leg and the creature escaped.[30]

In January and February 1992, Moscow Radio and two different newspapers reported an incredible encounter at a northern Russian military base. Thirty witnesses claimed to have seen two red-eyed "abominable snowmen" breaking into and entering an on-base building contractor's barracks. The larger one was described as being 6.5 feet (2 meters) tall and the "younger" companion as only half its size, measuring 3.2 feet (1 meter) tall. They were both covered in long, gray "wool," and the larger one howled before they both leaped onto the 9-foot-tall (2.7-meter) surrounding fence and ran away into the forest. Tufts of their hair were reportedly found left behind on the fence.[31]

Moving into the digital age, the Indian Army shared photos of footprints in the snow, tweeting to its nearly six million followers: "For the first time, an Indian Army Mountaineering Expedition Team has sited mysterious footprints of mythical beast Yeti measuring 32x15 inches close to Makalu Base Camp on 9 April, 2019. This elusive snowman has been sighted at Makalu-Barun National Park in the past." Reacting to disbelief and jokes on social media, army personnel said they made the discovery public only after analyzing the evidence and deciding that the prints matched theories about the Yeti. "We thought it prudent [to go public] to excite scientific temper and rekindle the interest."[32]

OPERATION ENDURING ALMAS

One thing every veteran of Afghanistan will attempt to explain to civilians—and usually fail for a loss of descriptive words—is the sheer magnitude of the geography there. If you read the excellent 2012 book *The Outpost* by Jake Tapper[33] and saw the 2020 film of the same name about Combat Outpost (COP) Keating and the 2009 Battle of Kamdesh, you can at least grasp what some of the elevation and terrain is like there.

COP Keating was in Afghanistan's least populated Nuristan Province, an area located on the southern slopes of the Hindu Kush mountains in the northeastern part of the country, most of it covered by mountainous forests with a rich biodiversity. The terrain is vertical, with dense old-growth forest like the Colorado Rockies on steroids. The region is full of mountain goats and bears, birds and small game, streams full of brown trout, and draws full of snow. The mountain valley villages raise livestock and grow barley, wheat, peas, millet, and wine grapes. Going beyond, up higher and deeper into the mountains, we encounter a very convincing tale from early in the Global War on Terror (GWOT).[34]

It was 2003 and "Chris" (aka "Jack") was a soldier working force protection on a Long Range Presence Patrol for a command group made up of government intelligence agents, an Afghan interpreter (Terp), and his Special Operations team. At this point in the conflict, the United States hadn't really established ground forces yet. For centuries, Afghan warriors had utilized winters to go up higher in the mountains and regroup, refit, and rearm themselves—somewhat like their own mini versions of Valley Forge. And, if nothing else, the Taliban certainly are traditional. Special Forces sent teams up there to show the Taliban that they had men who could and would pursue them anywhere. This team was on a high-stakes intelligence-gathering mission, and the CIA was exchanging huge amounts of cash for information and names.

The Green Berets had entered the hut where they were meeting a local Afghan warlord and sat down with him as he finished eating a meal of rice and flatbread. The atmosphere was tense, and a gregarious senior sergeant decided to try to lighten the mood. Flashing a grin, he told the Terp to ask the ancient-looking warlord if he had ever seen something like a Yeti up there before. The interpreter, taking him seriously, repeated the question in Pashto, and they all watched as the man replied quickly with a tone of aggravation. He essentially said, "Yes, I know this thing, I grew up with this thing, and we all hate it." The Terp explained that the word he used to describe it was like a cuss word meaning a pest or really dirty creature.

As he returned to his meal, the Americans looked at each other in shocked amazement. The sergeant, thinking his question was misunderstood, directed the Terp to clarify what he was talking about, and he asked the warlord again. Now very perturbed, the warlord pushed back from the meal, threw his arms up, and gave a lengthy response before glaring at the noncom. His annoyance and matter-of-factness was the most convincing aspect of what he said.

"When I was young it would come all the time and steal livestock and frighten our women. When we had chances we would shoot at it with our Kalasnikovs [AK-47s]. During the first Russian war, the loud X's in the sky [he meant fighter jets] would drop bombs and made the things disappear for a long time and we were happy because we hated them. After the war ended, they slowly started to return and become pests again. Now this war has started, and sometimes we see the X's in the sky dropping bombs again, and I have not seen one in a while."

The last part was delivered with passion.

"But, now I have a question for you, American. Why do you waste my time asking about this dirty thing when I am here to talk seriously about getting guns and money?"[35]

The Barmanu, meaning "muscled forest man" or "the big hairy man" depending on whom you ask, is the northwestern Pakistan and eastern Afghanistan version of the Almas. Although often reported to be a bit taller, their descriptions and behaviors match well. The Hindu Kush mountains and Upper Chitral District are their usual home, but they are known to come down from the hills during winter to prowl around remote houses and steal livestock.

An elderly man, Rahim Shah, of the remote Allai Valley in Pakistan's Battagram District, offers local knowledge of the Barmanu. "They are up there and only come down into the valley during heavy snows. I have been seeing them all my life, but this winter for the very first time, I saw a mother and child together, holding hands. They live up there and have always done so. They don't bother me and I don't bother them. They are mountain people too."[36]

Along with his favorable opinion of them, he offers the insight of believing they live in hidden caves or underground. This is because in all his years of wandering the mountains, he has never found one of their homes. His grandfather once saw five of them together, and Rahim claims he saw a group of three adults one time, but he feels there are fewer surviving now than during his great-grandfather and grandfather's lifetimes. He also suggests the devastating 2005 Kashmir earthquake as a reason, too. "They could have been killed in the quake or maybe they have moved to some other, safer place. Since then, more people have learnt of our valley and we now have a government presence, plus people go exploring in the mountains."[37] Rahim adds that Gujar nomads, who graze their herds during summer in the valley, have also reported seeing fewer Barmanu in the high pastures than ever before.

One night during a 2008 deployment in Kunar Province in Afghanistan, a U.S. Army Infantry team leader was manning an Observation Post (OP) overlooking a remote village.[38] Using a thermal-imaging Long Range Scout Surveillance System (LRAS), he clearly zoomed in on a very large heat signature on the crest of a mountain roughly parallel to him at the same altitude. The image was so large that he believed he was observing a group of four or five individuals huddled together, but there was little to no movement from any of them for quite some time. Suddenly, he watched the entire heat signature move as one, unfolding its legs and standing up—as though it had been sitting there cross-legged. Even more unsettling, based on the height of the trees near it, the man-like figure when fully standing upright was at least 10 feet tall (3 meters)! The heat signature suggested that it was not wearing clothing of any sort, which would have created darker patches on the body, and its coloration seemed to be a uniform white, the way exposed skin and hair appears. The soldier watched in disbelief as the enormous image turned, scaled the mountainside with a fast, easy stride, and disappeared over the crest of the hill.

It was well past midnight and below freezing on a November 2011 night outside the mountain valley village of Bargi Matal, in Nuristan Province, Afghanistan. A 26-year-old veteran U.S. Army sergeant was on watch for any potential Taliban attack on the COP, scanning the surrounding steep hillsides with a thermal scope. At a distance of 500 to 600 meters (547–656 yards), he suddenly spotted something so unexplainable that he felt compelled to wake up five of his fellow squad members to look at it too. For the next 10 to 15 minutes, all of them observed a creature scrambling up the sheer, loose granite and shale mountainside at an impossibly fast and sure pace that none of them could reasonably explain. "It looked like a big monkey or ape. It was big and beefy in the shoulders," the sergeant reported.[39] None of them had any idea of what it could be, as it was much too large to be a man and looked very apelike, to the point that one of the soldiers even half-jokingly suggested that a gorilla must have escaped a zoo and wandered out into the wilderness. When the men later talked to locals, they were told that what they had seen was probably a Barmanu.

Unconfirmed reports by soldiers claim that they observed local men in these remote mountain villages periodically dyeing both their beards and the hair of selected goats in their herd with a distinct color of orange. Within a short time, these colored goats would inexplicably disappear. While this was happening, the locals would tell the soldiers, "Don't go up in the mountains; the giants there will eat you."[40] Could this bizarre practice of marking certain goats be some form of offering or sacrifice to these things?

Sulaymaniyah Province is a mountainous governorate in the Kurdistan region of northeastern Iraq, bordering Iran. The region's Zagros mountain range includes extremely rugged terrain that makes the area very difficult to access. In 2005, an army Criminal Investigations Division (CID) agent was embedded within an infantry unit there.[41] As the U.S. Army's primary criminal investigative organization, the CID is responsible for conducting felony-level criminal investigations in which the army is, or may be, a party of interest. The agency was looking into disturbing activities reported by both isolated villagers and the Kurdish military concerning recent mysterious disappearances of people. The locals claimed that a tall, humanoid creature with unnaturally long arms and legs was stalking and hunting people for their flesh. Villagers believed this so strongly that many became afraid to leave their homes, even during daylight hours. The CID agent had been deployed to the region to conduct an inquiry, as one theory being put forth by his superiors was the possibility of an active serial killer operating out of the American ranks.

Using a squad of specially assigned infantrymen, several days of searching and conducting surveillance was completed with no activity witnessed or any evidence found. The agent began to conclude that the entire affair must have been caused by the stress of war and local super-stitions. But then, while preparing some reports with the squad leader one evening, both were stunned to hear a shrill and ghastly scream echo through the mountain pass nearby. Villagers immediately claimed that the terrifying shriek was from the monster that had been menacing them and started rushing toward the safety of their homes.

The squad mobilized and headed into the pass, hearing the unearthly, hair-raising howl several more times. As the sun dipped below the hori-zon and the alien landscape went black, the soldiers agreed the noise was unlike anything heard by any of them before. No known animal in the area could have made it. The heavily armed men suddenly found them-selves as frightened as the villagers and reluctant to meet the source of the vocalization in the night. Pushing past their fears, the well-disciplined troop spread out through the pass and patrolled.

After hours of searching using night vision and thermal imagers, nothing was encountered, and no footprints or evidence of any kind was found. After the men entered the mountain pass, the howl had not been heard again. The investigation was closed a few days later with nothing solved. The CID agent and the squad were extracted, but the question of what they had all heard that night would stay embedded in their minds forever.

GIANTS, GILGAMESH, AND GOVERNMENT EMAILS

A pretty fantastical story that has been circulating for a few years regard-ing the "Giant of Kandahar" deserves mention here, as it doesn't get much weirder than this. First reported by researcher L. A. Marzulli in the 2016 documentary *Watchers X*, there's a lot of holes to punch in the account, but it's fun to ponder nonetheless.

In 2002, according to eyewitness "Mister K," a Special Forces team was supposedly operating in a remote, mountainous area near Kandahar, Afghanistan, on a search to find a lost infantry patrol that headquar-ters had lost radio contact with for several hours.[42] The patrol had not reported a Troops In Contact (TIC) or indicated any kind of distress before becoming unaccounted for. The Special Forces team was inserted near the last known location of the missing soldiers, but several days of searching had produced nothing—until, following a noticeable goat trail up into the mountains, the Green Berets began to notice what looked like broken-off pieces of U.S. Army communications equipment and remnants of uniforms scattered across the ground. When they started to find pieces of unidentified bones, they went on high alert and continued onward, ascending to a kind of plateau where several large cave entrances led downward into the dark mountain. There were also several large, heavy rocks arranged in a strange though intentional way outside the cave entrances. Without warning, an enormous spear came flying out of the blackness, impaling and killing one of the soldiers, "Dan." The men watched in stunned disbelief as a 12- to 15-foot (3.7–4.5-meter) giant with long red hair and an unkempt red beard emerged from the darkness of the cavern, howling loudly and wearing animal skins. The towering humanoid quickly sprinted to the dead soldier and was in the act of removing his crude spear from Dan's limp body when the rest of the force started shooting. It required nearly half a minute of sustained fire to bring the creature down.

Upon receiving a call for extraction and to report the incident, the military reportedly sent two helicopters and retrieved the corpse for examination. An unknown C-130 pilot further claims that he flew the remains out of Afghanistan to an undisclosed base back in the United States, possibly Wright-Patterson Air Force Base near Dayton, Ohio. He provided a description that the giant was at least 12 feet (3.7 meters) tall, had six-fingered hands, and weighed a massive 1,100 pounds (499 kg). The witnesses claim that they were all debriefed and ordered to alter their reports on the engagement and transport of the cryptid, ensuring that the government would erase all evidence of the top-secret encounter.

Although this story may seem ridiculous to most of us, the existence of giants in Afghanistan is widely accepted within the culture of the people—and not just among the rural or uneducated population. An American reporter embedded with a patrol of Afghan policemen had an experience that demonstrates how seriously they take the subject.[43]

The patrol was passing a grave marker that had an unusual length of about 20 meters (65 feet). One of the policemen pointed at it and said it was the grave of a famous giant. When the female reporter responded with skepticism and insinuated that sometimes very tall people *can* grow to eight or nine feet tall and seem like giants, the Afghans were actually insulted. The whole squad of police began yelling at her, even her university-educated interpreter who had lived out of the country before.

The Afghans informed her that as recently as 80 years ago, there had been giants in the area. Not just exceptionally tall people, but an actual different human species. Some of their grandparents had seen them and told their grandchildren about them, so in their opinion it had to be true. Giants had roamed the earth within living memory, and just because some American couldn't believe it, didn't mean it wasn't the truth.

* * *

On April 13, 2017, the United States dropped a 20,000-pound bomb from the rear of an MC-130 cargo plane onto a cave complex in Nangarhar Province in eastern Afghanistan. Named MOAB—officially an acronym for Massive Ordnance Air Blast and unofficially for "Mother Of All Bombs"—it vaporized 94 entrenched ISIS fighters. This was the first time it had ever been used, and the explosion created a blast radius that stretched a mile in every direction. "The enemy had created bunkers, tunnels and extensive mine fields, and this weapon was used to reduce those obstacles so that we could continue our offensive in southern Nangarhar," said General John Nicholson.[44]

Several "unnamed" sources have reportedly come forward and made sensational claims that counter the U.S. military's mundane explanation for its use of the largest conventional bomb in the American arsenal.[45] These conspiracy theorists say it was actually released in order to destroy Afghan giants. They further claim that even the name MOAB is a specially selected moniker, not an acronym, and refers to the tribe Moab from the Old Testament. Turns out the Moabites battled a race of giants called the Emim, who were part of the Nephilim, and destroyed them to settle in their conquered lands. "They were regarded as giants, like the Anakim, but the Moabites call them Emim," reads Deuteronomy 2:10–12 (KJV).

Nimrod in the Bible was the great-grandson of Noah and the first of the "mighty men" (not a Nephilim) to appear on the earth after the

Great Flood. Besides being the founder of Babel and other cities, he was also believed to possess supernatural physical strength, power of will, and size—he was possibly a real giant. Like his antediluvian forefathers, Nimrod rebelled against God, building the infamous Tower of Babel and causing the Lord to respond by confusing the languages of humanity. He is a character in the ancient mythologies of the Greek, Arabic, Syrian, Armenian, and Hungarian cultures. There is evidence that both *The Epic of Gilgamesh* and the myth of Hercules find their origins in Nimrod.

The Epic of Gilgamesh, the world's first-known literature at over 4,000 years old, began as a series of Sumerian poems and tales completed later by the Babylonians around 1200 BCE. Written in cuneiform on 12 clay tablets, this epic story was discovered in 1853 among the ruins of the library of Ashurbanipal in Nineveh, which is now encircled by the modern Iraqi city of Mosul. The adventure centers on a Sumerian king named Gilgamesh, who is one-third man and two-thirds god, as he slays monsters, searches for the meaning of life, and grasps for the key to immortality. His capital city was Uruk (the biblical Erech), from which Iraq derives its name, and was about 186 miles (300 km) south of Baghdad near present-day Samawah in Iraq.

Gilgamesh was supposedly buried under the Euphrates River in a tomb constructed when the waters of the river parted following his death. A German archaeology team announced its possible discovery of the lost tomb of Gilgamesh (Nimrod) in April 2003, under the marshland of an ancient channel of the Euphrates River—just weeks after the Coalition forces had started bombing Iraq in late March.[46] "It looks very similar to that described in the Epic," said Joerg Fassbinder of the German Archaeological Institute.[47] Using a magnetometer to digitally map the layout of the ancient city of Uruk, the scientists had discovered numerous structures that confirmed details and descriptions found in the Epic. The partial mapping covered an area of more than 250 acres and included garden and field structures, Babylonian houses, and an incredibly sophisticated canal system. "We found, just outside the city an area in the middle of the former Euphrates river, the remains of such a building which could be interpreted as a burial," Fassbinder stated.[48] The archaeologists obviously had to evacuate because of the U.S.-led invasion, and had hoped to return when the political situation was resolved. Work was resumed in 2016, using high-resolution satellite imagery and core samples, and will hopefully lead to an actual excavation of the theorized tomb.

The reports of this discovery—coupled with several online-posted photographs, articles, and a very bizarre leaked government email—has created a popular internet-fueled conspiracy theory regarding the U.S. government's pursuit of Nimrod/Gilgamesh's tomb and the forbidden knowledge that it may contain.[49] The truth behind these images and accounts demonstrates how the simple misidentification of locations and situations can be completely misinterpreted and give life to these types of claims.

* * *

Ali Air Base (aka Imam Ali and formerly Tallil Air Base) is located in the southeastern city of Nasiriyah in Dhi Qar Province, Iraq. It was built for the Iraqi Air Force in the 1970s and encompasses a 12-square-mile (30-sq-km) area with a 14-mile-long (22-km) security perimeter. The awe-inspiring 4,000-year-old Great Ziggurat of Ur, one of the largest and best-preserved Sumerian structures, is located within the perimeter of the base.[50] Ur was an important Sumerian city-state in ancient Mesopotamia, and its partially excavated ruins can be found all around modern Nasiriyah. At the start of the Iraq War in 2003, Tallil Air Base was taken by the U.S. Air Force, renamed Camp Adder, and occupied by American and Coalition forces until their final withdrawal at the end of Operation New Dawn in December of 2011. After a few years of being left abandoned, the base reopened as Nasiriyah Airport, providing domestic and international flights.

Numerous photographs of U.S. soldiers climbing or descending the steps of the Great Ziggurat can easily be found online. Although tours of the historic site were often temporarily shut down (once because some soldiers were caught taking pictures of themselves urinating on it), many who were stationed there got to visit the temple during their days or shifts off. Members of the Texas Army National Guard can be seen posing in a group there on January 4, 2007. Colonel Dan Hokanson and Brigadier General Michael Lally were snapped together there while leading a troop of soldiers during a tour on July 31, 2009. Another image from May 18, 2010, shows artillerymen from the 17th Fires Brigade on the steps. These are documented and mundane U.S. Army photographs, yet they have been misrepresented in several places as showing proof of the American occupation of the then recently discovered "King Nimrod's Tomb." It seems a confusion of the ancient Sumerian "Ur," where Camp Adder was in Nasiriyah, and "Uruk," where the German Archaeological Institute *thinks* they discovered the tomb near Samawah, is also at play. These locations are separated by over 62 miles (100 km).

Another series of photographs manipulated for sensationalism (going viral on social media in 2019) claim to show some of the treasures recovered from "King Nimrod's Tomb," including skeletons wearing ornate gold jewelry, on display for U.S. Army officers and possible government agents. The problem is, these photographs (taken by army photographer Noreen Feeney) actually concern the "Treasure of Nimrud," a collection of hundreds of pieces of gold jewelry and precious stones from the height of the Assyrian civilization in 800 BCE.[51] A confusion of names is at play again. Originally unearthed in 1988 by Iraqi archaeologists and never seen outside Iraq, the Nimrud treasure—named for the ancient excavated Assyrian city in modern Iraq where it was uncovered—was an extraordinary find, containing gold and elite goods rivaling those of King Tutankhamun's tomb in Egypt.[52] Unfortunately, the discovery was made on the eve of the Persian Gulf War, which overshadowed the excavations. The artifacts survived the confusion and looting after the American invasion in a bombed-out Central Bank of Iraq vault, where the treasure had been put away for 12 years until it was "rediscovered" on June 5, 2003.[53] The Americans seen examining the treasure in the photos are a team of U.S. Customs agents and officials from the Coalition Provisional Authority.

As for Nimrud, it was destroyed in 2015 by the terrorist organization Islamic State of Iraq and the Levant (ISIL) because of its "un-Islamic" Assyrian nature. In November 2016, Iraqi forces retook the site and confirmed that only around 10 percent of the excavated portion of Nimrud remained.

The last piece of evidence reported to support the idea of a U.S. government cover-up concerning the discovery of the giant Nimrod's Tomb is by far the most intriguing and, at first glance, also the most unexplainable. Accessible through the Freedom of Information Act (FOIA) releases of State Department emails available on its website, within the file "Department of State FOIA log 2018," on page 470, number F-2019–02110, there is an email received on December 13, 2018, by a sender named Denetra D. Senigar. The subject of the document reads: "Requesting documents pertaining to the resurrection chamber of Gilgamesh, the location of his body and the location of the buried Nephilim." (Go look for yourself, using the link provided in the footnote.[54]) Something about seeing a statement like that on an official government website definitely makes the war immediately get weirder.

Purported to have only been discovered because of the 2015 Hillary Clinton controversy over her using a private email server during her time as Secretary of State, the subject of this email spawned a viral fever among the masses. Searches for the sender's name reveal no one of obvious significance, so many theorists claim it must be an alias. Some also believe there is the possibility that it is a cryptic discussion, using embedded code words. Others counter by questioning why someone would use a title that would clearly gain so much attention if it was meant to be hidden.

Yet, even for all the wild conjecture, it's really not that difficult to find an alternative, unsensational, rational explanation once again. First, this email is not from the Hillary Clinton releases, it's from a simple list of FOIA requests, and was clearly received in 2018, five years after her tenure as Secretary of State had ended. Literally all this email suggests is that someone (not even necessarily a federal employee) named Denetra submitted a request with this title and that the request is closed. If I had sent the Department of State an FOIA request that year and asked for "the location of recovered Sasquatch bodies in Area 51" and anyone searched for terms similar to that, my document would appear as a result. With FOIA requests, you have to ask for something specific—and of course, the information you request may not exist—or the request becomes closed.

As thrilling as the idea of our government invading Iraq to loot the recently discovered tomb of a fabled half-god giant who had unlocked the secrets of immortality may be, there just isn't any provable basis for it, like so many other fantastical conspiracies currently living in the minds of the gullible masses.

Let's get back to the truly unexplainable stuff.

GUERILLAS IN THE MIDST

American servicemen's experiences with hairy hominins aren't just limited to our Middle Eastern wars, as many Vietnam veterans will attest. The phenomenon of the "Rock Apes" continues to develop as more eyewitnesses come forward in their later years, becoming less concerned about being ridiculed or not believed, and staying the course about what they know they saw living in the mountainous jungles of Vietnam's Central Highlands.

These Rock Apes (named by the GIs for their tendency to throw stones) were consistently described as walking upright and between 4 and 6 feet tall (1.2–1.8 meters), with powerful builds, long limbs, and sometimes protruding stomachs, all covered in brown or reddish-brown hair similar to an orangutan, except for bare skin on the face and hands. Orangutans once did live in Vietnam, but they went extinct there thousands of years ago, and all the known primates native to the area are very small.[55] The Rock Apes' behavior demonstrated no regard or fear for humans, often surprising patrols in the jungle, attacking en masse with rocks, or screaming and shaking their fists in anger at troops in a very humanlike manner. Seen both solitary and in groups, during the day or night and almost always on the ground, their habitat was the most remote forested mountain areas stretching from Kon Tum Province near the border with Laos and Cambodia to Lam Dong Province in the south, which were regions disturbed for the first time by the American war. Known locally as the Batutut or Ngoui Rung—pronounced "newie run" and meaning "forest people"—they have been encountered and described in oral traditions for hundreds of years.[56]

Before the arrival of American soldiers, the Central Highlands of Indochina had barely been explored by westerners. Fierce hill tribes had always managed to keep the Vietnamese and French out. The few French explorers who did manage to penetrate the region often reported stories of and encounters with "wildmen" bearing consistent attributes, going all the way back to an 1820 account by a ship captain named El Rey.[57] In a report from 1947, a French officer with a force of indigenous troops encountered a creature he said was neither human nor ape. A native sergeant told the French officer that the creature was well known to the locals, and that they never hunted or ate them. The officer recorded that the indigenous men were filled with joy as a result of the encounter.[58]

The Vietnam War was intensifying in August 1965, when the U.S. Marines assumed responsibility for the defense of a base on the 2,200-foot (671-meter) peak of Son Tra Mountain, located near the Da Nang air base overlooking the harbor and China Beach. A divisional outpost, landing zone, and Signals Intelligence (SIGINT) gathering radio relay station, it would acquire the nickname "Monkey Mountain" due to the many close encounters there with Rock Apes.[59]

Vietnam veteran Mark Hegge was in the 1st Marine Division assigned to the area from 1969 to 1970 and provided me with the following account during an interview in November of 2021:

> The rock apes were not made up. But, very few Vietnam vets ever saw one during the day. The location of this apparent family of apes was northwest of Da Nang between there and Hue City, above the railroad tracks. We were guarding the tracks for a month or so when parts of the 2nd Battalion of the 26th Marines were deployed there. I was in Fox Company—a rifle company that did small outpost ambushes at night, guarded bridges and those tracks, and of course worked with local ARVN youngsters trying to give them some guidance. The apes were in some very dense jungle-like terrain all the time. I am sure they always knew when humans were anywhere close. I am positive they could smell us a mile away. Anyway, it was only a couple of times within a week that we were aware they were around.
>
> They did occasionally come out in the daytime to raid our food supplies, but were always gone before we got back from our patrols and ambushes. They would make sure no one was nearby and then go after

our C-rations by puncturing the cans with their canine teeth. If they hit something unsavory, they would simply drop it. The cans they did not open had large puncture holes in the tops, as if they were smelling for fruit or jelly, maybe. I believe a person could almost get a pinky finger tip in one of the holes I found in a ham and eggs can one day. They have jaws like baboons and made puncture holes in cans big enough to drop an M&M through without any problem. That's one big tooth! When they hit the peaches or peanut butter, they would actually rip off the top of the cans and scoop out the treats.

They sure liked to mess up our camp, to throw stuff around too. They also liked to poop in our camp to tell us we were not welcome. I don't think they appreciated us being there. I cannot describe one because I never saw one. But, one of the Marines I served with was bitten in the shoulder by an adult when the guy found a baby ape and picked it up. If all the Marines who went to Nam were interviewed . . . there would be a few who could sketch one from memory.[60]

Mark described what happened to the bitten soldier in more detail, saying:

[The Marine] found a baby one outside the perimeter on a hill his company was protecting and thought it was a lost chimpanzee. He picked it up, when out of nowhere, an ape the same size as him (he said), jumped on his back and bit him on his right shoulder, knocked him to the ground, and grabbed the little one all in about five seconds. All he saw was something brownish, as big as he was, and fast as hell heading into the underbrush, upright on its feet. He said it had a flat ape-like face but did not have those long dangling ape-like arms. The bite left four bruises, but were not severe enough to puncture the cloth on his shirt or his skin. He thought maybe this thing meant him no real harm, but wanted to send a message. Stories like this are everywhere. I had a fellow Marine (new in-country) light up a cigarette in the pitch black of night to find an ape eye-to-eye with him. Both let out a yell at the same time![61]

There was evidence of them everywhere. Excrement would be found on bunker roofs in the morning, and mysterious vocalizations could be heard throughout the night. The son of a deceased Vietnam veteran that I know related a story from the war that his father often repeated, saying, "Dad did time on Monkey Mountain. He said there were Rock Apes to deal with during the night that made a lot of noise and unearthly howls. One night while set up in an ambush position, a guy in his platoon went to check out a noise he kept hearing in front of him. A huge rock was hurtled at him from the jungle, knocking him out and leaving a serious dent in his helmet. Everyone wanted to shoot one because they pissed them off so much."[62]

Rock throwing is a known behavior in all the great ape species, possibly as a way to demonstrate dominance or mark their territory. In 1968, a company of the 3rd Battalion of the 5th Marine Division was in the jungle in the area around Monkey Mountain. The Marines reported that when they were in the mountains, apes would get above them and throw rocks down at them, ambushing the ambush teams.[63] There are also reports of grenades being collected from soldiers before they passed through known Rock Ape areas, to prevent them from being used and thrown back by the creatures.

Sergeant Kurt Boley of Company D, 1st Battalion, 26th Marines, offered this anecdote in a letter written home:

Another probe, I guess. Unless it was rock apes—there are a lot of them in the jungle around here. One of them actually came right through the perimeter once. It scared the guy who saw it so much that the kid almost passed out before firing a whole magazine at him. People laughed pretty hard about it the next day because even with all of those bullets at short range, he missed. No dead rock ape in front of his position. If the guy in the next hole hadn't seen the whole thing, I would have figured that the kid was making it all up. But I'd be really scared, too, if some huge, furry thing on two legs decided to lurch right up to me in the middle of the night.[64]

Early 1966 is when tensions seem to have come to a head, and the apes went on the offensive, engaging Marines in the infamous Battle of

Dong Den.[65] About 42 kilometers (26 miles) northwest from Monkey Mountain, a Marine observation post was established by blowing off the top of a 939-foot-tall (286-meter) jungle-covered hilltop named Dong Den. The strategic summit afforded sweeping views of the highlands and coastal plain around Da Nang. The Rock Apes living nearby possibly resented what had been done to flatten the top of the hill and objected to the new human presence in their habitat. When the Marines on the OP called their commander and told him they had movement in the foliage one day, everyone was thinking it was a possible force of Viet Cong. They were ordered to "stay in place," and that they could call in artillery if necessary. It wasn't long before the Marines realized it actually wasn't a unit of the enemy, but a large group of Rock Apes who were surrounding them and moving in closer. Ordered to not reveal their positions by discharging weapons, the men were told to throw rocks and scare them away.

As might be imagined, the apes responded by throwing the rocks back, only much harder and more accurately. Loud thumps were followed by screams, curses, and threats. Denied the request to open fire again, bayonets were fixed and hand-to-hand combat ensued. The radio at headquarters crackled with the screams of pain and anger from both sides. Suddenly, the hill exploded into a full-fledged firefight, the sounds of American weapons echoing through the valley. When the relief squad dispatched to assess the situation finally reached the battlefield, they found Marines and Rock Apes strewn all over. They called the captain and told him that most of the creatures were dead and most of the Marines were very pissed off. The encounter left four serious medevacs— and not one of them for a Rock Ape.

In 1969, Delta Company, 1st of the 502nd Infantry, 101st Airborne Division, was on Nui Mo Tau Ridge northwest of Da Nang, about 10 miles (16 km) south of Hue City.[66] As they were eating lunch, a squad of what they took to be eight NVA soldiers in khaki uniforms came around a bend in the trail and surprised them. The unsuspecting Americans opened fire on the group, quickly realizing they were actually Rock Apes, not enemy troops. The alpha male was reported to be very dark, almost black in color, while the others were reddish and light brown.

He went up in the trees and would repeatedly rush the GIs and then retreat. He did this several times, apparently covering the withdrawal of his troops, which is similar to the actions of silverback gorillas. "He was flying through the branches and rushing the men with his teeth bared," veteran Michael Kelley remembered in 2000.[67] As realization dawned on the paratroopers, the shooting stopped instantaneously, and they all just stood silent in shock for a while.

Lance Corporal Alfonso Villarreal, of Refugio, Texas, was drafted and served in Vietnam from 1967 to 1968 with 3rd Battalion, 5th Marines. He was wounded twice and participated in 23 major battles. He was out with his platoon one night when off in the distance, they saw what looked like a large "medicine ball" moving toward them through a ravine. The object kept rolling toward them until it was right at the end of a Marine's rifle, who tapped it lightly. The "thing" uncurled and began screaming, yelling, and waving its arms before running away. "It was a baby rock ape," Villarreal said.[68] Then, from the tops of the steep sides of the ravine, large boulders started falling. The 300- to 400-pound boulders were being launched by the adult Rock Apes, who fearlessly started coming down the path toward the platoon. "They were like gorillas," Villarreal said. He noted the animals had four- to five-inch fangs. "We had to shoot them. I think there were about 17 of them. I've never seen anything like it."[69] When it was over, the juvenile ape was not found among the dead.

Sergeant Gary Linderer and five paratroopers of the 101st Airborne were in the field on a Long Range Reconnaissance Patrol (LRRP).[70] At dawn on the second morning, while set up on a hillside with a huge patch of 12-foot-high (3.7-meter) brush behind them, the squad heard a commotion in the brush. As they all turned to face the threat, the vegetation suddenly parted and a creature stepped through. It stood 5 feet 10 inches to 6 feet (1.8 meters) tall, with extremely long, muscular arms, broad shoulders, and a heavy torso, walking upright. The face and hands had no hair on them, and the incredibly humanlike eyes were deep-set on a prominent brow and seemed to reflect intelligence. They all saw it clearly, as it was only 10 to 15 yards (9–14 meters) away, its left arm holding a branch back while it looked downhill at them. The cryptid didn't make a sound as it cocked its head a couple times, never changing its surprised expression. After 7 to 10 seconds, it turned around and disappeared up the steep rise, leaving the stunned soldiers frozen in place.

Army Sergeant Thomas M. Jenkins reported his platoon was attacked with stones while on recon in 1969.[71] He had previously become aware of the Rock Apes after hearing that a Marine had been thrown off a location known as the Rock Pile by one. The creatures would burst out of the jungle at dawn, awakening the soldiers with screams, yelling, and fist-shaking. He was amazed at the expressive, humanlike emotions and how displeased they were with the Americans' presence in their jungle. He described them as being more stocky and muscular than other apes, with a darker color.

Even pilots got a view of the cryptids once in a while. Larry Wilson was flying his helicopter in a convoy mission down a stream valley somewhere in western Vietnam in November or December 1970.[72] As the Huey ascended a ridgeline, he witnessed a defoliated tree shaking and wiggling violently. Very clearly, he spotted an apeman on top of it, shaking it aggressively. He described the creature's soccer ball–size head as being flat on top, with facial features like a man. He swears he had an unobstructed view and is certain he saw an apeman.

When a dark figure continued to advance into the far end of a restricted zone late one night, overwhelming fire was directed at it. A reporting witness stated, "When daylight came, we realized we had blown the living shit out of a large seven-foot ape. It was a male, with the face of a wild man, and not much else left of it to describe the stinkin' thing. We poured fuel over the remains and set it afire."[73]

A Special Forces team laid up for several days waiting to ambush the enemy deep in the Central Highlands jungle heard mysterious choking and gurgling noises continue off and on nearby for three consecutive nights.[74] As they were moving out at dawn on the fourth day, they found a decomposing apeman nearly blown completely in half by what appeared to be a mine. The open body cavity was already crawling with bugs. The creature had shorter hair on its huge head, eyes set back an inch and a half deep from the prominent brow line, a flat nose, and long arms with large and lengthy fingers. One hand was still wrapped around a tree branch it was clutching when it had died. The teeth included flat, well-formed molars and long, pointed canines.

During a lecture at the Naval War College in the mid-2000s, Medal of Honor recipient and Special Forces/Delta Force Command Sergeant-Major Jon Robert Cavaiani told a fascinating Vietnam War anecdote.[75] While out on a trail ambush, one of his soldiers had attempted to knife what he believed was a Viet Cong guerilla walking on the pathway. Cavaiani said that he watched his team member run up to the "man" from behind with his knife. Just before reaching his intended target, the Green Beret abruptly "about-faced" and started running away in retreat. The "man" suddenly turned, too, and ran after the American on two feet, jumping on his back and biting into him. Cavaiani and the team opened fire and killed the attacker, only afterward realizing it was a man-size "orangutan-like" creature covered in reddish-colored, long hair. The bitten Special Forces soldier survived, but they had to sever the dead ape's head to remove it from his shoulder.

Corroborating Sergeant Thomas Jenkins's earlier testimony, veteran Philip Bello was near the Rock Pile in September 1968. This landmark was a rock pillar standing over 75 feet (23 meters) tall that was used as an observation post by the army. One night, he and his platoon heard screaming and shouting coming from the top of it, followed by gunfire. As they gazed upward, the troopers witnessed some men falling from the heights. The following morning, Bello claims the unit that was up there said the soldiers had been thrown off the Rock Pile by "hairy creatures they thought were some type of ape."[76] The confrontation had supposedly escalated when the creatures began throwing sticks and rocks and were subsequently shot at. The soldiers killed a few, but it was such a large group of Rock Apes that they were able to overrun the position and snatch up a few soldiers. Bello claims his unit left the area too fast the next morning to learn more information.

Sometimes the cryptids apparently fought for our side too. One report claims that while Americans were engaged in a firefight with a unit of Viet Cong, one of these creatures went running on two legs at tremendous speed right through the middle of the opposing forces. It disappeared into the forest where the Viet Cong were hiding, and a lot of unusual cries and screams were heard by the Americans. The fighting soon stopped. After the battle, the GIs supposedly found several dead Viet Cong that had been physically beaten to death, with a few actually physically torn apart in gruesome ways.

During research, I discovered that another term popularly used by GIs to describe these creatures was "Powell's Apes." An article published in the April 27, 1970, *Army Reporter* explained why. The headline read: "Ape Story Lingers, Cam Ranh Bay, Vietnam." The article stated:

> Guards at the depot here keep a watch for Powell's Ape. It has been nearly three years since the monster was almost seen by a bleary-eyed guard. Detecting movement on the perimeter, the guard fired and the beast fled. When morning came the area was examined and a footprint and trail of blood were found. The footprint was neither human nor ape. A picture was taken of the track but no one could decide who or what had made it. It wasn't long before Captain Powell, then a depot company commander, found his name associated with the monster. All that remains now is a small photograph on the ammunition area's orderly room wall. Perhaps the legend of Powell's Ape is all there ever was, but the guards at the ammunition area here still have something to think about besides Charlie.[77]

The Battle at Khe Sanh occurred between January and July of 1968. Locals believe today that the Rock Apes of that area still inhabit the caves at Khe Sanh and its underground tunnels, called "rat holes" by the soldiers. Riflemen in Company D, 1st Battalion, 26th Marines, reported that the road to Khe Sanh was riddled with caves that were inhabited by both "maniac hair-covered rock apes" and the NVA.[78] "I believe that the Viet Cong built hundreds of miles of tunnels to run their operations in relative secrecy which played into the needs of the Rock Ape perfectly. Like 'Charlie' the apes were tucked away from harm during the day and had the run of the place all night long," said veteran Mark Hegge.[79] The creatures were also known to the Marines during the siege at Khe Sanh. Perimeter sensors around military outposts were often activated by random wildlife, and once in a while by the hairy wildmen. A Marine in the security platoon of the 26th Marines HQ stated, "Khe

Sanh Combat Base was to the south of us. That night a trip flare went off on the north side of us. Castillo went to see what he thought would be the VC, as the flares had been going off for weeks. When he got there, he was told it was furry Rock Apes that seemed to have manes going down their backs."[80]

Sightings by Viet Cong and NVA troops were also common enough that the Communist Party secretariat ordered an NVA general to organize an expedition in 1974 to try to capture or kill one. No hard evidence was retrieved. In 1982, another government-sponsored project to locate the possible relict hominid was launched. The research team discovered and cast more than 10 humanlike footprints in a remote mountain pass in Kon Tum Province.[81] They were wider than a human foot and too big to be an ape. As a result of this evidence, the government designated over 87,000 acres of the Mom Ray Mountain region's forest to protect and study this mystery species further. As of 2002, it has been designated the Chu Mom Ray National Park. It remains little explored due to its remoteness and hazards, which include many remaining landmines.

Even if our own nation won't believe our Vietnam veterans, at least the people of Vietnam seem to.

BANZAI BIGFOOT

Across the Pacific Ocean 3,915 miles (6,300 km) to the southeast of Vietnam are the Solomon Islands, a sovereign state in Oceania, consisting of nearly 1,000 islets grouped in an area smaller than the state of Maryland. Isolated biologically, over half of the mammals living there are found nowhere else on the planet. As recently as 2017, legends about a giant, possum-like rat that lived in trees and could crack open coconuts with its teeth were proven true with the spectacular discovery there of the new species *Uromys vika*.[82]

Guadalcanal, one of the largest islands of the Solomon chain, was the main scene of the bloody World War II campaign fought between the United States and Japan between August 1942 and February 1943. The mountain peaks of the island are overgrown with foreboding, moss-covered jungle forests that have been barely explored by world science. Requiring no validation of that sort, the local Uluna-Sutuhuri tribe have always known the humid, cloud-draped mountain ranges as the home of the Mumu, Sasquatch-like giant creatures covered in long black, brown, or reddish hair.[83] Generations of children have been told and retold the stories of abduction and cannibalism inflicted by these aggressive creatures upon their villages in the past. True giants, ranging between 10 and 15 feet tall (3–4.5 meters), their physical traits include protruding double eyebrows, bulging red eyes, flat noses, and wide-gaping mouths. The creatures seem to resemble ones found in Malaysian folklore, known as the Orang Mawas or Orang Dalam, that are said to inhabit the dense jungle of Johor in Malaysia. They are similarly described as being about 10 feet (3 meters) tall, bipedal, and covered in black fur.

During their occupation, Japanese soldiers infiltrated all of Guadalcanal's remote rain forests and reported encountering these terrifying creatures on several occasions. Units described them suddenly crashing through the vegetation to aggressively attack squads of soldiers, sometimes even using crude clubs and seemingly not seriously wounded by bullets. They were also reported to snap thick trees and branches in half—as threatening displays of immense power—and would keep the Japanese awake at night with their impossibly loud, ghoulish wailing. Besides the large canon of regional folklore, sightings and footprint evidence of these giant hominids are reported even today.

The Solomon Giants weren't the only hairy cryptids encountered by the Imperial Japanese Army during the war. While occupying the Bukit Timah rain forest region of Singapore, reports of bipedal, apelike creatures standing between 3 and 5.5 feet (1–1.7 meters) tall with grayish skin and hair were collected. Already identified in old Malay folklore, the first recorded sighting of the "Monkey Man" was in 1805.[84] This proto-pygmy, or miniature hominid, also resembles a more humanlike creature from Indonesian folklore called the Orang Pendek ("short person"), who is said to inhabit the remote, mountainous forests on the island of Sumatra.

The Ryukyu Islands consist of 55 islets covering a 1,193-square-mile (3,090-sq-km) area, with Okinawa ranking as the largest landmass. While occupying the southern reaches of these islands, soldiers of the Rising Sun encountered yet another short, primate-like hominid during the war. The Kijimuna were vividly described as being the size of a human three- or four-year-old child, sparsely covered in kinky reddish hair, with disproportionately long arms and a large head.[85] They also possessed a distinctive and powerfully offensive odor. Seemingly nocturnal, their reflective catlike eyes would spook soldiers on the beach at night; the creatures were often encountered as they appeared to be foraging for their favorite seafoods. Mysterious piles of discarded empty shells were considered to be a sure sign of a nearby Kijimuna. Reported to be agile climbers, they were often seen in banyan trees during the day.

Much like the eyewitness American veterans from Vietnam to the Middle East, the Japanese soldiers who returned home with stories about their weird war encounters with these unknown creatures were often laughed at and found their observations and experiences discredited and dismissed by a society that hadn't even been there. But is it truly possible that so many accounts are all just nonsense?

Respected and world-famous conservationists and scientists, including primatologist Dr. Jane Goodall, field biologist Dr. George Schaller, and professor of anatomy and anthropology Dr. Jeffrey Meldrum, have gone on record that they are open-minded about the possible existence of these kinds of cryptid beings. Wildlife expert and author Gareth Patterson, known internationally for his work to protect the lions and elephants of Africa, released a book in 2020, *Beyond the Secret Elephants*.[86] Although it centers on his nearly two decades of research and rediscovery of the secretive South African Knysna elephants, it also slyly and reluctantly reveals his startling discovery of a much more mysterious species: a relict hominin known to the indigenous Knysna forest people as the Otang. Gareth had long heard about the existence of the bipedal, russet hair-covered, 6- to 7-foot-tall (1.8–2.1-meter), humanlike Otang from the local people before actually observing them multiple times himself. Those aware of these types of documented recent discoveries know that science is truly on the verge of something absolutely extraordinary. Perhaps it will be a member of the armed forces who finally settles the issue with a well-placed round, which will surely be considered another "shot heard round the world" in the annals of human history.

CHAPTER 2

Unexpected Enemies

TEAM ROCK MAT WAS ON THE FIRST OF A FIVE-DAY RECON ON MAY 5, 1970. The seven-man squad from the 1st Reconnaissance Battalion of the 1st Marine Division had been inserted into the combat zone by helicopter about 25 miles (40 km) northwest of Da Nang.[1] Sergeant Robert C. Phleger—newly married to his high school sweetheart and just returned from R&R in Hawaii—was the team leader. As the men prepared to sleep on the first night of the mission, they spaced themselves widely apart, spreading their poncho liners on the jungle floor, completely unaware that they had been stalked all day by a silent killer. Around 2000 hours, the Marine on watch duty thought he heard a slight disturbance near Sergeant Phleger's unseen position—vegetation moving, branches breaking, maybe a muffled cry, then silence. The man radioed headquarters, and the company commander ordered him to sit tight and stay on high alert until daybreak. Nothing else happened through the long night.

At dawn, the squad prepared to move to another location, but none of the six men could locate their team leader. Chills went down their spines when they found Sergeant Phleger's rifle and equipment, his blood spilled on the ground, and the compressed grass where he had been dragged away by something big into the dense jungle. The men gathered their collective courage and followed the trail, finding the dead Marine 164 feet (50 meters) away, pushed up against a tree with his neck broken and one side of his body bitten into and deeply lacerated.

A sudden movement from the trees revealed an enraged 400-pound (181-kg) tiger, ready to protect its fresh kill. The team opened fire wildly, missing the animal, and it retreated. As they quickly gathered up their sergeant's remains in a poncho and requested immediate extraction, the Marines could hear the monster cat moving around them, refusing to leave. The beast charged again, and they threw a grenade and opened fire, causing it to finally run off, still unharmed. The traumatized recon team was successfully extracted, disappointed at being unable to achieve vengeance for their unexpected loss.

Any soldier deployed in the field has an endless amount of inconveniences, irritations, and discomforts to deal with. Weather and temperature extremes; unforgiving terrain and fauna of all types; abrasions, cuts, and muscle injuries; blisters and trench foot . . . the list is endless and unique to the setting of each training or combat mission. And then there are the unexpected enemies that are rarely acknowledged and discussed throughout history: the poisonous plant life, insects and spiders, amphibians and reptiles, vermin, and dangerous mammals that all exist and will be encountered in the bush.

I was on an extended field exercise at Fort Polk, Louisiana, attached to an infantry battalion in preparation for an upcoming rotation at the National Training Center (NTC) at Fort Irwin, California. As the S2 intelligence sergeant, operations continued 24 hours a day, and I would grab a few hours of shut-eye at any given opportunity. I had strung up a hammock between two tall pine trees a short distance from the Tactical Operations Center (TOC) and had fallen asleep around dusk one evening. My next shift began at midnight, and I remember at some point during my slumber waking up after something had bitten me on my arm, but because it was so dark I couldn't see what the pinprick sensation had been inflicted by. I unsuccessfully felt for anything on me and then dozed off again, waking up about an hour later in serious trouble.

The pain I experienced over the next few hours is still the most intense discomfort I've ever endured. A few years later, I was accidentally shot in my left foot with a Soviet .380 Makarov pistol by a Green Beret Vietnam veteran, and that pain wasn't even close to the effects this bite had on me. People will often ask how it feels to be shot, and I can attest that surprisingly the most excruciating part of it is the burning caused by the hot lead of the bullet. I would describe the way my gunshot wound felt as similar to that of a giant wasp sting—that kind of intense burning and throbbing. I would describe the effects of the mystery insect bite as similar to having a heart attack coupled with the worst muscular aches imaginable. At intervals of a few seconds, it felt like all the muscles and organs of my body were seizing and locking up—especially my heart and lungs—causing me to take short, quick breaths like a dog panting. Along with the breathing difficulty and increased blood pressure, the aching pain was centered in my abdomen and lower back, and was coupled with nausea, cold sweating, and tremors. Though still unknown to me at that moment, I had been bitten by a black widow spider, the most toxic spider in the United States. The venom of the black widow is composed of neurotoxins that affect the nervous system, which is used to paralyze their prey—hence the symptoms I was experiencing. Although I was too large to be paralyzed, the venom was still attacking my muscles and organs.

I stumbled through the pitch-black woods to the TOC and tried to describe what was happening to me to my lieutenant. He sent me to find the company medic station somewhere in the darkness, and I still remember the fearful agony I felt as I desperately wandered the woods alone. After locating them, the medics immediately administered a shot of epinephrine (adrenaline) to reduce the effects of what they believed to be an anaphylaxis allergic reaction. It calmed everything down for a few minutes, but then the symptoms slowly returned and intensified again. This cycle was repeated between the two more injections they dispensed, followed by my transport to the battalion aid station for further evaluation and treatment. Within a couple hours, the muscle and organ seizure feelings finally subsided, but were replaced by the worst muscular cramps I have ever felt. I'll never be able to thank the nameless medic who massaged my back and legs through that endless night, providing the only relief that worked.

By dawn, the major reactions had subsided and the bite was visible on my upper left arm, having swelled and turned red, forming a target-shaped lesion. Although I never saw the culprit, the doctor said that the particular symptoms, coupled with the appearance of the bite, suggested a black widow. I returned to my unit but wasn't myself for another 24 hours, and still experienced muscular aches and cramps throughout my body, which centered in my lower legs and feet before subsiding. To this day, I can't believe the bite of a small spider caused me so much torment!

NEVER GET OUT OF THE BOAT

Among the multitude of threats and deadly dangers faced by American servicemen in Vietnam, imagine adding in the fact that you might be silently stalked, dragged off in your sleep, and eaten alive by a tiger. The most comprehensive study of deaths due to tiger attacks estimates that there have been at least 373,000 victims between 1800 and 2009. The majority of these man-eaters live in South and Southeast Asia.[2] The number of tigers and tiger attacks in the jungle increased dramatically during the Vietnam War. It is believed that a contributing factor was the opportunity presented by multitudes of unburied bodies and wounded casualties caused by the violent conflict. Tigers will scavenge and feed at old kills that are not their own. After developing a taste for human flesh, the tigers of Vietnam became eager to stalk and attack soldiers on both sides of the conflict. The jungle nights were often dark, starless, and misty—perfect tiger weather in which to prowl. Using their speed and the dense vegetation of the jungle to stay silently hidden, they were apex ambush predators and dragged several American soldiers away in the dark, including Sergeant Phleger of Team Rock Mat.

On December 22, 1968, a man-eating tiger stalked an element of the 3rd Marine Reconnaissance Battalion while out on an observation patrol in Quang Tri Province, about 10 miles south of the Demilitarized Zone (DMZ) and 6 miles east of the border with Laos. It was near a spot where a young Marine had been killed the previous month, on November 12. A small team consisting of Marines and two professional South Vietnamese tiger hunters had been sent out to find the man-eater and three other big cats believed to be in the area, but the hunt had failed. The six-man recon team now operating in the same vicinity had accomplished their mission and were awaiting extraction due to bad weather conditions. Posting a two-man radio watch, the four others tried to get some sleep. The patient predator recognized an opportunity and pounced swiftly and silently.

Private First Class Thomas E. Shainline recounted, "Suddenly I heard somebody scream, then somebody else was yelling, 'It's a tiger, it's a tiger!'"[3] The Marine who had been asleep next to the victim, Private First Class Roy Regan, said, "I jumped up and saw the tiger with his mouth around my partner. All I could think about was to get the tiger away from him. I jumped at the tiger and the cat jerked his head and jumped into a bomb crater 10 meters away, still holding his prey."[4]

The Marines all opened fire on the beast, and it released the dazed and wounded man, then was killed in a hail of gunfire. The injured rifleman, Sergeant Goolden, staggered out of the bomb crater, asking the others what had happened to him. He was suffering from lacerations and bite wounds on the neck, but would survive. The tiger measured nine feet from head to tail and weighed approximately 400 pounds. The CH-46 transport helicopter finally arrived, extracting the team and the dead tiger to the 3rd Reconnaissance Battalion headquarters, and the mauled Marine to the military hospital at Quang Tri.

Veteran Mark Koons recounted, "In the 26 months I served at the 249th Medevac, we had at least two survivors who had been wounded and then carried off by tigers. In both cases, the tiger took them by the knee to drag them to someplace quieter."[5] Some of our servicemen would not be as lucky.

In late May 1970, the U.S. Army's B Company, 1st Battalion (Mechanized), 50th Infantry Regiment, was operating out of LZ Betty, a firebase south of Phan Thiet in Bình Thuan Province in southern Vietnam. One night on watch, Frenchy Lagimoniere heard some noise coming from in front of the bunker he occupied. Searching carefully with a starlight scope, he observed a tiger crouched low in the elephant grass. For the next 30 minutes, Frenchy and the others watched the tiger "playing" with a six-foot-long lizard, pouncing on it and slapping it around like a toy animal. Then the feline was suddenly gone.

Two days later, while on patrol in their Armored Personnel Carriers (APCs) in an area of dense woods and underbrush about 25 kilometers (15.5 miles) outside the wire of LZ Betty, veteran Rick Leland recalled his lieutenant seeing something up ahead and ordering the convoy to halt. "I remember seeing a flash of orange and we all agreed that it was a tiger! Man, we were excited and we thought and talked about it all the rest of the day."[6] The patrol set out a mechanical ambush on a jungle trail that night, which usually consisted of a half dozen Claymore mines rigged to fire simultaneously, and it triggered. At dawn, they found a blood trail and decided to stay in the area. Day patrols turned up nothing, so they set up another mechanic ambush near the first one. The soldiers heard it explode again.

The APC dispatched to investigate in the morning radioed back that they had a dead tiger. It had walked into the trip wire and been killed on the spot. "Soon the word spread and we had a bunch of choppers carrying brass and other higher-ups flying in all morning long. We all took pictures and then hauled the tiger off on an APC," Frenchy stated.[7] Could it have been the same tiger that had entertained him at the bunker a few days previously?

B Company APC driver, John (The Mole) Williams, continued the tale: "We wanted to take it back to base on the APC, but they made us take it off the track. By the time we got to camp dragging it with a cable, all we had left was a tiger tail to talk about."[8] Rick Leland noted the tragedy of the experience, adding, "I was excited and sad at the same time to see such a beautiful animal dead. It left me thinking that nothing escapes war."

Staff Sergeant Darwin "Scotty" Stamper and his platoon leader, First Lieutenant James MacQueen, experienced a similar incident. After an evening of setting up several mechanical ambushes along trails, their unit heard an explosion overnight. The next morning they discovered the mangled corpse of a Viet Cong fighter. They left the body where it was, setting up a new ambush around it in hopes of eliminating anyone who might come to recover their dead friend.

Sure enough, another explosion was heard early in the morning, and when the sun rose they discovered the remains of a very large tiger in the kill zone. It had apparently triggered the Claymores while trying to drag off the dead VC, but the undamaged, beautiful pelt suggested the concussion of the mines is what had killed it. Claiming the role of trophy hunters, the soldiers planned to take the carnivore back, make a rug out of the skin, and hang it up in the base club. They secured the beast to the front of an M113 APC and started home.

Staff Sergeant Stamper said, "Well, by about 10 a.m. he started getting pretty ripe and we did not have anyone that could dress him out, or wanted to. Just as I was considering dumping him, a chopper started circling over us and the pilot called on our frequency to ask if that was a tiger on the front of the APC. I told him it was and he asked me what we wanted for it. I told him he could have it for 15 cases of beer to be delivered when we got back to Phan Thiet."[9]

The deal was agreed on and the soldiers secured a landing zone for the helicopter, which swooped down and picked the coveted animal up. Later, when the force got back to the company area, they had 15 cases of beer waiting for them.

During an anxious night of zero visibility in 1968, a six-man U.S. Marine patrol was taking turns sleeping. Something hidden in the darkness suddenly pulled on the leg of one of the reclining men, and he glimpsed a large silhouette standing before him before it slipped away. The patrol leader confirmed they had movement around them. The black shadow returned, grabbing at another Marine, and the team opened fire on it. The mystery menace was killed and immediately identified as a jungle cat.

Having revealed their position, the team was advised to immediately clear the area and head to the extraction landing zone (LZ). Although at first determined to take the heavy animal with them, a combination of rugged terrain, monsoonal weather, and the danger of having to evade enemy patrols made it impossible. A decision was made to skin the cat. The team hustled to the LZ only to be told the helicopter was unable to fly due to the weather. For two more humid days, the Marines had to stay on the move, and their prized tiger pelt was beginning to deteriorate.

The next radio exchange between the patrol and base involved desperate requests for intelligence regarding how to tan an animal hide. A Marine back at base near the radio said he had grown up on a farm and that you had to use tannic acid to preserve the skin. When the team leader asked where in the hell he was supposed to get tannic acid out there, the response was, "Urine has tannic acid in it. Piss on the tiger!"[10] Finally extracted back to base the next day, the men posed for photos with the remains. Within two more days it was too rotted and horrible smelling to keep.

To set the record straight, urine is actually a rich source of urea—a nitrogen-based organic compound—which when stored for long periods of time decays into ammonia. Its high pH breaks down organic material, making urine the perfect substance for ancients to use in softening and tanning animal hides. Soaking animal skins in urine also made it easier for leather workers to remove hair and bits of flesh from the skin.[11] So the farm boy was correct about urine being useful on animal skins, just not about what ingredient from it actually works.

THE GREEN INFERNO

As we all know, a tropical jungle environment seems to have just about everything weird things need to survive and flourish. And Vietnam contained just about every variety of natural danger that exists, lying in wait to torture the unsuspecting Americans from the moment they arrived in-country. Twisted cord flowers, flame lilies, bark cloth trees, heartbreak grass—all examples of beautiful indigenous fauna that are also dangerous, with the power to kill or cause blindness upon contact or ingestion. Troops were occasionally even lifted out of their vehicles and APCs by low-hanging "wait-a-minute" vines that seemed harmless at first, but when touched actually constricted around the men, grabbing them by the arms or neck as they screamed in shock. The vines acted like strings or ropes, and were usually not seen until they were snatching the trooper or their weapon away. Point men on foot patrol suffered the most, with the "wait-a-minutes" pulling their rifles out of their hands in a different direction than they were moving, often causing them to fall. The grunts would have to cut away the vines in order to get up and then attack the ones that held their weapons, causing quick exhaustion in the unforgiving heat.

Reptiles and amphibians love the heat, humidity, and shade provided by the jungle, and Vietnam has so many varieties of snakes (cobras, vipers, kraits, and giant constrictors) that Americans were advised to just consider them all deadly. The list of things that could and would bite or sting was ridiculous—tarantulas and other bizarre spiders, red ants, black horseflies, bees, wasps, hornets, scorpions, land and water leeches, hordes of mosquitoes—causing a soldier's heart to stop when something was felt moving across their body in the dark. When there's no light to switch on and you can't risk giving away your position by using a flashlight, the only options are to risk brushing it away, swatting it, jumping around to make it fall off, or simply leaving it alone and hoping for the best. These creatures also seem to always be found in the most unexpected places in the morning, making a search and destroy mission top priority before breakfast, checking under your poncho liner blanket and inside your boots and pockets, helmet, rucksack, canteen cup, and any other place you can imagine they could be.

Viet Cong guerillas are reported to have even carefully relocated wild hives of *Apis dorsata*, the Asian giant honeybee, alongside the trails used by American patrols. One fighter would hide and wait until an enemy squad approached, then set off a small firework to aggravate the bees and cause them to attack. These bees are known to be aggressive and will viciously sting humans, with at least one verified fatal defensive attack on a human.[12]

Scolopendra subspinipes, the Vietnamese giant centipede in the class Chilopoda, is a local creepy crawler of particular note. Growing up to 10 inches (25 cm) long, this super-venomous monster is easily disturbed and extremely aggressive, with a bite that generates extreme pain. Also known as the Chinese redhead or jungle centipede, this species is responsible for the only human fatality attributed to a centipede bite—likely an allergic reaction to the toxin. Their bodies grow into 21 elongated and segmented sections, appearing reddish brown in color, with yellow or yellow-orange multiple legs. The venom is located in glands attached to the sharp claw tips of two modified legs, called the forcipules, which sit on top of the head, separate from the creature's two antennae. This terrestrial invertebrate lives under the litter of the jungle floor or beneath stones, fallen logs, and inside crevices, usually only emerging on cloudy days to prey on insects or even frogs, lizards, and rodents. Unfortunately for our soldiers, one of their favorite places to call home was inside troop bunkers, hiding in the nooks and cracks of the walls and ceilings. Veteran John Fish remembered lying on his cot one night in a bunker, horrified as he watched a centipede fall from a ceiling rafter and land right on his stomach. The soldier across from him reacted quickly, using his knife to flip it off and decapitate it, preventing what would have been a very painful bite.[13]

There has been a photograph from the Vietnam War circulating on the internet for several years now depicting a young, blonde, shirtless soldier dangling an extremely large centipede from his hand, with the jungle highlands in the background. The length of the creature appears to be around 3 feet (1 meter) long, making it absolutely terrifying. Although one veteran I talked to claimed he encountered one over a foot long and 1.5 inches wide, common sense should tell us that the picture can't be real. The truth is, the picture *is* real, but the centipede isn't as large as it appears. The photo is an example of forced perspective, a type of optical illusion that makes objects appear larger or smaller due to their proximity to the camera and the other objects in the frame. The son of the soldier in the picture reported that the centipede was actually only 10 inches long, saying, "My dad and his buddies put it on a string and stood behind it to make it look bigger."[14]

Another bunker mate of American troops in Vietnam that caused a lot of anxiety was the large and aggressive rats. Having served in the 5th Infantry Division, I belong to several alumni groups with fellow Red Devils, many who served in Vietnam between 1968 and 1971 with elements of the 1st Brigade when it was deployed after the Tet Offensive. They were tasked with defending the Vietnamese Demilitarized Zone (DMZ) in northern Quang Tri Province and spent time at the bases Con Thien and Dong Ha. Veteran Joe Ivey described encountering a rat in the crew bunker that was the size of a house cat, biting him on his big toe. Seeking retribution, he baited his attacker with crackers, waiting over an hour until the rat reappeared. Joe shot it with his .45 pistol, and it crawled out of the bunker and finally died about 30 feet distant, screaming all the way.[15] Bites were common and required getting several vaccine shots to protect against possibly getting a transmitted disease. Eric Ball remembered a rat running across his face in the darkness one night, and Ted

Nordin had one walk very slowly across his left shoulder and face. After an agonizing 30 seconds of cold sweating, he finally flung it off when it moved onto his right arm. Veteran Jay Mahn was bitten in the back by a giant rat while sleeping in the platoon bunker, and Robert Urso was bitten on his left foot. Ron Perron remembered his first night in-country, lying awake on his bunk and feeling very anxious about what was to come. He finally fell asleep eating some M&Ms his mother had packed for him. He was awakened by the biggest rat he had ever seen just sitting on his chest, nonchalantly finishing off his chocolate snack for him.

Veteran Lee Aanonsen described dealing with rats the size of footballs in the bunkers. They would stay hidden until all the lights went out, emerging then and making scurrying sounds in the pitch-black darkness. Soldiers would create all forms of improvised lamps to keep burning, holding the vermin at bay. Lee used empty soda cans filled with fuel oil and stuffed with a knotted bandolier strap as a wick. The fumes would rise and settle at the ceiling, forcing occupants to crouch in order to breathe. The fumes also created a new, worse problem: It drove out the giant centipedes that lived in the nooks and crannies of the ceiling and walls, which began dropping down on the soldiers as they tried to fall asleep. Joe Prince, to avoid fuel fumes, used pieces of cardboard soaked with melted wax and rolled up inside empty C-ration cans for night-burning lamps that worked very well. Al Groller reported that in the bunkers at Dong Ha Mountain, they burned the wax that the artillery shells were packed in to keep the rats away. When that sputtered out, he was forced to just cover his head with a poncho liner and let them run all over him. Al also once had to kill a pit viper found right outside his bunker door. Larry Carr remembered how some soldiers had taken empty artillery crates and filled them with dirt, using them to form a bunker within the bunker, big enough for two or three cots to fit inside. The rats would burrow tunnels right through the crates anyway, and Larry could hear them running back and forth all night. "Sometimes one would scoot across your legs, chest, or head and scare the living hell out of you! One guy got bit on the nose and had to get shots," he said.[16] Larry would just roll himself into a ball inside his poncho liner too.

A veteran who calls himself Marcus Tiberius reported that the seemingly indestructible rats at Con Thien chewed their way into six large cans of rat poison—"pink, sawdust-looking stuff"—eating it all and then sitting around looking "high."[17] He designed a trap by placing his .45 pistol in a vise with a string attached to the trigger, which was baited with C-ration caraway seed cheese spread. When Bill Dodge woke up one night to find a staring rat only six inches away from his face, he started to design his own booby traps, setting cheese-baited trip wire and blasting cap ambushes on the bunker rafters. He also replaced the slugs in M16 rounds with large pieces of bar soap or grease pencil, enabling Bill to blast away at the rats at night, "like a cool carnival shooting gallery," although he said the makeshift rounds wouldn't kill them and "you better be wearing ear plugs."[18] Tired of dealing with the nightmare bunkers full of rats and centipedes, he decided to take his chances and sleep outside on top of one of the perimeter sandbag bunkers. He changed his mind when the biggest scorpion he had ever seen walked up onto his chest. There was no escape from this particular hell.

These stories of rats in Vietnam are actually mild compared with the experiences of soldiers on both sides of the lines during World War I. The piles of corpses and discarded food scraps that littered their trenches attracted swarming masses of huge rats. They became so bold that they would steal food from the pockets of sleeping men and would eat alive any wounded soldiers who couldn't defend themselves. One British officer described hearing a scuffling in the night and shining his light to find two rats on his bed fighting over possession of a severed hand. Multiple rats would always be on dead bodies, going for the eyes first and burrowing their way into the corpse. Another soldier described, "I saw some rats running from under the dead men's greatcoats, enormous rats, fat with human flesh. My heart pounded as we edged toward one of the bodies. His helmet had rolled off. The man displayed a grimacing face, stripped of flesh; the skull bare, the eyes devoured and from the yawning mouth leapt a rat."[19]

A Cacophony of Hell

Most people know the horror story created for the 900 floating survivors of the Japanese submarine attack on the USS *Indianapolis* on July 28, 1945. Immortalized by a powerful scene in the 1975 film *Jaws*, the dwindling group of sailors would endure four days of dehydration, exposure, hunger, and deadly mass shark attacks before the surviving 317 were finally pulled out of the seawater. Fewer people are aware of a similar nightmare involving a very different predator that happened to the Japanese in the saltwater mangrove swamps of Ramree Island a few months earlier in February 1945.

The Imperial Japanese Army had captured the island, which lies just off the coast of the country of Myanmar, formerly Burma, in the Bay of Bengal, from the British navy in 1942. In late January 1945, the Limeys came back. Needing to establish an airfield supply point for troops operating on the mainland of Burma, British and Indian forces were dropped on the beach of the muddy landmass, tasked with a do-or-die mission dubbed Operation Matador. The primitive island had no harbor. "The navy said they didn't know how we would get off the island, so it was a case of get rid of the [Japanese] or be taken prisoner," remembered artilleryman Robert Duff.[20] Caught off-guard, the initial fierce resistance of the Japanese beach defense faded away when their main position at Ramree Town fell to the bloodied invaders on February 8. Of the original 1,200 to 1,500 Japanese, around 900 defenders refused to dishonor themselves by surrendering, instead attempting to unite with another battalion of the Imperial Army across the island. The route to get there went directly through 10 miles (16 km) of mangrove swamp forest. The British troops chose not to pursue, and instead encircled the impenetrable swamp, used loudspeakers to continue to offer surrender, and waited on any survivors to emerge.

The acres of thick forest lacked any solid ground and were a mass of deep, slimy black mud. Offering no fresh water to drink, the Pacific hellhole was a breeding ground for tropical diseases, swarms of mosquitoes, scorpions, biting flies, venomous spiders, and deadly snakes. Worse than all these terrors put together was a waiting predator that thrived in the coastal swamp habitat—the monstrous saltwater crocodile. Prehistoric holdovers, the world's largest reptilian killer (*Crocodylus porosus*) can grow over 23 feet long and weigh more than 2,000 pounds, easily able to kill and devour a human adult in minutes. "Salties" will eat prey dead or alive, swallowing their catch whole whenever possible, and have the strongest bite pressure of any animal in the world. Ramree Island is their natural habitat, and humans who have risked venturing into crocodile territories have a long history of being taken, seen as nothing more than taller, easy meals. British soldiers in India and Burma had already learned by brutal experience to protect themselves from ambushes during movements across inland freshwater canals and waterways. "When we swam in . . . small tributaries . . . a soldier or one of your group stood by with a rifle with .303 ammunition in case of attack by a small type of crocodile called a mugger," recalled Burma campaign veteran Lieutenant Colonel William Albert Weightman, in a 1990 interview with the Imperial War Museum in London.[21]

Dripping the scent of blood and sweat into the fetid water, the wounded and sick were the first victims, picked off one by one as they entered the mangrove at sunset. Monsters appeared seemingly out of nowhere, dragging the Japanese under the water to be drowned and then eaten. Veteran and Canadian naturalist Bruce Stanley Wright, in his 1962 book, *Wildlife Sketches Near and Far*, provides a bloodcurdling description of what he witnessed next. "That night [of February 19, 1945] was the most horrible that any member of the M.L. [motor launch] crews ever experienced. The crocodiles, alerted by the din of warfare and smell of blood, gathered among the mangroves, lying with their eyes above the water, watchfully alert for their next meal. With the ebb of the tide, the crocodiles moved in on the dead, wounded, and uninjured men who had become mired in the mud."[22] Of the approximately 900 Japanese who entered the swamp, around half are believed to have slipped out going east by using *chaungs* (small streams) and escaped to the mainland, and the other 450 . . . well, they simply disappeared.

Wright continues: "The scattered rifle shots in the pitch black swamp punctured by the screams of the wounded men crushed in the jaws of huge reptiles, and the blurred worrying sound of spinning crocodiles made a cacophony of hell that has rarely been duplicated on Earth. At dawn, the vultures arrived to clean up what the crocodiles had left."[23] The giant reptiles had the feast of their lives, attacking in frenzied feeding masses, turning the stagnant pools of swamp water crimson red for weeks afterward. Aside from the croc attacks, dehydration from being forced to drink brackish water and a lack of food made it virtually impossible for any Japanese to have survived there for long. Only 20 of them actually did, emerging traumatized and stumbling into the British perimeter that surrounded the slaughter grounds by the end of the conflict on February 22. The incident is included in the Guinness Book of World Records as having the highest number of fatalities ever recorded in a crocodile attack.[24] There are an estimated 1,000 deadly crocodile attacks every year worldwide, with the majority being Nile crocodiles in Africa and salties in Asia and Australia.[25]

DESERTS OF DEATH

The dry deserts of the Middle East and the rugged mountains of Central Asia as theaters of war contrast sharply with the rain-soaked jungles of Southeast Asia. Yet one shared characteristic of all three is the prevalence of natural dangers and poisonous creatures—hostile, heavily armed, and always ready to crawl inside available bedding or boots.

The arid landscape surrounding Kandahar airbase in southern Afghanistan is home to many hidden enemies besides the Taliban, including ants, spiders, scorpions, millipedes, centipedes, and snakes. Specialist Michael Kubik, a base pest controller, was tasked with keeping troops safe from the multitude of natural hazards there. While some of the tents at the airbase had wooden floors, others were provided only with canvas groundsheets that pests could easily crawl in. "The biggest threat now is that soldiers are digging foxholes, they're digging fighting positions, and they're not realizing how close they are coming to some of these creatures like snakes and scorpions. These are nocturnal creatures and when they go into their foxholes, they may have company, and they may not realize that until it's too late," he explained.[26] And while most bites or stings are just extremely painful, there's always the chance of an allergic reaction causing death.

The most lethal creature in the area is the *Echis*, also known as the carpet or saw-scaled viper. These vipers have a characteristic threat display called stridulation, where they rub sections of their body together to produce a "sizzling" warning sound, resembling water on a hot plate. Highly aggressive and striking to bite, they can be as small as 12 inches (30 cm) long. Medics at Kandahar are supplied with the specific antivenin used to treat the highly lethal toxin of this species that is held responsible for the most snakebite cases and deaths in the world.

Scorpion species thrive in the dry desert landscape of the Middle East. Throughout the wars in Afghanistan and Iraq, scorpion sting rates among troops remained high. Soldiers returning from both areas self-reported spider and scorpion stings equaling 46.1 out of only 10,000, and were largely unaware of these ever-present threats in the region before deployment.[27] During the Persian Gulf War of 1990–1991, 2,400 Americans out of 100,000 stationed in Saudi Arabia suffered scorpion stings. As an example of how local knowledge of these creatures helps prevent being struck, in the neighboring nation of Oman, only an average of 16 out of 100,000 residents are stung yearly.[28]

Antivenins that counter the most lethal indigenous scorpion stings are relatively rare in the Middle East. The fat-tailed scorpion, of the genus *Androctonus*, is one of the most dangerous scorpion species in the world. The common name is derived from its distinctly fat metasoma, or tail, while the Latin name originates from Greek and means "man killer." This four-inch (10 cm) monster's venom contains powerful neurotoxins and is especially potent, known to cause several human deaths each year. Injections from its stingers can also result in shock, respiratory failure, pulmonary edema, or coma.

Back in 198 BCE, the Atrenians of the Mesopotamian city-state of Hatra (near Mosul in modern Iraq) were under siege by the powerful Roman army. If you've ever watched *The Exorcist*, the ruins being excavated at the beginning of the film is Hatra. The walls of the city still stand today, but due to the Islamic State of Iraq and the Levant's (ISIL) systematic destruction of all the graven images of the ancient world, it's not nearly as impressive as it once was. The besieged defenders utilized a very unique weapon against the Romans under their walls, filling hundreds of clay pots with scorpions and hurling them down to shatter on the attackers. These scorpion grenades were both physically and psychologically effective, as recorded by the scribe Herodian of Syria: "The insects fell into the Romans' eyes and on all the unprotected parts of their bodies, digging in before they were noticed, they bit and stung the soldiers," he wrote.[29] This tactic certainly contributed to the Romans lifting the siege and packing up to go home. Folklore credits the Atrenians with having perfected a method of handling the scorpions without getting stung by spitting on their tails, but it is more logical that they just bred them right in the jars.

Giant camel spiders have become the subject of much myth and lore, originally told by servicemen who had deployed during the Persian Gulf War and continuing throughout the wars in Afghanistan and Iraq that began in 2001. More forced-perspective photography, like the giant centipedes in Vietnam, quickly made these creatures an internet sensation. New arrivals in-country were warned about their mythic evil and told harrowing stories about how the creatures aggressively sought out soldiers to bite in the night. As a kind of hazing and bonding ritual, camel spider stories quickly became incorporated into soldiers' belief systems and part of a common military worldview. They could grow as large as dinner plates, make screaming sounds, chase you at speeds of 25 miles per hour, leap several feet into the air, and latch onto the stomachs of camels to eat their way through and lay their eggs inside. Their venom was said to contain a powerful anesthetic, allowing them to unknowingly gnaw away chunks of flesh from sleeping soldiers through the desert nights. All of these claims are false.[30]

Although they belong to the same class as spiders (Arachnida), camel spiders are actually a type of arthropod from the order known as Solifugae, which in Latin means "those that flee from the sun."[31] Solifugae, neither a true spider nor a scorpion, contains over 1,000 described species. During World War I and II, British troops stationed in Egypt and Libya would stage fights between captive scorpions and "jerrymanders," as they called them, and place bets on the outcome. In southern Africa, they are known by a host of names, including red Romans, haarskeerders ("hair cutters"), and baardskeerders ("beard cutters")—relating to another myth that they used their formidable jaws to clip hair from humans and animals to line their subterranean nests with. They actually use their powerful jaws to feed on small prey such as other arthropods, lizards, snakes, mice, and birds, using speed and stealth to seize a victim and then turn it into pulp by chopping or sawing the bodies. Being nonvenomous, they use digestive fluids to liquefy the flesh, making it easier to suck up the remains. Although they appear to have five pairs of legs, only the hind four pairs actually are, with the front pair usually held aloft and not touching the ground. These are called pedipalps and function partly as sense organs similar to insects' antennae, detecting obstacles and prey. The spiders generally hide during the day and shun the sun—hence their Latin name—coming out to hunt at night.

Camel spiders are common throughout the Middle East and have been found often hiding in sleeping bags and equipment of American servicemen. Normally fairly passive, they can become vicious when provoked, and bites can penetrate human skin, be very painful, and be prone to terrible infection. They produce no venom or anesthetic. By rubbing their jaws together, camel spiders can produce a hissing sound (not a scream) as a defensive behavior. Despite the legends and trick photography, camel spiders usually only have about a 5- or 6-inch (12–15 cm) leg span, with a few outliers reported being as large as 10 inches long. Although still exceptionally quick compared to other arthropods, they can only run about 10 miles per hour (16 km/h) and don't do any significant jumping. Lacking the book lungs of most arachnids, a well-developed tracheal system that inhales and exhales large amounts of air allows them to move faster than most other insects.

One trait often recounted in the legends is indeed true—they will chase you in the daylight—but the real reason is because they are following your shadow, trying to stay in the shade you create and escape the hot sun. If the person stands still, the camel spider will stop moving too, enjoying the cooler ground. The creature supposedly got its name because they can often be seen gathered under camels. Again, they do this for the shade the animals provide, not to eat through their stomachs. Finally, at night they will often run toward lights because they are attracted to them.

Because of their unfamiliar appearance and rapid movements, encountering any Solifugae can be an extremely frightening experience.

The danger of animal bites in the war zone was highlighted in 2011, when the only rabies death in America was a 24-year-old army specialist named Kevin Shumaker, eight months after getting bitten by a stray dog in Afghanistan.[32] He died in a hospital after returning to Fort Drum, New York. After news of his death spread, the number of reported past attacks rose, showing that the number of animal bites among troops had been undercounted. "We felt like this was an unrecognized risk," said Captain Luke Mease, a medical investigator for the U.S. Army.[33] Between the start of hostilities in Afghanistan in 2001 through 2011, 643 animal bites had been recorded—half from dogs; the rest were cat, rat, and monkey attacks. Afghan National Security Forces, civilians, and American troops often adopted monkeys for pets and unit mascots. The most common monkey bites were from the rhesus macaque (*Macaca mulatta*) species. Captain Mease continued, "Bites from macaques can cause serious infections. Monkey bites can spread rabies, tetanus, or Herpes B virus to humans." Because of regulations prohibiting deployed U.S. servicemen from keeping pet animals, the bites are often not reported in order to protect the pet. "In talking to people overseas, my experience is that they are often protecting the mascot. The human-animal bond is a very strong thing," Mease reported. Field medics are often unprepared to handle these types of injuries.

Many varieties of wild mammals inhabit Afghanistan, roaming the mountains and foothills, including wolves, foxes, striped hyenas, and jackals. Gazelles, wild dogs, and big cats are widespread. Accounts of American patrols being harassed by these creatures abound, and an Afghan soldier was reportedly killed by an elusive and endangered snow leopard. Iraq also has its share of dangerous animals. In 2017, three Islamic State militants were mauled to death (and another five injured) by a pack of stampeding wild boars in northern Iraq. While setting up to ambush a band of local Ubaid tribesmen on the edge of a field about 50 miles (80 km) southwest of Kirkuk, they were overwhelmed. "It is likely their movement disturbed a herd of wild pigs, which inhabit the area as well as nearby cornfields. The area is dense with reeds, which are good for hiding in," said Sheikh Anwar al-Assi, chief of the tribesmen and leader of anti-ISIS forces.[34] It seems karma was at play, as the incident occurred after the Islamic State fighters had mass-executed 25 people for trying to escape from the town of Hawija.

In the chaotic and confusing days immediately following the collapse of Saddam Hussein's regime in Iraq, the hundreds of animals in the Baghdad Zoo were either stolen or let loose by looters. Only the big cats—seven lions and two tigers—were left untouched, obviously too intimidating for the robbers to approach. Going unfed for more than 10 days and desperate, one lion and three lionesses clawed their way out of their pen through a crumbling wall. Two of them charged at American soldiers of the 3rd Infantry Division, and all four big cats were shot dead. The zoo was then occupied by U.S. forces and protected by four APCs, allowing anxious zoo staff to return and begin caring for and feeding the few remaining animals. This included Mandor the Siberian tiger, which belonged to Saddam's oldest son, Uday, and a lioness named Sudqa. Baghdad residents returned two hybrid wild dogs, and there were also two brown bears, left out of their cages by looters, that wandered back to the zoo on their own. Soldiers nicknamed them Boo Boo and Alfred. Sergeant Matthew Oliver of the 3rd Infantry remarked, "Boo Boo is half blind and was damn near half dead when she came back."[35] The Kuwait government donated the meat to continue feeding them.

One of the two surviving tigers at the zoo later became a victim to a group of disgraceful and ignorant U.S. soldiers. The off-duty Americans were spotted by a night watchman as they arrived in military vehicles, casually dressed and drinking alcohol. At some point, one of them entered the first cage intended for zookeepers and pressed up against the inner cage of the tiger enclosure. The zoo's manager, Adil Salman Musa, explained, "Someone was trying to feed the tigers. The tiger bit his finger off and clawed his arm. So his colleague took a gun and shot the tiger."[36] U.S. officials investigated the incident, and hopefully the responsible soldiers were punished. A similar incident had happened in the early 1990s at the Kabul Zoo in Afghanistan, involving a young Afghan fighter. Attempting to show off to his friends, the man entered the cage of a lion named Marjan. The giant cat pounced and easily bit his arm off, resulting in his death later at a hospital. A friend of the dead man returned to the zoo seeking revenge and threw a grenade at poor Marjan, which tore into its legs and blew off one side of its muzzle, blinding the lion in the left eye. Marjan survived the attack, finally dying of old age at 45 years old in late 2001.

ANIMAL ASSAULT CORPS

Exotic animal attacks on soldiers seem to be more common worldwide than most people are aware of. An Australian Special Air Service (SAS) lance corporal, Paul Harold Denehey, was attacked and mortally wounded by a wild elephant on June 6, 1965.[37] He was part of a four-man patrol from the 1 Squadron SAS Regiment conducting reconnaissance in north Borneo along the Sabah border during the confrontation that stemmed from Indonesia's opposition to the creation of the Federation of Malaysia. The special forces unit was part of the British Commonwealth's Operation Claret, a cross-border operation tasked with stopping Indonesian infiltration into Malaysia. The rogue elephant apparently attacked without warning, violently goring the corporal while he was alone in the jungle, but not killing him outright. No elephant populations were known in that region of the island until this tragic event, which required medic Lance Corporal Bloomfield being left for three days with the injured soldier while the rest of the SAS patrol sought help. Unable to be reached in the remote inland mountains, he was the first ever fatality of the Australian SAS Regiment.

A teenage soldier, Private Stuart Edgar, was conducting training exercises with the 3rd Battalion, Royal Regiment in Kenya in October 2008. The legendary light infantry unit known as the Black Watch was preparing for an upcoming deployment to Afghanistan. He and his mates were pausing to take photographs of a herd of wild elephants when a gigantic male charged them. As the men started to run away, Edgar tripped and fell. "I thought I was going to die. All I could see was this huge, terrifying shape bearing down on me as it struck me again and again," he said.[38] The rampaging bull elephant kicked him around, battered him with his trunk, and tore at him with his lethal tusks. Possibly saving him from death, the sharp tip of one tusk was broken off and missing from some earlier incident in the pachyderm's life. The rucksack he was wearing also helped protect his body. The beast finally broke contact, turning and wandering off into the bush. Luckily, Private Edgar only suffered some lacerations, bruising, and muscle damage. Local tribesmen revealed to the unit that three men had been killed by the elephant in the past six months.

Another British soldier in Africa, Private Steven Wishart, survived a vicious attack in 2011 by something he never saw during a dark night in the field. He had been in-country for three weeks, conducting exercises at the British Army's Training Unit Kenya, and was pulled awake and bitten by something with powerful jaws. "Only one person saw it, and it wasn't Steven, who only felt it," remarked Major Peter Starkey, a medical officer with the Royal Gurkha Rifles (RGR) Regiment in Nairobi.[39] He treated the Scotsman for rabies and other possibly transmitted diseases. "Given the wildlife in the area, a hyena is most likely. The punctures indicate it's a canine," he continued. One other soldier witnessed the attack and was able to frighten the beast away by shining a light in its face, but was unable to identify it. "[It] made me think about where I sleep and to be more aware of what is out there," Private Wishart commented.

It seems the African continent has always provided unexpected enemies for the Limeys. Back in World War I, the Battle of Tanga—also known as the Battle of the Bees—was an unsuccessful attack by the British Indian Expeditionary Force to capture German East Africa (present-day Tanzania). It was the first major event of the war there and saw the British defeated by a significantly smaller force of German askaris (native soldiers) and colonial volunteers. While skirmishing amid the coconut and palm oil plantations surrounding the town of Tanga, the 98th Infantry Regiment of the British Indian Army were attacked by swarms of angry bees and broke apart, causing the assault to fail. The bees also attacked the Germans—hence the battle's name. British propaganda claimed the bee attack was a fiendish plot by the Germans, who were said to have used hidden trip wires to disturb and anger the hives.[40]

Moving across the ocean to Guantanamo Bay, Cuba, American soldier James Alexander-Rodriguez related a somewhat humorous tale, although maybe not so much to him at the time. Stationed there in 1965, he was on overnight guard duty at one of the gates, checking credentials of anyone entering the base. Provided with only a nightstick and no radio, his only line of communication to base security headquarters was an EE-8 field telephone in the guard shack. Standing outside in the humid air, he noticed a single black cat the size of a dog suddenly appear from out of the darkness. The scruffy feline sat down and started making some hellish yowls. Slowly, more than a dozen more feral cats answered its call, moving in on James together. Making shushing noises to try to scare them away, he started to retreat to the shack and drew his only weapon. As he turned toward the door, he found his path to safety blocked by another feline, which was aggressively hissing and snarling. The circle grew tighter. "Instantly I bolted for a chair leaning against the shack, jumped and clambered to the roof waving the stick in the air, yelling, cursing, and barking like an anxious dog," James said.[41] His relief finally arrived a tense hour later, the headlights of the Jeep finally scattering the gang of diabolical beasts into the night.

Animal-borne bomb attacks involve using animals as delivery systems for explosives. Strapped to pack animals like horses, mules, or donkeys, the blast can be set off in a crowd of people for devastating effect. One of the first attempts to do this occurred during the 1862 New Mexico Campaign of the American Civil War. A Confederate force approached a ford on the Rio Grande at Valverde, six miles north of Fort Craig, with the mission of cutting off Union communications to its headquarters at Santa Fe. Around midnight on February 21, federal Captain James Craydon attempted to blow up rebel picket posts by sending two mules loaded with fused gunpowder barrels into their lines. The faithful old army mules instead wandered back, blowing themselves to pieces in the Union camp. Although the only casualties were the poor mules, the explosions did cause the nearby herd of Confederate beef cattle and horses to stampede away, depriving the rebels of the last of their dwindling meat and transportation.

During the Iraqi insurgency following the U.S. occupation that began in 2003, the use of Improvised Explosive Devices (IEDs) hidden inside dead animal carcasses was a common tactic. Graduating to the use of live animals, in 2004 a donkey was loaded with explosives and set off toward a

U.S. checkpoint in Ramadi.[42] Thankfully, it exploded before getting close enough to injure or kill anyone. This incident, along with several more involving dogs in 2005, was successful at creating a new fear during the war. Donkeys became the preferred delivery platform, as they were often loaded down with sacks and did not look suspicious when carrying large amounts of explosives. The Taliban in Afghanistan used the same tactic, strapping an IED device to a donkey in 2009 and sending it toward a camp of the British armed forces in Helmand Province. In April 2013, a bomb attached to a donkey blew up in front of a police security post in Kabul, killing a policeman and injuring three civilians.[43]

During World War II, the United States and the Soviet Union explored plenty of weird war strategies involving animals, actions that today would have anti-cruelty groups up in arms. Between 1941 and 1943, anti-tank dogs were trained and used by the Russians against German tanks. Initially the dogs were trained to drop off a timer-detonated bomb and retreat, but this routine was replaced by an impact-detonation procedure that killed the poor dog in the process. The U.S. military started training anti-tank dogs in 1943 in the same way the Soviets used them, but problems encountered during training thankfully led to the program quickly being eliminated. The Soviet dogs were loaded with a 22- to 26-pound (10–12-kg) mine carried in two canvas pouches with a safety pin that was pulled out right before their deployment. A wooden lever extended out of the pouches, and when the dog dove under a tank as they were trained, the lever struck the bottom and detonated the charge.

The first group of 30 anti-armor dogs arrived at the front line in 1941, with only four managing to detonate their bombs near German tanks.[44] Six canines exploded upon returning to the Soviet trenches, killing and injuring their own soldiers. The Nazis considered this Red Army tactic both desperate and inefficient. They produced a propaganda campaign against the Soviets, saying that their soldiers refused to fight and sent their dogs instead. Several documented cases of success countered the Nazis' opinion, including at the front near Hlukhiv in Ukraine, where 6 dogs damaged 5 German tanks. Near the Stalingrad airport, anti-tank dogs destroyed 13 tanks, and 16 dogs disabled 12 German tanks at the Battle of Kursk.[45]

U.S. President Roosevelt approved the development of a bizarre experimental weapon in 1942, and the military spent over $2 million trying to get it to work. The "bat bomb" was designed to start thousands of fires in cities across Japan and involved housing 1,000 bats inside a casing that could be dropped from warplanes. A tiny incendiary device was attached to each chiropteran, with the idea that when released they would contribute to the American war effort by seeking wooden Japanese homes and buildings to roost in and start fires. More than 6,000 bats were used in the bomb tests, with most of them plunging straight to the ground or just flying away.[46] Some actually did their job, setting fires in a mock Japanese village, a U.S. Army hangar, and a general's car. Not too surprisingly, the program was abandoned and forgotten.

Another off-the-wall World War II program was renowned American psychologist/behaviorist B. F. Skinner's plan to develop a pigeon-guided missile system that would be effective against surface ships.[47] The size of the primitive automatic guidance systems available at the time made them impractical to use. The ingenious "Project Pigeon" was developed to answer the need for a simple and effective guidance system. An unpowered airframe (basically a small glider with wings and a tail surface) had an explosive warhead section in the center and a guidance section in the nose cone. Within the nose cone were three separate compartments, each containing a pigeon that would act as pilots of the missile and had been trained by operant conditioning to recognize the target. Lenses projected an image of distant objects onto a hinged screen in front of each bird, so that when its missile was launched from an aircraft within sight of an enemy ship, an image of the ship would appear there. The screen was mounted on pivots and fitted with sensors that measured any angular movement. Each time the birds pecked at the recognized image, seeds would be dispersed, and as long as the target remained in the center of the screen, it would not move. If the bomb did begin to move off-track, the image would too, and the pecks made to follow it would be detected by sensors that sent signals to the control surfaces. The bomb would then be steered in the direction the screen had moved, effectively allowing the pigeons to correct deviations and steer the bomb to the target.

Despite an effective demonstration, the project was considered impractical and eccentric, and it was abandoned in 1944. Skinner complained, "Our problem was no one would take us seriously." Project Pigeon was resurrected by the U.S. Navy in 1948 as "Project Orcon"—meaning "organic control"—but was canceled again in 1953, as the reliability of electronic guidance systems was established.

Cetaceans and pinnipeds, including bottlenose dolphins, seals, sea lions, and beluga whales, have all been trained for various military uses. U.S. and Soviet forces have both trained and employed marine mammals to rescue swimmers, guard navy ships against enemy divers, locate and flag mines, and aid in locating and recovering classified equipment lost on the deep seabed. The U.S. Navy Marine Mammal Training Program began in 1960, and during the Vietnam War five dolphins were deployed to Cam Ranh Bay to perform underwater surveillance and guard boats and submarines from enemy swimmers.[48] During the late 1980s, six dolphins were used in the Persian Gulf, patrolling the harbor in Bahrain to protect U.S. flagships from saboteurs and mines. Rumors later circulated about a "swimmer nullification program" in which dolphins were being trained to attack and kill enemy divers. Richard L. Trout, a former civilian mammal trainer for the U.S. Navy, told the *New York Times* in 1990 that navy dolphins "were learning to kill enemy divers."[49] Brandon Webb, an ex–Navy SEAL, described a kill mechanism in his memoir where mounted hypodermic needles full of compressed gas were placed over the dolphin's nose.[50] The dolphins were trained to head-butt enemy swimmers and inject the needles, causing a fatal embolism. The military denies such a program ever existed and claims that training dolphins to fight or kill humans is impossible—which may indicate that they did indeed try. Today, the San Diego–based Marine Mammal Program musters about 75 dolphins and 30 sea lions, just half of its peak troop strength during the Cold War.

In 1965, the Soviet Navy responded by opening its own marine life program on the Black Sea, based near Sevastopol on the Crimean Peninsula. A second center on the Arctic Ocean, the Murmansk Marine Biological Institute, was opened in 1984. Similar to the United States, only object retrieval and reconnaissance was reported to be the purpose of the

Soviet program. However, also similar, former Russian dolphin instructors have repeatedly stated that "combat dolphins" were trained for lethal attacks. Scientist Gennady Matishov said, "Their main role is to protect the waters of the fleet's principal base against underwater saboteurs. For instance, the bottlenose dolphins graze at the entrance of the bay and, on detecting an intruder, immediately signal to an operator at a coastal surveillance point. After that, in response to the relevant command, they're capable of killing an enemy on their own with a special dolphin muzzle with a spike."[51] Russia also allegedly trained kamikaze dolphins to deposit limpet mines onto enemy submarines. A former handler, Colonel Victor Baranets, told the BBC that they were trained to distinguish the difference between the sounds of Soviet and American submarines.[52] When the Soviet Union dissolved in 1991, the Crimea-based combat dolphin program passed to Ukraine. In 2001 the program's manager sold the animals to Iran, claiming he lacked the finances to give them proper care.[53] Twenty-six marine mammals were transported by cargo plane to Iran, but it's unknown whether that country was seeking a military use for them. Official statements claim they were acquired for civilian enjoyment and that all reside at the Kish Island Dolphin Park, a huge recreational and tourist complex located off the southern coast of Iran. In 2012, Ukraine reopened its combat dolphin program, training 10 new dolphins to attack intruders with "special knives or pistols fixed to their heads." Two years later, the program was acquired by Russian forces when they seized the Crimean Peninsula. Their media has reported on the new dolphin training program and confirmed its application for lethal attacks.

It's one thing to train and use animals in military operations, but what about one that actually earned rank, was paid, and survived combat alongside his fellow soldiers? Wojtek (meaning "happy warrior" and pronounced VOY-tek) was a male Syrian brown bear (*Ursus arctos syriacus*) purchased as a young cub by Polish II Corps soldiers, who had been evacuated from the Soviet Union in 1942.[54] While at a railway station in Iran, the Poles encountered a young boy selling the cub, who said its mother had been shot by hunters. Adopted by the men of the 22nd Artillery Supply Company, he was raised drinking condensed milk from empty vodka bottles. Just like any other grunt, Wojtek enjoyed drinking coffee in the mornings, smoking (or eating) cigarettes, and drinking copious amounts of beer when off-duty. He would sleep with the other soldiers (keeping them warm on cold nights), enjoyed wrestling with them, learned how to salute when greeted, and could even march alongside them on his hind legs. With the 22nd Company, he moved throughout the Middle East, serving in Iraq, Syria, Palestine, and Egypt. From there, the Polish II Corps was deployed to fight alongside the British 8th Army in the Italian campaign. British regulations on the transport ship outlawed mascot and pet animals. To circumvent this problem, the bruin was officially drafted into the Polish Army as a private and rostered with the 22nd Artillery Supply Company. His pay was used to provide for his rations.

During the bloody 1944 Battle of Monte Cassino, Wojtek earned his combat stripes, being promoted to corporal after moving crates of ammunition while under fire. He carried boxes that would have required four men, even having learned to stack them onto trucks or in piles. In recognition of Wojtek's popularity, a new unit patch of a bear carrying an artillery shell was adopted by the 22nd Company. He became a celebrity with visiting Allied generals and statesmen. At the end of the war in 1945, the Poles were stationed in Berwickshire, Scotland, where Wojtek was mustered out of the army. He lived out the rest of his life at the Edinburgh Zoo. Maintaining his celebrity status, the old veteran bruin was a frequent guest on a BBC children's television program called *Blue Peter*. Wojtek passed away in December 1963 at the age of 21, weighing nearly 1,100 pounds (500 kg) and standing over 5.9 feet (1.8 meters) tall. He is immortalized in several statues and sculptures around the world.

THE GREAT EMU INSURGENCY

The island continent of Australia was the setting for one of the most bizarre episodes in military history, and perhaps the only time animals were able to out-strategize humans on a mass scale—the Great Emu War of 1932.

Returning home after serving in World War I, over 5,000 Australian veterans took advantage of a new government program offering them plots of land in agriculturally marginal areas in the west. They were to convert the undeveloped tracts into working farms for growing wheat or breeding sheep, by clearing the land and supplying water. Emus (*Dromaius novaehollandiae*) were an indigenous species already living there, and found these newly cultivated lands to be a perfect habitat. Brown, soft-feathered, flightless birds with long necks and powerful legs, this relative of the ostrich stands around 6 feet (1.8 meters) tall and averages between 69 and 82 pounds (31.5–37 kg). Emus can travel great distances and sprint at an impressive 31 miles per hour (50 km/h). The giant birds regularly migrated through Western Australia after their breeding season, heading to the coast from inland regions. October 1932 saw an influx of at least 20,000 emus massing about 200 miles (322 km) east of Perth in the Wheatbelt region around Chandler and Walgoolan. Like Native American Comanche warriors out of the wasteland, the birds began raiding the remote farms, flattening fields of crops and eating the wheat down to stubs. They used their legs—among the strongest in the animal world—to tear down fencing, leaving large gaps where other vermin could access the remaining crops. Using their rifle training, the veterans shot thousands of emus, but could not reduce the population significantly, or afford the ammunition required.

A delegation was sent to meet with the Minister of Defense, Sir George Pearce. Seeing an opportunity to demonstrate that the distrusted government (during a time when a Western Australia secession movement was brewing) was willing to help struggling veteran farmers, Pearce agreed to deploy the military and two of their Lewis machine guns along with 10,000 rounds. If nothing else, it would be great target practice for the bored troops.

The war commenced on November 2, 1932, under the command of Major G. P. W. Meredith of the 7th Heavy Battery of the Royal Australian Artillery. Having been delayed by a period of rainfall that caused the emus to disperse over a wide area, his immediate objective was to collect 100 emu scalps . . . er, skins . . . to provide feather plumes for the hats of Australian light horsemen. Fifty birds had been spotted near the town of Campion, and the soldiers moved in formation to get behind them. Using their speed to stay out of range, the birds used superior guerilla tactics and scattered into small groups, minimizing their casualties to only about a dozen killed in this first engagement. Two days later the

Australians set up in a concealed ambush near a local dam and observed a large force of 1,000 emus approach unaware. Waiting until they were in point-blank range, the machine gun suddenly erupted—and promptly jammed only seconds later. A few dead birds littered the ground, but the force scattered to the winds and none were seen the rest of the day.

By November 5, now the fourth frustrating day of the campaign, one of the soldiers remarked, "Each mob has its leader, always an enormous black-plumed bird standing fully six feet high, who keeps watch while his fellows busy themselves with the wheat. At the first suspicious sign, he gives the signal, and dozens of heads stretch up out of the crop. A few birds will take flight, starting a headlong stampede for the scrub, the leader always remaining until his followers have reached safety."[55]

Searching for solutions, Major Meredith ordered a Lewis gun to be mounted on an army truck, but the emus could outrun the rough-riding vehicle. One of the only kills they did get became tangled up in the truck's steering when they ran over the corpse, causing the driver to veer off and destroy a length of some poor farmer's fence. By November 8, it was reported that 2,500 rounds of ammunition (25 percent of the allotment) had been expended with only around 200 emus having been killed in action. The Australian Army had suffered no casualties, except wounded pride. Following negative press coverage, the House of Representatives had to address the failing operation. When one politician jokingly asked if "a medal was to be struck for those taking part in this war," a representative from Western Australia responded that it should go to the emus, which "have won every round so far."[56]

Crestfallen, Pearce withdrew from the field on November 8. Commenting on the birds' uncanny ability to maneuver, even when badly wounded, he said, "If we had a military division with the bullet-carrying capacity of these birds it would face any army in the world. They can face machine guns with the invulnerability of tanks. They are like Zulus who even dum-dum bullets could not stop."[57] (Dum-dum bullets are slang for rounds that expand on impact.)

The emu raids on crops continued without interruption, and the farmers again asked for support, enlisting Western Australia's Lieutenant-Governor James Mitchell to petition for help. Five days after withdrawing, Major Meredith was ordered back, resuming the hunt on November 13 and collecting 40 kills. By December 2, the army was killing an average of 100 emus per week, but at a high cost in ammunition. At the official end of hostilities, declared on December 10, 1932, a final war report claimed 986 emus killed in action by 9,860 bullets—a rate of exactly 1 kill for every 10 rounds. An additional 2,500 wounded birds were believed to have eventually died of their injuries.

Farmers of the region would request military assistance again in 1934, 1943, and 1948—all denied, perhaps the fear of further defeat preventing any future operations. The bounty system that had been in place since 1923 honestly proved more effective, bringing in more than 57,000 birds over a six-month period in 1934. The use of exclusion barrier fencing from 1930 onward also helped the problem. In 1950 the issue was raised with the government once again, and the army responded by providing 500,000 rounds of .303 ammunition for the beleaguered farmers to use on their own.

In modern times, the emus are much less hated and are protected again. Unofficially considered the national bird of Australia, the gangly cassowary appears as a shield bearer on the nation's coat of arms along with the red kangaroo. The current total population hovers around 650,000 and is not endangered, outside of a few local populations affected by human encroachment.[58]

CHAPTER 3

Nazi Necronomicon, the Cannibal Corps, and Wandering Souls

TIME AND AGAIN, IT HAS BEEN PROVEN THAT THE GREATEST MONSTERS inhabiting this planet are our own kind. War can take an already twisted and disturbed mind and make it even worse, providing a once-in-a-lifetime setting where limits no longer exist and progressive atrocities can go unchecked and unpunished. Prolonged exposure to combat and death, combined with powerful feelings of desired revenge for fallen comrades, can be an alchemy for sadism. The supernatural and paranormal realm may seem frightening and mysterious, but human beings offer no mystery as to the level of violence and disturbingly evil acts we are capable of performing. When you have the knowledge that you have come into contact with a real monster, the memory stays with you forever.

While I was attending college in Pensacola, Florida, after my honorable discharge from active duty, the G.I. Bill was hardly even covering my beer and frozen soft pretzel diet. In addition to serving one weekend a month with the Alabama National Guard in Birmingham, I always had a part-time job to provide a livable income. While working as a salesman at an unfinished furniture store near campus, I encountered a very interesting customer who came in and purchased all of our largest oak bookcases, which stood nearly seven feet tall and together could have housed an extremely large library.

Intrigued, I struck up a conversation with the white-haired elderly gentleman and discovered he had a thick German accent. I inferred that he must have an incredible book collection, and he confirmed that indeed he did. Before too long, he also revealed that he was a native German and had actually served during World War II, later coming to America. I shared that in a documentary film class I was currently enrolled in, we were examining all the films of the controversial German director Leni Riefenstahl. She is known for having directed the Nazi-sponsored films *Triumph of the Will* (1935), showcasing the 1934 Nazi party rally in Nuremberg, and *Olympia* (1938), about the 1936 Summer Olympics in Berlin. Both are considered to be the most technically innovative and effective propaganda films ever made. Imagine my surprise when the well-dressed and distinguished man replied, "I am in her film. Around 40 minutes into *Triumph of the Will*, when Hitler is reviewing the Hitler Youth, I am one of the drummers. I was later in the Waffen-SS."

As a passionate military historian, I could hardly contain my excitement. I mean, here was a piece of living history, a former SS trooper, right in front of me and willing to talk about it. Yet another emotion lurked underneath my initial thrill—an immediate feeling of dread, disgust, and apprehension. I can usually separate a soldier from the actual war-starting politicians and bureaucracies that profess and enact hateful ideologies, as so many soldiers throughout history have been forced to serve for a variety of reasons and a lack of options. But I also knew what it meant to be a fanatical member of the Schutzstaffel (SS) during Hitler's reign of blood, the organization most responsible for the genocidal murders of the Holocaust. In the judgment of the Nuremberg trials, the SS was responsible for the majority of Nazi war crimes, and was declared a criminal organization by the International Military Tribunal in 1946. At a loss for words, I exclaimed, "Wow, that's incredible!" and awkwardly completed his order, having him select the color of finish he wanted on his bookcases and saying that I hoped we could talk more about it next time, while secretly hoping there wouldn't be one. The name on his invoice was "Hans Schmidt."

Time passed, and one afternoon a few weeks later I recognized him coming through the door. I could see he had some papers or magazines with him. He approached the counter, smiling, and we exchanged greetings. He inquired about the progress with his furniture and I provided an update, and then he set the papers down in front of me.

"I publish several German-American newsletters and magazines that I thought you might be interested in. Publications that tell the truth. You can have these and after you read them, if you want to discuss anything further, you are welcome to come to my home for dinner."

My eyes darted down, scanning the front pages of the documents, and quickly locked in on one hard-to-miss headline written in bold, block letters: "The Holocaust Never Happened—Truth of Global Conspiracy Revealed!" I was immediately thrust into the plot of Stephen King's 1982 novella (and 1998 film) *Apt Pupil* where a college student studying the Holocaust discovers that his neighbor is a death camp criminal hiding out in America. Hans was totally living up to all the stereotypes! I quickly explained to him that I believed he had misjudged my interest and intentions, and pushed the hateful pamphlets back across the counter. His congenial mood immediately shifted to a cold, hard stare of disgust. I saw the old Nazi in him with that hateful glare. He gathered up his papers and walked out without saying a word.

The couple times he came back, Hans would look past me, asking my co-worker questions and arranging delivery of his finished bookcases through him. I was thankful, as I was honestly uncomfortable in his presence now. I forgot about him and the incident until a short time later, in 1995, when I recognized his name in a headline spotted while browsing the *Pensacola News Journal*. Hans Schmidt, who was born on April 24, 1927, in Volklingen, Germany, had been arrested at the Frankfurt airport by German authorities on "incitement to hate" charges after copies of his newsletter *USA-Bericht* were discovered on August 9, 1995. I couldn't believe it!

Later research showed he was released on bail in January 1996, due to poor health. The sly old Nazi promptly fled Germany and returned to America to avoid further prosecution. It turns out he was the founder of the German-American National Political Action Committee (GAN-PAC) and the German-American Information and Education Association (GIEA), organizations dubbed "openly anti-Semitic" by the *New York Times* and "virulently anti-Semitic" by the Anti-Defamation League.

It seems Hans was well known for his promotion of white separatism, Nazism, anti-Semitism, and Holocaust denial—all of which I could personally verify. He had, in fact, been a member of the Hitler Youth before enlisting in 1943 with the Waffen-SS at the age of 16, serving as a corporal in the SS Division Leibstandarte.[1] Schmidt was wounded twice during combat in Hungary, Austria, and the Battle of the Bulge. He escaped Germany in 1947, arrived in the United States in 1949, and became a naturalized citizen in 1955 in Chicago. He may have come to the United States under the guise of being a refugee, as many former SS soldiers did, sometimes using forged documents. The experience of meeting him and later realizing who he actually was may have been the closest I've ever been to pure evil—and it happened in a furniture store because he was looking for bookcases. I still wonder what was in his library . . .

WAFFEN WITCH HUNT

In 2016, a massive collection of 13,000 books reportedly related to witchcraft and the occult was discovered in a depot belonging to the National Library of the Czech Republic in Prague.[2] Forgotten since the 1950s, the collection known as the "witch library" is believed to have been compiled at the behest of SS commander Heinrich Himmler. In 1935, he tasked a special unit called the H-Sonderkommando to search occupied countries for literature connected to the occult, sorcery, the supernatural, and witch-hunt trials. The "H" referred to *Hexe*, the German word for witch. The SS troops ravaged over 260 libraries, archives, and Freemason lodges across Europe, accumulating a compilation of books on witches and their persecution in medieval Germany. Himmler personally believed that the Catholic Church's Inquisition had been a conspiracy that attempted to eradicate an indigenous Aryan nature-based pagan religion called Volkisch. He also claimed that one of his own ancestors had been burned as a witch, hence his bizarre obsession.[3] Other researchers counter that the real reason the SS collected these books was because they believed the material posed a threat to Nazism, not because they believed in it themselves. It is a fact that the party banned all forms of expression that might question its ideology, and used censorship, seizure, and propaganda to suppress any opposing views.

Appointed Reichsführer-SS by Adolf Hitler in 1929, Himmler controlled the infamous Schutzstaffel for 16 years. Having always been interested in mysticism, astrology, and the occult, he combined these interests with his racist philosophy, looking for proof of Aryan and Nordic racial superiority from ancient times. He believed that the power of the old occult masters and the reemergence of the prehistoric pagan nature religion would help the Nazis rule the planet. He seems to have been influenced greatly by the witch-cult hypothesis presented by archaeologist Margaret Murray in her 1921 book, *The Witch-Cult in Western Europe*,[4] and further explored in her following publication, *The God of the Witches*.[5] Murray proposed that the witches persecuted in European history were actually followers of an old-world established religion with highly developed beliefs, rituals, and organization. She referred to the witches' deity as the Horned God, an entity that had been worshiped in Europe since the Paleolithic Age. Murray demonstrated that the Horned God was represented by Pan in Greece, Faunus in Rome, and Cernunnos in Gaul, and had been declared the Devil by Christian authorities. Esoteric Hitlerism was Himmler's new pseudo-Germanic neo-pagan religion, based on a cult created in his imagination. He directed his staff to begin planning a cultural framework designed to replace Christianity, with a new moral code that rejected humanitarianism.

This new SS esotericism included Germanic mysticism, an ancestor cult, worship of runes, and racial doctrines. SS members were expected to renounce their Christian faith, and Christmas was replaced with a solstice celebration and seasonal festivals. Church weddings were frowned upon in favor of a "marriage consecration" ceremony, called Eheweihen. Esoteric rituals and the awarding of symbolic regalia and insignia for milestones in SS troopers' careers were incorporated. Himmler's pseudo-religious rites and ceremonies took place near SS-dedicated monuments or in special SS-designated places. Aleister Crowley, the infamous English occultist and magician, recognized what was happening, saying, "His magical technique was indescribably admirable; he adopted the swastika, the Hammer of Thor, the distinctive dress, the slogan, the gestures, the greeting; he even imposed a Sacred Book upon the people."[6]

The "Great Beast," Crowley contributed his own footnotes to Weird War history, with claims that he was recruited by high-ranking British intelligence officer Maxwell Knight at the onset of World War II.[7] Knight was an eccentric who lived with a pet baboon and a bear, and he harbored a keen fascination for the occult sciences and their secret societies. He and another member of the United Kingdom's MI5, Ian Fleming (the creator of James Bond), are believed to have formulated a plan to use Crowley as an occult disinformation agent, utilizing his reputation to influence and capture one of the Nazi high command. The bizarre solo flight to Scotland undertaken by Hitler's deputy führer, Rudolf Hess, on May 10, 1941, and his subsequent capture is claimed by some accounts to have been the successful result. Mister Crowley also contributed to the Allied war effort by performing his "magick" rituals in Ashdown Forest, burning Nazi effigies to ensure England was protected from invasion. Another famous British occultist and magician, Miss Dion Fortune, conducted ceremonies to repel the Luftwaffe during the Battle of Britain. Aleister Crowley additionally took credit for inventing the "V for Victory" sign, having previously used the symbol in his occult work and intending to use the "V" as the sigil for a proposed "Union of Men—an association of magicians that would help defend Britain against the Axis powers."[8]

THE REAL CASTLE WOLFENSTEIN

The most important location for Himmler and the SS to conduct their quasi-magic rituals was at their headquarters in the German castle of Wewelsburg, in the Westphalia region. Considered the spiritual center of their new beliefs, this "Black Camelot" was revered as a source of mystical power. Located near the site of the Battle of Teutoburg Forest, where an alliance of Germanic tribes defeated the Roman army in the year 9 CE, it had been built in the 17th century and belonged to the prince-bishops of Paderborn and then the Kings of Prussia.[9] Two witch trials had taken place there in 1631, utilizing an inquisition room located in the basement of the east tower, and prisoners had been kept there during the Seven Years War between 1756 and 1763. Himmler had signed a 100-year lease (costing just one Reichsmark annually) on the triangle-shaped hilltop castle from the Landrat of Buren in 1933, and immediately began restoring the badly decayed interior in his own unique style. The next year, the fortress opened as the SS Leadership School, but in 1935 was renamed SS School, House Wewelsburg. The training had shifted from military leadership to pseudo-scientific courses on racial superiority through lessons on Germanic history, folklore, and genealogy. Eventually the castle became the premier venue for lavish SS dinners and the occult-based, neo-pagan rituals of the new Nazi mysticism that even Hitler himself participated in.

Himmler imagined Wewelsburg as the Grail Castle and named the redesigned rooms after legendary characters and Teutonic military heroes. The walls and ceilings were adorned with swastikas, ancient Germanic runes and symbols, and works of art glorifying the Aryan people. On the ground floor of the north tower, a hall with 12 pillars, each guarded by an ever-burning flame, represented the Knights of the Round Table. The room featured a dark green sun wheel of 12 radial sig runes (the Sonnenrad) that symbolized "the center of the new world." Twelve highest-ranking SS generals, the Obergruppenführer, became his court of occult knights and would meet at a specially built round table to spiritually prepare before military campaigns.[10] Many unknown rituals were conducted at the castle, as well as baptism-like ceremonies and internments in the former cistern, which was converted into a vaulted crypt for cremated SS heroes. Reportedly believing himself to be the reincarnation of Heinrich I—founder and first king of the medieval German state—Himmler dedicated the vault to him. When any SS soldier died, his issued "death's head" ring would be delivered to Wewelsburg Castle and placed in a chest. These approximately 11,500 Totenkopfring rings—adorned with engraved skulls and mystic symbols—have never been found and are believed to still be buried in a nearby mountain.

Himmler only lasted 12 years before having to break his 100-year lease, and his grand plans for Wewelsburg were far from realized. He had planned to add a circular wall with 18 towers around the hill and an enormous moat. To construct the moat, the SS had ordered the evacuation of the entire town, with plans to completely flood the surrounding valley. Due to the massive amount of physical labor the reconstruction of the castle entailed, Himmler had set up his own private concentration camp, called Niederhagen. Over 4,000 inhabitants—with a core of Jehovah's Witnesses and Soviet prisoners of war—would struggle to endure the inhuman living conditions and brutal abuse of the labor camp, with at least half of them dying there. Work on the castle ceased in early 1943, when Germany was defeated by the Soviets at Stalingrad. Three days before the U.S. Army's 3rd Armored Division arrived, on March 31, 1945, Himmler ordered the castle demolished. Explosives and tank mines were set off, and SS Major Heinz Macher set fires inside to destroy the interior, but the exterior walls survived. Restoration started only three years later, and today it is open to tour as a war memorial and museum.

RAIDERS OF THE LOST ARTIFACTS

In Himmler's fevered vision, once the Third Reich ruled the entire world, the magical books and artifacts collected by the SS from every conquered culture would radiate mystical power from inside the castle. Locating and retrieving these occult treasures would require a very specially trained and equipped unit of the Schutzstaffel. Thus, in 1935 he created the German Ancestral Heritage Society for the Study of the History of Primeval Ideas.[11] The Nazi think tank, composed of scientists and scholars, quickly became known simply as Ahnenerbe (AH-nen-AIR-buh), a German term for "something inherited from the forefathers." Their mission task was researching the archaeological and historical roots of the Aryan race to ultimately prove that all Germans were descended from a god-like advanced species of Nordics—survivors of Atlantis—that had once ruled the world. Teams were dispatched across the world to locate physical evidence of this original, ancient Nordic culture, with their discoveries being used to justify the Nazis' distorted racial policies and the coming genocide of all those they deemed inferior. In addition, members of Ahnenerbe were ordered to search for and seize important cultural relics, investigate mythical places, and obtain occult manuscripts and legendary tomes.

The top-secret organization was always under SS control, and eventually grew to include 51 "Institutes" divided into two broad categories of "Social" and "Natural" sciences. Besides expected subjects like language, archaeology, and history, some of the stranger institutes included divisions dedicated to researching "Folktales, Fairy Tales, and Myths," "Landscape Science," "Folk Medicine," and "Secret Societies." Excavations and explorations were made throughout Nazi-occupied Europe, Crimea and Ukraine, the Middle East, Tibet, and even Antarctica. Ahnenerbe also conducted top-secret experiments with new technologies, some of which involved the use of discovered artifacts and ancient texts. Sanctioned studies of the paranormal, ancient aliens, and necromancy reflected Himmler's bizarre interests and beliefs.

Aside from searching the world for the Holy Grail, Excalibur, and the location of Atlantis, the organization also conducted horrific experiments on living human beings. Similar to the Imperial Japanese Army's notorious medical Unit 731, which subjected men, women, and children to gruesome medical experiments, SS doctors performed immoral investigations in the name of science, too. Concentration camp inmates were placed in vacuum chambers to determine the effects of high-altitude pressure, left in ice water or outside naked to see how long it would take them to freeze to death, and were shot or had limbs amputated to be administered an experimental blood coagulant made from beets and apple pectin called Polygal. Ahnenerbe was also responsible for an event dubbed the "Jewish Skeleton Collection," where 86 men and women prisoners from Auschwitz were gassed and collected for their bones in August 1943. The corpses were never finished being de-fleshed as planned and were discovered by the sickened Allies; the bodies had been preserved in formalin, with some beheaded in an attempt to conceal the war crime.

After the witch library was collected by that special unit of Ahnenerbe in 1935, another team set off in June of 1936 on an expedition through the Karelia region of Finland to locate pagan sorcerers and witches.[12] Musicologist Fritz von Bose brought along a magnetophon to record their pagan chants. The SS team successfully located Miron-Aku, a legendary soothsayer believed to be a witch by locals. Upon meeting the Nazis, she claimed to have foreseen their arrival. Miron-Aku performed a ritual for the camera and recorder in which she summoned the spirits of ancestors and told the Germans a prophecy of the future. Other pagan chants and ceremonies were recorded to learn and be used later in Nazi cult rituals.

A prized artifact was seized by the organization from a museum in Vienna after Germany annexed Austria in 1938. The weapon that reportedly wounded Christ on the cross, the Spear of Longinus, was delivered to Hitler himself. He claimed that when he held it for the first time, it showed him visions of his future. Another small team was inserted into Krakow, Poland, in 1939, to obtain the 15th-century Veit Stoss altarpiece. The Poles had feared German interest in their national treasure and had already disassembled it into 32 pieces, which had been shipped to different locations. The SS unit was ruthless in its pursuit, eventually locating every piece for a mission accomplished.

After analyzing the two medieval Icelandic works known collectively as the Eddas, Nazi researchers claimed passages described long-forgotten advanced weaponry and sophisticated medicines. Himmler desired the discovery of Thor's hammer as one such weapon that could be manipulated by the Third Reich, saying, "I am convinced that this is not based on natural thunder and lightning, but rather that it is an early, highly developed form of war weapon of our forefathers."[13]

The Ahnenerbe investigated the concept of landscape alignments, now known as ley lines, linking sacred sites of the ancient Germanic people. Following the theories of Wilhelm Teudt, who believed in an ancient, highly developed Germanic civilization, the Nazis excavated several prehistoric "star temples." These structures were reported to be aligned with important positions of the sun, moon, and stars. The sacred center was believed to be the Externsteine, located in the Teutoburg Forest near the town of Horn-Bad Meinberg. Dubbed the "Germanic Stonehenge" by Teudt, it is a natural outcropping of 13 free-standing sandstone pillars, unique and bizarre in a region devoid of rocks. The SS studied the imposing stones for their value to Germanic folklore and history.

The majority of the intensive and expansive classified work completed by the Ahnenerbe may never be known. Throughout the war, the organization would often destroy or hide its collections and records as Allied forces approached. When the last headquarters in the village of Waischenfeld, Bavaria, was taken by the Allies in 1945, most of its secrets had already been lost, and only a small cache of records was discovered hidden in a nearby cave. However, a recent discovery made in another mountain cave by a team of scientific explorers in southern Russia has shed some light on possibly one of the most bizarre artifacts the Nazi organization had obtained.

An almost perfectly preserved brown chest, unmistakably bearing the official emblem of the Ahnenerbe, was found in a 256-foot-deep (78-meter) cave in the Caucasus mountain range of the Adygea Republic in Russia.[14] Discovered near the same area in 2015 were the remains of a company of 200 Nazi Gebirgsjäger, bearing the elite Edelweiss patch of the First Mountain Division, which showed signs of having been suddenly buried long ago by a devastating avalanche. The Ahnenerbe is known to have had teams in Crimea seizing artifacts and investigating the ancient mountain fortress of Mangup Kale in 1942 and also in Ukraine during 1943. According to Professor Ivan Bormotov, of the local Maikop State Technological University, the SS unit had sent teams into the Caucasus Mountains of Adygea, trying to locate several items of interest.[15] One was a mystical substance called "living water" that they believed could be used to produce human blood plasma. Hydrologists in the secret organization had previously decided that water from a cave under beautiful Lake Ritsa, in the Abkhazia region of Georgia, was a source. Silver canisters filled with the "living water" from Abkhazia were transported overland to the Black Sea, taken across by submarines to a coastal base in Constanta, Romania, and then finally flown to Germany for experimental use.

Another subject of Ahnenerbe interest was the study of neolithic dolmens—gigantic stone slab structures with a round opening in the side—believed to be connected to Atlanteans and erected in geographically anomalous places of mysterious power. The impossibly stacked and balanced megaliths are often found built over fault lines and other aberrations in the Earth's crust. The SS located them scattered around the south of Russia and in a diverse host of other countries including China, Korea, North Africa, France, and Spain. They desired to find proof that these primeval structures were the work of their ancient Aryan ancestors, which would confirm a worldwide influence on all cultures and early civilizations. Who actually built the dolmens—with the oldest dating back to 7,000 years ago—and what their purpose was remains an unsolved mystery of the world.

The disturbing contents found within the lost Ahnenerbe chest suggest that SS members were also looking for something else in the enigmatic, remote mountains of Russia. The explorer team, led by scientist Vladimir Melikov, was shocked to discover two peculiar horned skulls of creatures seemingly unknown to zoology. At first believing them to be some kind of fossilized animal remains, a closer examination of the skulls left them all shaken. "They are unlike anything known to man," said Melikov.[16] The position of a round hole at the bottom of the skulls, called the foramen magnum, shows the location of the spinal cord, impossibly indicating a bipedal creature. Anthropologists confirm a direct link between upright, two-legged walking and the position of this hole. The cryptids also seemed to possess unusually large eye sockets, nostrils, and two organic hornlike protuberances, but lacked a cranial vault, jaws, and an opening for a mouth. The facial bones are flat, as in hominids, with humanlike features, but several small holes arranged in a circle replace where a mouth should be. It seems probable that the skulls were collected as mystical artifacts to be shipped back to Germany, and Ahnenerbe mythologists may have seen them as proof of the existence of their Horned God, to be used in occult SS rituals and magic ceremonies.

Although he hasn't actually inspected the evidence himself, Nikolay Ovodov, a paleontologist and senior research fellow at the Russian Institute of Archeology and Ethnography, offers a less exciting explanation. They could be something as common as ram skulls. "It is probably a skull that spent some time in running water with sand and pebbles and changed shape over a period of years," he stated.[17] This still wouldn't explain how two separate skulls, if deformed or weathered, ended up looking so similar. Besides the disturbing bones, the only other item in the chest was an accurately detailed, full-color map of the Adygea region made by the Germans in 1941. Adding to the weirdness, the chest and skulls are now supposedly being studied and stored at an archaeological complex in southeastern Europe, where a team is excavating the 7,000-year-old settlement of Belovode, in Serbia. Makes you wonder what the connection could be. Ironically, Belovode now stands as the world's oldest-known copper-making site, a discovery that would surely have aligned with Ahnenerbe ideology concerning who invented everything first, and would have been manipulated to their advantage.

THE KEEP

Pagan rituals paying homage to the Horned God may have taken place at another Nazi-occupied place of mystery—Houska Castle—located about 29 miles (47 km) north of Prague in the Czech Republic. Perfect for the setting of a horror movie, this forest-surrounded, gothic-style castle perched on the edge of a steep limestone cliff has a long history of weirdness. Built between 1270 and 1280, during the reign of King Ottokar II of Bohemia, possibly as an administration center from which to manage his extensive lands, Hrad Houska was remote and surrounded by forests, swamps, and mountains. It was in a place of no strategic importance, removed from trade routes and borders, with no external fortifications, no source of fresh water except a rainwater cistern, no kitchen, and no occupants when it was completed. Even stranger, the defenses of the square stone structure were seemingly built backwards, facing toward the inner courtyard as if to keep something in rather than out. There were also no stairs leading from the upper floors of the castle down into the courtyard. What was going on here?

Early historian Vaclav Hajek first recorded the legend of the land Houska Castle was built on in his 1541 history called *Czech Chronicle*.[18] Apparently it was originally the site of a small wooden pagan fort in the ninth century. The first inhabitants of the area had discovered a strange crack in the top of the limestone cliff there, a bottomless hole in the earth reaching unimaginable depths—a literal gateway to Hell. Villagers avoided passing near it, especially after dark, and told tales of strange creatures that were half-human and half-animal crawling out of it to kill their livestock and terrorize their homes. Dark-winged, otherworldly creatures were seen flying in the air around the portal. They attempted to fill the fissure with gigantic stones, but all were swallowed to no effect. The local duke finally devised a plan to learn more about the hole to Hell, offering prisoners that were sentenced to death a pardon if they agreed to be lowered down as far as possible by rope and report back on what they saw. When the first prisoner who volunteered descended, he began screaming from deep within the ground, and when pulled out he had instantly aged, his hair had turned white, and he was suddenly and completely insane. He died within a few hours.

The crack in the limestone was ordered to be covered with thick stone slabs, and a chapel was constructed on top of it. The chapel was dedicated to the Archangel Michael, leader of God's angel armies versus Satan's demons from Hell. Faded frescoes on the chapel's walls, some of the oldest in Europe, depict Michael in two scenes. He fights a dragon in one, the medieval symbol of evil, and in the other holds a sword and a set of scales, weighing souls at the Last Judgment. On another chapel wall can be seen a bizarre figure unlike any other found on paintings of the time period. A creature of pagan mythology, a female centaur, is depicted holding a bow in her right hand and aiming an arrow at a human figure with her left. Left-handedness was associated with Satan in the Middle Ages, so researchers agree the image must be linked to the legends surrounding the hole buried beneath the chapel's floor.

The castle was then built around the chapel, appearing to have not been intended as either a residence or as a wartime sanctuary, but as a defense against what evil could crawl out of the hole. By constructing the protective walls facing inward, the defenders seemed to be attempting to keep the demons inside the courtyard, trapped within the lower level's thickest walls. These walls are not visible today because after the Thirty Years War, fought between Catholic and Protestant states in the mid-1600s, Holy Roman Emperor Ferdinand III ordered all private castles to be made less defensible.[19] Houska's tower, moat, earthen ramparts, and other defenses were completely dismantled.

During the vicious war, a rogue Swedish mercenary commander and black magician named Oronto is said to have occupied the vacant castle around 1639 with his band of brigands. The alchemist is rumored to have performed immoral experiments on locals in his makeshift laboratory in an attempt to discover the elixir of life. After living in constant fear of unprovoked violence and rape from Oronto's outlaw army, two brave villagers who were hunters crept up in the darkness to Houska Castle and shot him dead through an open window. The castle later remained in possession of various nobles until the beginning of the 18th century when it was remodeled into a Renaissance chateau.

Immediately following the occupation of Czechoslovakia in 1939, the SS moved in and occupied Castle Houska, despite it having no apparent strategic significance for the German war effort. The Ahnenerbe is believed to have begun conducting experimental research on the legendary gateway to Hell and any other occult connections the location may have had. Researchers were searching for supernatural weapons and a way to harness the enigmatic power present there. The team investigated the theory that the structure had been built according to the principles of sacred geometry, and that the portal in the earth could be used for teleportation or inter-dimensional travel. They stayed until they were forced to vacate in 1945, retreating from Bohemia ahead of the advancing Allied armies. We will never know exactly what they were doing there for all those years or what secrets they may have discovered, as the Nazis methodically destroyed all records and evidence of their activities at Houska. The perimeter of the castle was protected by landmines, which had to be cleared after the war.

The fear of unexploded munitions is the excuse the current owners give when asked why they will not allow any excavations inside the castle or beneath the chapel floor that covers the crack in the earth. The same family has retained ownership of the property since 1924, and despite the castle being in a constant process of repair and renovation, it has been open to visitors since 1999.[20] Tourists can view the highly vaulted ceilings of the bizarre gothic chapel and examine the fading frescoes and murals of pagan demon-like figures and human-animal hybrids. There is also a green chamber adorned with late-Gothic 15th-century paintings and a knight's drawing room.

As for the paranormal attributes of the location: The chapel walls stay moist even during terrible droughts, dead birds are often found in the inner courtyard, cars will sometimes not start near the castle, and howling screams have been heard coming from the deep forest at night. Visitors have detected what they describe as "a chorus of screams" coming from beneath the floor of the chapel and the scratching of claws when it is deathly silent.[21] Castle Houska is also reputed to have various types of ghosts lurking around and a unique cryptid frog-human-dog creature that has been witnessed several times.

As for Heinrich Himmler, the man who directed the troopers of Ahnenerbe to manifest his demented dreams, he was dismissed from all posts by Hitler in April 1945, after attempting to negotiate peace with the Allies on his own in order to escape war crimes. Himmler went into hiding but was captured and identified by the British, finally biting down on a hidden cyanide capsule to commit suicide on May 23, 1945. With his death, an untold amount of top-secret knowledge collected by his team of occult Nazis was forever lost. Perhaps it's better that way.

THE LONG PIG

"And they will eat one another's flesh during the stress of the siege imposed on them by the enemies who seek their lives," states the Old Testament Book of Jeremiah, chapter 19, verse 9.

I think most people can understand eating another human being due to the desperation of starvation, even if they can't imagine themselves ever being hungry enough to do it. But, someone choosing to eat another human being just because they *want* to do it will usually elicit a response of disgust and horror. But ritualized cannibalism was practiced by the Imperial Japanese Army in several different places, and in one instance, a future American president was the one little piggy who got away.

Japanese historian Yuki Tanaka, in his 1996 book about war crimes, revealed more than 100 cases of cannibalism committed by Japanese troops in Papua New Guinea.[22] Victims included Australian soldiers, Asian laborers, and indigenous people of the islands. In some situations, unit supply lines were indeed cut off and it was practiced for survival, but in other cases, officers ordered their men to eat human flesh to manifest victory and power over their enemies.

Australians fighting in the New Guinea Campaign in August 1942 had been chasing desperate Japanese troops across the rugged central highlands. Arriving at their recently abandoned jungle camp, they hoped to find evidence of their mates lost earlier in the fighting. They certainly found it. Australian Corporal Bill Hedges described, "The Japanese had cannibalized our wounded and dead soldiers. We found them with meat stripped off their legs and half-cooked meat in the Japanese dishes. I was heartily disgusted and disappointed to see my good friend lying there, with the flesh stripped off his arms and legs, his uniform torn off him. We found dumps with rice and a lot of tinned food. So they weren't starving and having to eat flesh because they were hungry."[23] Other mutilated bodies were found, with only their hands and feet untouched. An Australian lieutenant verified what had transpired there: "In all cases, the condition of the remains were such that there can be no doubt that the bodies had been dismembered and portions of flesh cooked."[24] Testifying at a war crimes trial after the conflict, a young Japanese veteran confessed that he had shot and eaten an Australian soldier "out of intense hatred and intense hunger."[25] Another Japanese veteran claimed that many isolated and starving soldiers were reduced to cannibalism. He claimed they first tried to eat the local natives, but found them too difficult to catch. Australian soldiers on the island were then hunted, and when all was lost, they finally turned on each other, picking their victims based on personality. Cannibalization-for-sustenance—amputating limbs only as needed, to keep the meat fresh—was used to keep prisoners alive over the course of several days and ensure fresh flesh.

A surviving Pakistani corporal who had been held as a prisoner of war on Papua New Guinea testified that he had witnessed his Japanese captors kill and eat one prisoner a day over the course of 100 days. Another Indian POW verified what happened, saying, "The Japanese started selecting prisoners and everyday one prisoner was taken out and killed and eaten by the soldiers. I personally saw this happen and about 100 prisoners were eaten at this place by the Japanese. The remainder of us were taken to another spot 50 miles away where 10 prisoners died of sickness. At this place, the Japanese again started selecting prisoners to eat. Those selected were taken to a hut where their flesh was cut from their bodies while they were alive and they were thrown into a ditch where they later died."[26] A gruesome description regarding the fate of a captured American pilot, provided by Indian captive Havilar Changdi Ram, reads like a horror film: "About a half an hour from the time of the forced landing, the Kempeitai [military police] beheaded the pilot. I saw this from behind a tree and watched some of the Japanese cut the flesh from his arms, legs, hips, and buttocks and carry it back to the quarters. I was so shocked at the scene and I followed the Japanese just to see what they would do with the flesh. They cut it in small pieces and fried it. Later that evening, a very senior Japanese officer, of the rank of Major General, addressed a large number of officers. At the conclusion of the speech, a piece of fried flesh was given to all present, who ate it on the spot."[27]

The existence of a cannibalistic cult within the Japanese army, or at least a loose association of senior officers with a shared belief structure, is suggested by the evidence. It seemed that once the line was crossed, it could quickly grow into an accepted practice. One example tells of an American pilot who was captured by the Japanese in the Philippines, executed, and had his liver removed. As the cooked organ was served to his officers, their commander, Masanobu Tsuji, professed, "The more we consume, the more we shall be inspired by a hostile spirit toward the enemy."[28] In Japanese folklore, the liver is the organ where power and courage dwell, and some soldiers of the Rising Sun apparently believed that eating the liver of their enemy would transfer and bolster those traits in them. Australian troops also told stories of finding defected Japanese soldiers who obviously didn't feel the same way, deserting their units when other soldiers had started eating prisoners.

On the morning of September 2, 1944, a group of anxious American torpedo bomber pilots headed toward two Japanese radio towers on Chichijima, in the Bonin Islands, with a mission to destroy them. The tiny island, about 620 miles (1,000 km) south of Tokyo, was ferociously defended by anti-aircraft defenses and 25,000 troops. Nearing his objective after an hour of flight, a 20-year-old U.S. Navy lieutenant named George H. W. Bush felt the massive punch of a hit in the belly of his plane, a Grumman TBF Avenger. "Smoke poured into the cockpit, and I could see flames rippling across the crease of the wing, edging toward the fuel tanks," Bush later wrote.[29] He pushed onward, dropping two 500-pound bombs from 3,000 feet (914 meters) directly onto his targeted radio tower before pulling back out toward the open ocean. To give himself and his crew their best chance of evading capture, he flew the deteriorating bomber as far away from the island as it would go. Bush finally ordered his radio operator and the gunner to jump, but floated down to the water alone, a failed parachute killing one and the other being unable to eject from the doomed aircraft. Once in the waves, he endured painful jellyfish stings and constant vomiting from swallowing too much seawater, but managed to swim to the life raft from his plane wreckage. Japanese patrol boats attempted to pursue and capture him, but were driven back by American fighter planes. "I was crying, throwing up, and swimming like hell," he recalled, feeling guilty over the deaths of his crew and realizing the gravity of his situation.[30] Afloat for four terrifying hours, the submarine crew of the USS *Finback* suddenly surfaced near him and pulled Bush from the saltwater. "Happy to be aboard," was all the shocked pilot could manage to say.[31]

Eight other American airmen had ditched their planes and ended up in the ocean near Chichijima, but none of them would ever know that feeling of gratitude, as they were all immediately captured by the Japanese and brought to the island. They suffered greatly in their last months alive, enduring beatings and sadistic torture before being executed in gruesome ways. Sharpened bamboo spears and bayonets, clubbings, and beheadings by samurai sword were methods used. But the real horrors began after their death.

Marvell "Marve" Mershon, a 19-year-old from California, was the first to be selected. After having been tied to a tree all day in the center of the Japanese camp and enduring hours of constant beatings, he was taken out into the jungle and beheaded with a sword. The event remembered as the "Chichijima Incident" was then set in motion when Japanese Lieutenant General Yoshio Tachibana—a sadistic, alcoholic commander—gave the drunken order to dig up the recently executed American airman and use the body for meat. He insisted that all his officers had to participate, to prove their "fighting spirit."

Surgeons removed the liver, gallbladder, and six pounds of thigh meat, and the body was butchered by the division's medical orderlies. The officers dined on the liver, while the enlisted men were served the cuts of thigh. Vice Admiral Mori Kunizo would later testify that a chef "had [the liver] pierced with bamboo sticks and cooked with soy sauce and vegetables."[32] Accompanied by hot sake, the meal was considered a delicacy that Mori Kunizo considered "good for the stomach." The admiral and a Major Sueo Matoba leaned hard on the other officers to eat the livers, calling them out if they did not intend to participate. Mori reminded the timid officers that during the Sino-Japanese War, their troops had dined regularly on human flesh, using it as a medicine to make them invincible in battle. Matoba said he ate the liver "to gain the strength of a tiger" and later tried to explain, "These incidents occurred when Japan was meeting defeat after defeat. The personnel became excited, agitated and seething with uncontrollable rage. Yes, I was a madman due to the war, and that is the only reason I can give for being a cannibal."[33]

About a month later, the remaining seven prisoners of war were taken out to the Japanese rifle range. Floyd Hall, a 25-year-old from Missouri, was suddenly snatched from the group and tied to a wooden stake in the ground. His comrades were forced to watch as he was used for bayonet practice and stabbed repeatedly. After enduring his slow and agonizing death, they were further traumatized to witness the unit surgeon immediately cut Hall open and freshly harvest his liver and gallbladder.

A document was captured during the war and authenticated by Major Matoba at his war crimes trial in 1946. It was an official order "regarding eating flesh of American flyers." Instructions stated three points: that the battalion wanted to eat the flesh of the aviator Lieutenant Hall, that First Lieutenant Kanamuri would see to the rationing of the flesh, and that Cadet Sakabe would attend the execution and have the liver and gallbladder removed.[34]

Requiring even more human meat and organs for their planned feast, the Japanese soldiers now grabbed 22-year-old Texan Warren Earl Vaughn, and he decided to fight back. Knowing what was in store for him and that his situation was hopeless, he continued to struggle while also extending his neck for his captors, indicating his request for a quick death. Unable to tie him up, he was finally beheaded and then also promptly butchered for the troops' meal that evening.

The five remaining airmen would all eventually be executed one by one, and two of them would also be eaten by their Japanese captors. Their names were Lloyd Woellhof, Grady York, James "Jimmy" Dye, Glenn Frazier Jr., and an unknown American. One of them was horrifically used as cannibalization-for-sustenance, literally being eaten alive over the course of several days through amputations and surgical removals, in order to keep the meat fresh.

It wasn't until 2003, with the publication of James Bradley's book *Flyboys: A True Story of Courage*, that the 41st president learned how close he had come to being eaten.[35] The U.S. Navy had made the horrifying truth top secret after post-war military trials in Guam revealed the events. The investigators didn't want the families back home to know their sons had been eaten, fearing it would ultimately just cause further trauma. Bush survived the war as a highly decorated pilot who flew 58 combat missions and was blessed to live for 94 years. Throughout life he often felt survivor's guilt and ruminated on his lone rescue, wondering, "Why had I been spared, and what did God have in store for me? In my own view, there's got to be some kind of destiny, and I was being spared for something on Earth."[36] I think we can all agree that he made the most of his second chance in life.

General Tachibana and his staff stood trial in August 1946, and 34 Japanese were found guilty of war crimes and sentenced to death by hanging, including the general, Major Matoba, and two other officers. They were all buried in unmarked graves. Vice Admiral Mori Kunizo would be sentenced to death and hanged in a separate trial for war crimes committed in the Dutch East Indies.

A Japanese unit that did not surrender for more than a year after the war ended in 1945, the so-called "Suzuki Unit," was deployed to the humid mountain jungles of the Philippines to combat native and American resistance to the Japanese occupation. Led by Colonel Fumio Suzuki of the 15th Debarkation Unit, the force began foraging for wild food and stealing corn and livestock from local villages when rations began to run low. Many were getting sick and dying, with tropical diseases like malaria and dysentery taking their toll. Suzuki believed his soldiers needed meat to stay healthy. A trooper named Rikimi Yamamoto later testified, "We frequently ate human meat as our dinner. Boiled it with vegetables and ate it. The meat was brought into camp by patrols who had cut it up and dressed it. Sometimes the meat was dried and sun-cured. Since no other meat was available, we had to eat human flesh. For this reason, Filipinos were captured and butchered. I was so hungry I ate it, although I would have preferred pork."[37]

Relatives of Filipinos cannibalized by these soldiers solicited compensation from the government of Japan in 1993.[38] Members of a mountain tribe on the southern island of Mindanao, the group claimed that at least 77 of their relatives—45 males and 32 females, including six children—were butchered and eaten by Japanese soldiers between 1945 and February 1947. Two women, then teenagers, said soldiers killed their father in October 1946 and forced them to eat his flesh before raping them repeatedly during a month of captivity.

When the remaining 34 Japanese cannibal holdouts were finally rounded up by military police led by Captain Alejandro Sale, their encampment truly looked like a set for an underground snuff film. They found human bones and flesh in the process of cooking, with human skulls and pieces of bodies scattered everywhere. Evidence of cannibalism was found in and around all of their shelters, proving full participation of the entire demented group. Suzuki committed suicide before 13 of the captured men confessed to eating at least 16 Filipinos and some of their own slain comrades. When the soldiers tried to claim starvation drove them to the taboo practice, Captain Sale countered by saying there were plenty of wild pigs and monkeys in the area, as well as edible plants. The military policeman also testified that the Japanese had been found robust and healthy. A war crimes tribunal sentenced 10 of the Japanese soldiers to death by hanging.

* * *

During World War I, stories circulated about a gang of murderous deserters joining together from the various armed forces—Australian, Austrian, British, Canadian, French, German, and Italian—who lived hidden deep in the earth below abandoned trenches. These ghoulish scavengers would emerge at night, ravaging the fresh victims of the day's fighting for clothing, food, weapons, and their flesh, sometimes fighting among themselves for the prime portions. In his 1920 memoir, *The Squadroon*, British cavalry officer Ardern Arthur Hulme Beaman recounts witnessing more than 25 German prisoners of war suddenly vanish into the ground of the bloody marshes of the Somme in northern France.[39] When he wanted to order a search party into the labyrinth of abandoned trenches, he was advised that the area was the territory of underground-dwelling deserter wild men who came out at night to plunder and kill. A fellow officer told him that "mingled with the snarling of carrion dogs, they often heard inhuman cries and rifle shots coming from that awful wilderness as though the bestial denizens were fighting among themselves."[40] War veteran Sir Osbert Sitwell, in his autobiography *Laughter in the Next Room*," wrote, "Outlawed, these men lived—at least, they lived—in caves and grottoes under certain parts of the front line . . . they would issue forth, it was said, from their secret lairs, after each of the interminable checkmate battles, to rob the dying of their few possessions."[41] He also shared what may have been the fate of these derelict troops, saying that British troops believed "that the General Staff could find no way of dealing with these bandits until the war was over, and that in the end they [the deserters] had to be gassed."

During the occupation of Iraq, rumors circulated of an Islamic extremist fighter who gathered a brigade-size cult of followers that ate the hearts and livers of their enemies. He preached that the ritualistic act transferred the power and knowledge of the slain enemy into the eater of the dead. He validated the atrocities by citing a Fatwa where the Arab woman Hind ate the liver and heart of Hamza, the uncle of the prophet Muhammad, in retribution for him having killed her father, son, brother, and uncle at the Battle of Badr in 624 CE. Originally opposed to the prophet, she converted to Islam in the year 630. The unidentified modern Iraqi militant was also whispered to conduct rituals that summon supernatural Djinn (more on them later), channeling specific spirits that would help them fight the infidel, such as ones that target travelers or strangers in their lands.[42]

* * *

Unless you're pretty twisted or a serial killer, it's hard to imagine becoming a cannibal if there are any other options available. Is it possible that the degenerate men of the Suzuki Unit actually grew so accustomed to the taste that they began to crave human meat? People are overwhelmingly reported to taste like pork, which is likely why the culinary term for it is "long pig."[43] The phrase comes from a translation of what a Pacific island cannibal tribe called human flesh in the mid-1800s. Experienced cannibals have described human meat as odorless and not gamey, and tasting quite good, although a bit more bitter and robust than pig flesh. Be warned though, as science claims the mass consumption of human anatomy isn't too good for you. Devouring the nutritious brain presents a risk with its high concentration of prions—the infected proteins that cause the human equivalent of Mad Cow Disease—bringing on the symptoms of brain deterioration, loss of muscle and motor control, and eventually death. Many New Guinea tribes that practiced ritualistic cannibalism began dying en masse from this brain and nervous system disease that they call Kuru.[44] A healthy cannibal should also avoid eating the liver and kidneys, as they are filtering organs that are actually loaded with waste products, not power and courage. Eyeballs contain an acidic secretion that will make humans sick, fingers and toes are filled with indigestible cartilage, and penises are spongy and contain little nutritional value.

I think I'll just stick with beef.

AMERICAN VAMPIRES

The psychological effects of taboo practices like Nazi occultism and Japanese cannibalism on Allied soldiers has never really been evaluated. The fear of such bizarre beliefs and extreme behaviors surely must have weighed on the minds of some servicemen who were exposed to them. During the war, the United States had begun to develop its own Psychological Operations (PSYOP) branch within the Office of Strategic Services (OSS), recognizing the power of such tactics. Edward G. Lansdale was an Army Air Force intelligence officer who cut his teeth in the OSS, and when the U.S. Air Force was formed in 1947, he became one of their first captains. Quickly promoted to lieutenant colonel, by 1950 he found himself assigned to the Joint U.S. Military Assistance Group advising the armed forces of the Philippines in their war against an indigenous guerilla army in Central Luzon: the Hukbalahap.

The "Huks" (which peaked at around 13,000 soldiers) were a Communist-sponsored insurgency made up of veteran peasant farmers who had previously maintained a fierce resistance to the Japanese during World War II, and then against the Philippine government until 1954. Lansdale believed guerrilla wars could be won by studying the enemy's psychology, and he was aware of a local Filipino belief in supernatural creatures known as the Aswang. As far back as the 16th century, Spanish colonists had noted that the Aswang were feared in the Philippines.[45] The name actually refers to a multitude of shape-shifting monsters, including vampires, weredogs, witches, and ghouls. The common behavior that links them all is their need for blood and their tendency to stalk and hunt human victims who find themselves alone in the jungle.

The Huks of the more remote provinces like Pampanga, Nueva Ecija, and Tarlac were especially susceptible to superstition, and Lansdale began circulating rumors in their villages about recent Aswang sightings in the area, claiming that the creature had been seen living in the nearby hills.[46] The next phase was leaving piles of dead Huk fighters by the sides of busy roads; all the corpses were marked with two small puncture holes resembling fang marks in their necks. The news started to spread quickly, coming in from numerous locations and involving the same patterns of bodies with holes.

The final and most effective phase was sending covert teams to lie in wait for passing Huk patrols and silently snatch the last man, or grab lone Huks who were on guard duty at night. Lansdale, in his memoir, described how they would puncture the insurgent's neck with two holes, hang his body by the heels to completely drain it of blood, and then return the corpse to the trail or near the position he had originally disappeared from.[47] When the deceased man's comrades discovered the mangled remains, they would usually pack up and go home, or at least relocate to a different area, allowing an objective to be secured.

Another PSYOP tactic employed by Lansdale and his team was using the "Eye of God," an image that would be painted on a wall facing the house of suspected Huk insurgents during the dead of night. Finding the mysterious presence of the malevolent eyes the next morning staring at their home and family would terrify fighters into laying down their arms.

PSYOP HORROR SHOW #10

This type of strategy would be employed again by American PSYOP in Vietnam, exploiting Buddhist beliefs regarding the suffering and wandering souls of the unburied dead. According to indigenous folklore, the spirits of the dead who are not returned to their homes for proper burial are cursed to remain on earth in torment until their remains are located and ceremoniously laid to rest. On the anniversary of the death of these lost souls, a spiritual rift between our reality and the afterlife briefly opens for contact and communications to be made.

Imagine sitting alone in the pitch-dark remote jungle at midnight, when suddenly a cacophony of mournful wailing, sobbing, and tortured shrieking shatters the silence. A disembodied voice gargles out a message in your native tongue: "My friends, I come back to let you know that I am dead . . . I am dead! I am in Hell . . . just Hell. It was a senseless death, but when I realized the truth, it was too late . . . too late. Friends, while you are still alive, there is still a chance that you can be reunited with your loved ones. Do you hear what I say? Go home! Go home friends! Hurry . . . if not, you will end up like me. Go home my friends, before it is too late!"[48] This was followed by banging gongs, Buddhist funeral music, women sobbing, and a young girl's mournful cries calling out for her father, "Daddy, daddy, come home with me, come home. Daddy! Daddy!" The effect—even if quickly recognized as an enemy ruse—had to be chilling and effectively damaging to any homesick soldier's morale. Go check it out at the link on the endnote and listen to it by yourself with the lights off.[49]

These eerie sounds, known collectively as Ghost Tape Number 10, were broadcast across South Vietnam in late 1969 through early 1970 as part of a top-secret psychological warfare campaign dubbed Operation Wandering Soul. Organized by the U.S. Army's 6th PSYOP Battalion, it was intended to frighten Viet Cong fighters and to hopefully demoralize them enough to cause more desertions. The session was recorded over several weeks in a Saigon sound studio, bringing in South Vietnamese allies to record the dialogue as slain Viet Cong soldiers amid the horror movie background of distorted effects and other weird audio. The tapes were then broadcast at night in areas of recent Viet Cong activity by GIs equipped with portable loudspeakers, speakers mounted on helicopters, or patrol boats moving up and down the rivers. Special Forces teams would infiltrate enemy lines and play the recording too. The sounds were hard to ignore and loud enough to even penetrate the underground tunnels used by the insurgents.

There is little evidence that many enemy fighters subjected to the sounds actually believed they were hearing authentic ghosts, but the Ghost Tape was known to have unintentionally terrified our uninformed South Vietnamese allies and many civilians. U.S. forces were instructed not to play it within earshot of them, because they were just as susceptible to the psychological effects. A few desertions and the surrender of some Viet Cong or North Vietnamese Army prisoners were documented after having played the recordings, but the best effect it actually had was causing angry and irritated enemy soldiers to reveal their hidden positions by firing at the sources of the broadcast. After an HC-47 (basically a civilian DC-3 airliner outfitted with twice the fuel load) of the 9th Special Operations Squadron came under heavy fire while broadcasting the tape, the pilot swore he'd never play it again. Despite his oath, he was sent on the same mission to the same spot the next night, but this time with "Spooky," an AC-130 gunship, in support, flying in opposing orbit and all blacked out.[50] The sophisticated ground-targeting systems on the aircraft annihilated everything that attacked the broadcasting crew this time.

The most success experienced with this project didn't involve wandering spirits at all. When an insurgent defector shared intelligence that Viet Cong forces that controlled Nui Ba Den Mountain were being repeatedly stalked and attacked by a tiger, the 6th PSYOP Battalion got creative and went to work again in 1970.[51] They recorded a captive tiger's growl and roar at a zoo in Bangkok, and mixed a recording that was taken behind enemy lines by a specially tasked two-man force. The sound was amplified up through an occupied mountain pass. Reportedly, within a few days, 150 Viet Cong had abandoned their positions from fear of being eaten alive by the ferocious and agitated tigers.[52] Psychological warfare had proved to be a powerful tool in Weird War again.

CHAPTER 4

The Things That Should Not Be

FOLLOWING THE DECEMBER 2001 BATTLE OF TORA BORA IN THE DEEP caves of the White Mountains near the Khyber Pass in Afghanistan, U.S. Marine Operational Detachment Alpha (ODA) 561 and 572 were tasked with cleaning up and gathering any intelligence left behind by al-Qaeda fighters. Tora Bora was a system of small natural caves that had housed around 200 of the enemy, along with stores of arms and ammunition. While using sonar equipment to map out the cave network, the Marines encountered some type of unknown signal causing interference that seemed to originate from deep in the earth somewhere. A team was quickly assembled, consisting of Sergeant Carlos Ramos and two corporals, Derek Sawyer and Latrel Wade, to investigate the possible jamming device.[1]

On point and a few steps ahead in the subterranean darkness, Corporal Wade reportedly fell into a lower chamber and injured his spine. When the other two Marines reached him, he was in great pain but actually more concerned about what he claimed he had seen while lying helpless on the cave floor. He said something large had flown over him, and that it looked like a humanoid woman with wings. Thinking he might just be in some sort of shock, the Marines radioed his location and the need for the corpsmen to bring a backboard down and carry him out. They moved on, as the interfering signal was now registering nearby, but became unsettled when it unexpectedly started to dart around. Suddenly, gunfire and screams exploded from back at Wade's position. The two Marines raced back to find him dead from fresh wounds, and then witnessed several humanoid beings with bat-like wings and feminine features lingering in the shadows. The Marines opened fire wildly, sending the things scurrying back to whatever depths they had emerged from. When the rescue force arrived, there was no evidence of what the two surviving men said they had seen. Since the interfering signal had disappeared, they were ordered to immediately vacate the caverns.

* * *

The human imagination is an amazing generator of experiences you may not really be having. Nervous anxiety, heated emotions, lack of sleep, hunger and thirst, and preconceived ideas can all contribute to altering our perception and interpretation of any event. We rely on our senses to confirm our reality. When we see or experience something that seems unreal, our brains have a hard time processing the information.

Soldiers, sailors, Marines, and airmen are often on duty for extended amounts of time, especially during intense training schools or while performing actual combat missions. Sleep deprivation and lack of comfort are accepted characteristics of most military service, and things can get pretty weird in the dark times of the witching hours. Odd sounds or feelings can all contribute to suddenly seeing or hearing things that aren't really there, or misinterpreting events or something seen as a different thing entirely.

After graduating college, I worked as a lead instructor for Escambia River Outward Bound in north Florida, a residential wilderness-based program for adjudicated juveniles that used challenging outdoor expeditions and experiential education to foster character development, responsibility, and self-reliance. Ten repeat offenders, ages 10 through 16, and three adult instructors would pack out everything needed for a 15-day river trip, traveling isolated and living primitively. We were midway through an August expedition in 1997, and after a hard day of avoiding strainers and dealing with behavior issues, we had set up camp on a river sandbar across from an abandoned state park. There was a well pump with drinkable water up on the bluffs of the old park overlooking us, but the shoreline on that side of the river was deep water and vertical banks. You had to exit the canoe carefully to jump onto the narrow strip of dry earth and grab onto the cliff, anchor the boat by tying it to any available tree branch, and then ascend the fairly easy route to the top. Two of the kids and I successfully negotiated the challenge before sunset, refilling our group's five-gallon jugs of water and the personal gallon jugs we all carried. We were in remote central Alabama, and a local man in his 20s was also filling up jugs at the sulfurous-smelling pump.

I was a recent newlywed, having been married just a couple months before this river trip, and I missed my new bride terribly. This was in the years immediately before cell phones started to become commonplace, and there was no way for me to easily call and talk with her. Seeing an opportunity, I asked the man if he knew of any pay phones in the area. He told me there was a gas station with a phone booth about two miles down the road that paralleled the river. I thanked him for the crucial intelligence and began to formulate a plan.

About an hour after the group had gone to bed, I left the other two instructors as previously arranged and quietly paddled a canoe across the dark waters. I brought the boat in as close to the shoreline as I could, then put one hand on each gunwale to carefully walk down the boat's center-line to the bow, staying low to prevent tipping. Turning around, I stepped out backwards onto the thin shore, being careful not to push the canoe back into the water before I could secure the rope. I pulled myself up to the bluff again and headed for the darkened road, a moonless night making it especially hard to see. We ran every morning in Outward Bound, so I thought nothing of immediately launching into a fast-paced jog.

And so I ran. And ran . . . and ran. I knew I had passed the two-mile mark, and now was starting to question how far this damn gas station actually was or if the local man had just been messing with me. I spotted no signs or lights ahead, but the twisting road was completely enclosed under the gothic tree canopy. Behind me, I suddenly saw the glow of headlights and heard the slow idle of a rough-running old and battered truck. My anxiety grew as it pulled up beside me and stopped.

"What the hell are you doing out here, son?" was the old man's greeting, sizing me up and genuinely curious. I sized him up, too, as I told him all the details he needed. He replied that he had seen us coming down the river while he was fishing earlier that afternoon. He also told me that the gas station was still several miles away and to get in and he would take me there, wait for me to finish my call home, and then return me to where I had come up off the river. Despite the chance of ending up in Farmer Vincent's sausage garden from the movie *Motel Hell*, I just couldn't refuse.

My new friend lived by his word and delivered me safely to the distant, darkened service station. I would have definitely given up running there at some point. I made the phone call and was ecstatic to surprise and finally speak with my lady. It was the morale booster I needed to finish the course. After several minutes, I reluctantly said farewell and returned to the fisherman and his waiting truck, and we started back. He asked me where I had come up from the river, and I told him from underneath the bluffs of the old state park.

"Ole' boy, you best be careful messing around in the water right down there. There's a huge momma gator with a couple month-old hatchlings that she's still protecting that stays right there. I got too close the other day fishing and the she-devil almost knocked me out of my jon boat with her damn tail!"

A wave of stark fear washed away the lingering happiness from the phone call and I sat in silence, wondering again if this was another local just messing with me or if he was telling me the truth.

"She's a mean one, alright. And big! Not trying to scare you now, just giving you a heads up, is all."

I didn't say much the rest of the ride, my mind reeling with adrenaline. He dropped me off at the site of the water pump, I thanked him graciously, and he wished me good luck a little too sincerely. As he pulled away and the darkness closed in, my heart began to race and my breathing increased. I cursed myself for wanting to travel light and not bringing a flashlight. I looked down at the water beneath the bluff and squinted to try to scan for any long, floating shapes in the water, but it was too dark and I knew I had to get down to the canoe. The next few seconds of my life were a terrifying sequence of frenzied actions.

Alligators had been our constant companions on the Outward Bound trip as we journeyed farther south toward the Gulf of Mexico. The boys would point them out floating in the shaded bends of the dark river, or when groups of them were out in the open, lying across sun-drenched sandbars. They became so routine that most of us thought nothing of jumping overboard to cool off in the refreshing river waters when the blistering summer sun burned too hot. Sometimes on hazy mornings, we even found their tracks imprinted in the sand, showing where they had disturbingly circled our campsite the night before.

I was thinking about all of that and much more as I scrambled down the incline, almost sliding right into the water in my nervous haste to get in the canoe. Every darkened shape in the water was now the attacking mother alligator, and she was everywhere. I threw caution to the wind—untying the rope, leaping into the boat, and literally running down the gunwales—nearly capsizing in my terrified frenzy. As I sat down in the stern and fumbled for the paddle, the canoe seemed lower in the water than normal, and I just knew that gator was the dark shape looming beside me. I shoved off and made record time crossing the river, escaping certain death with power strokes, gliding up onto the sandy beach of our campsite still in one piece. Exhausted as I was from the whole experience, I couldn't sleep for another hour, the power of my imagination having put me in a state of fear that made me irrational and overstimulated my senses. The fisherman's account had planted a seed of suggestion in my mind that made me see alligators in half-submerged logs, floating groups of leaves, and shadows—which, in the moment, I would have sworn was the monster I feared.

Sometimes we see and perceive things that just aren't there, and so much of our individual reality is based on a singular perspective and our belief system. If that perspective or belief system is showing us something unnatural or paranormal, can we still trust what we think we see with our own eyes? Many servicemen have witnessed unexplainable creature sightings, and remain adamant that they know exactly what they saw. These rarely seen and undiscovered cryptids and monsters are just another reality in the history of Weird War.

Sea Monsters and Submarines

Off the Irish coast during World War I, on April 30, 1918, the German submarine UB-85 was on the prowl for merchant ships. The sub commander, Kapitänleutnant Günther Krech, was standing on the conning tower when suddenly there was a powerful surge on the starboard side, followed by a resounding "thud" as something landed on the deck. Krech and his fellow officers looked down and watched what could only be described as a gigantic sea monster climbing up from the water onto the submarine. He reportedly stated, "This beast had large eyes, set in a horny sort of skull. It had a small head, but with teeth that could be seen glistening in the moonlight. Every man on watch began firing a sidearm at the beast, but the animal had hold of the forward gun mount and refused to let go."[2] The massive weight of the monster was forcing the craft under the water with the hatch still open. Perhaps in pain from the continuing hail of bullets, the cryptid slipped back into the depths. The forward deck was so damaged, however, that the U-boat was incapable of diving.

A patrolling drifter of the Royal Navy, *Coreopsis II*, spotted and cautiously approached the damaged submarine as it helplessly floated in the water. The Germans standing on the deck had their hands up, offering a peaceful surrender, appearing to the British to be happy to become prisoners. Under interrogation, Krech told his tale. The crew of the *Coreopsis* were not sure whether to believe it or not, but were thrilled to scuttle and sink the German submarine either way. The story of the sea monster and UB-85 was retold and became a lasting maritime legend. Krech died of unknown causes soon after, in March 1919, at the age of 33.

The wreck of the submarine was discovered by the energy firm Scottish Power in October 2016, while a company vessel was laying undersea cables.[3] The sonar image wasn't detailed enough to show whether the foredeck could have been damaged by a sea monster in the way described. A believer is Gary Campbell, the keeper of the Official Loch Ness Monster Sightings Register, who said, "The area of sea where the attack took place has a history of sea-monster sightings—they have ranged from the north coast of Wales to Liverpool Bay. It's great to see how Nessie's saltwater cousin clearly got involved in helping with the war effort."[4]

Discovered records of the German navy contain an interview with one of the UB-85 crew, senior stoker Julius Göttschammer, who claimed that the real fault for the submarine's damage was due to Krech insisting on the installation of a heater in the officers' compartment. The power cables had to be run into the control room through the conning tower, compromising its ability to be completely sealed. After spotting Royal Navy patrol boats, Krech ordered a crash-dive of the U-boat without removing the cables. Heavy flooding occurred through the slightly open hatch, causing the pumps, batteries, and electric motors to fail. The only option was to surface, and Krech ordered the ballast tanks to be blown. Humiliated, it appears he chose to create an outlandish story of a sea monster attack to cover up his own incompetence.

I have no doubt that an earlier and somewhat more reliable sea monster sighting, reported in the same area by another German U-boat, had influenced Krech's story heavily. On July 30, 1915, the British merchant ship SS *Iberian* was torpedoed by a German U-28 off the coast of Ireland. The *Iberian* sank stern first beneath the waves so quickly that its bow was brought up almost vertically into the air before disappearing. Five of the crew were killed, while the other 61 escaped into boats and were rescued.

The German commander, Freiherr Georg-Günther von Forstner, reported:

> The wreckage remained beneath the water for approximately twenty-five seconds, at a depth that was clearly impossible to assess, when suddenly there was a violent explosion, which shot pieces of debris—among them a gigantic aquatic animal—out of the water to a height of approximately 80 feet. At that moment I had with me in the conning tower six of my officers of the watch, including the chief engineer, the navigator, and the helmsman. Simultaneously we all drew one another's attention to this wonder of the seas, which was writhing and struggling among the debris. We were unable to identify the creature, but all of us agreed that it resembled an aquatic crocodile, which was about 60 feet long, with four limbs resembling large webbed feet, a long, pointed tail and a head which also tapered to a point. Unfortunately we were not able to take a photograph, for the animal sank out of sight after ten or fifteen seconds.[5]

In a 1933 German newspaper interview, he later added that the cryptid was viewed from about 300 to 500 feet (90–150 meters) away in clear, bright sunshine.

It is theorized that the creature could have been a surviving Thalatto-suchia, a clade of marine crocodylomorph from the Early Jurassic to the Early Cretaceous period. Although often called marine or sea crocodiles, the reptiles are actually not members of the order Crocodilia. No one ever challenged von Forstner's account, although all the other eyewitnesses died during the war and the survivors of the *Iberian* were probably a bit too busy to take notice of any sea monsters.

* * *

Like the plot of some undiscovered H. P. Lovecraft story, the Japanese soldiers assigned to surveillance duty in 1943 on the surreally beautiful Kei Islands of Indonesia reported multiple encounters with bizarre man-fish creatures known by the local villagers as Orang Ikan.[6]

The cryptids were described as being around 5 feet (1.5 meters) tall with prominent spikes or spines on their head and shoulders, pink-salmon-colored skin, and a carp-like mouth filled with tiny, needle-sharp teeth. The faces were reported to be humanlike, and the creatures had arms and legs with webbed hands and feet, both of which ended in long, translucent talons. They reportedly smelled like rotting fish. Locals, who stated that they occasionally caught one in their fishing nets, warned the Japanese that they were highly territorial and would attack if approached too closely. Shocked soldiers claimed to have encountered this species on land and in the water, swimming and playfully splashing on the beaches and at inland lagoons.

One report claims a troop of Japanese were reconnoitering an unknown land area and came upon a natural lagoon. Hearing a strange thrashing in the water, the men were stunned to witness an Orang Ikan jump out of the water onto a nearby rock. It turned and clearly stared at the soldiers before emitting a bizarre "gurgling burping" vocalization that felt like a warning.[7] It may have been a call for backup, as they then spotted a second creature underwater, swimming fast and fluidly directly toward them. In stark fear and panic, the soldiers of the Rising Sun opened fire on the rocks and into the water, causing both man-fish to quickly disappear. Another soldier patrolling the beach one night thought he saw a human child, until it turned and the man saw its unnatural features displayed in the moonlight. The thing ran and dove into the ocean, never resurfacing.

When villagers found a dead Orang Ikan washed up on the beach, they laid it out on the grass in front of the village chief's house and invited the ranking Japanese noncommissioned officer of the unit, Sergeant Taro Horiba, to come inspect it for himself.[8] He recorded his life-changing experience and described the mystery species as being five feet two inches (1.6 meters) tall, with red-brown hair reaching to its shoulders. The face was a mix of human and apelike features, with a broad forehead and prominent brow, a low short nose, small ears, and a lipless mouth. The wide, fish-like mouth was indeed filled with many spiny teeth, and there were spines running along its neck and five long and webbed fingers and toes on each limb. Sergeant Horiba was deeply affected by this event, and upon returning to Japan after the war, he unsuccessfully sought any scientists who would be interested in investigating the phenomenon further.

* * *

In October of 1986, the Soviet submarine K-219 was patrolling near Bermuda when seawater began pouring into the vessel from a puncture in the torpedo room. A damaged torpedo suddenly exploded, several crew members were killed, and K-219 was barely able to surface. Captain Nikolai Tushin inspected the outside of his ship, finding two mysterious massive and distinct scratch marks along the side of the submarine. The Soviets later officially claimed a collision with a U.S. sub in the same area was the cause, although no American craft was near when the incident occurred.[9] In 2010, Tushin revealed during an interview that K-219 had made radar contact with an unidentified object dubbed a "Quacker" prior to the chaos. An unknown sound resembling a raspy "quack" crossed with a frog croak came from what he believed had collided with the submarine and caused its destruction. These same noises were heard by several other Soviet ballistic missile submarines in other locations throughout the Cold War, indicating that the sounds originated from intelligent objects that recognized the existence of the Soviet crafts. They believed this because the entities frequently appeared to be following, circling, or observing them while consistently emitting the bizarre croaking sound. The objects themselves could not be detected on normal sonar and appeared to maneuver to avoid the pulses.[10] When any contact with the objects was attempted, the mysterious things changed their movement and the pitch of the disturbing sound. Soviet sailors feared that prolonged listening to the noise would cause insanity.

According to the National Oceanic and Atmospheric Administration (NOAA), more than 80 percent of the world's oceans remain unmapped, unobserved, and unexplored.[11] Honestly, we still just don't know what could be existing in our underwater realms.

GREMLINS, SNAKES SEEN FROM A PLANE, ATTACK OF THE CRAB MONSTERS

The gremlin phenomenon that plagued aviators beginning in the 1920s involved reports of bizarre, impish creatures that infested aircraft and inflicted enough mechanical damage to cause many planes to crash and burn. The term comes from the Old English word *greme*, meaning "to vex or annoy," and was used to describe a type of mischievous gnome-like demon that had its roots in old folklore concerning fairies and goblins.[12] Vaguely reptilian, gremlins are usually depicted as being a foot tall, with long noses and brightly colored green or blue skin, and displaying wild and devious facial expressions. The modern version resurfaced with British airmen in 1923, when a crashed pilot reported tiny creatures had followed him aboard his plane, sabotaged the engine, and manipulated his flight controls. Other British pilots began to claim being harassed in the air by miniature troll-like beings with a mastery of technology and machinery, which ultimately would cause aircraft failure. In his 1953 autobiography *The Spirit of St. Louis*, the famed military aviator Charles Lindbergh revealed that during the 21st hour of his 1927 nonstop solo flight over the Atlantic, he suddenly felt detached from reality. "The fuselage behind me becomes filled with ghostly presences . . . transparent, moving, riding weightless in the plane," Lindbergh wrote.[13] They spoke to him and demonstrated incredibly complex knowledge of navigation and flight equipment, helping to keep him alert and reassuring him that he would safely complete his journey from New York to Paris. "These phantoms speak with human voices—friendly, vapor-like shapes, able to vanish or appear at will, to pass in and out through the walls of the fuselage as though no walls were there."[14]

The most intense alleged gremlin activity was in the violent skies of World War II, reaching prolific levels within the United Kingdom's Royal Air Force. High-altitude Photographic Reconnaissance Units (PRU), operating over enemy territory in bitterly cold conditions, regularly reported seeing the little monsters and blaming them for all types of technical troubles. During the Battle of Britain between the summer and fall of 1940, the multitude of gremlin reports caused the British Air Ministry to make serious attempts to investigate the phenomenon. The agency even produced an official service manual to instruct pilots and air crews on how to deal with them. Originally rumored by the British to be in league with the enemy, this theory was scrapped when German airmen started reporting encounters with the same types of creatures. U.S. pilots also described observing strange beings on the wings of their planes, often seen messing with the aileron—the movable part of the wing that is controlled by the pilot to roll and bank. Their fiddling with this hinge was so persistent that Americans began to call the cryptids "Yehudis," for a famous violinist of the time, Yehudi Menuhin.[15]

An American Boeing B17 pilot named L. W. was on a combat mission during World War II.[16] As he took the enormous Flying Fortress higher, a strange engine sound began, and he looked outside the cabin window to his right. He was startled to view a freakish three-foot-tall entity staring back at him, with long arms, gray hairless skin, a gaping teeth-filled mouth, red eyes, and pointed "owl" ears. L. W. spotted another creature on the nose of the plane, pounding away gleefully at the fuselage. He felt sharply aware and in control of his senses, dispelling the idea of it being a hallucination or some kind of disorientation. The gremlins tore at the aircraft, obviously attempting to bring it down, and L. W. maneuvered the plane and finally shook them off. He didn't know if they had actually fallen to their deaths or onto other planes. He didn't want to tell anyone about the disturbing ordeal, but when he broke down and revealed it to his gunner, the man responded that he had seen similar creatures on a training mission just a few days before.

Several veterans from the war remained adamant that they had no doubts the gremlins they saw were very real and not just a legend created to explain human errors and boost morale, or a hallucination caused by a lack of adequate pressurization and oxygen. Either way, reports of gremlin attacks on aircraft disappeared after the war ended.

* * *

During the Vietnam War, a crew member on a C-130 cargo plane related a bizarre experience that happened while flying off the coast of South Vietnam. Robert L. Pollock remembered, "I noticed movement at the rear of the boxcar-sized empty cargo compartment. I looked and was stunned to see a whirling, gray, cloudy mass forming at the rear right trapdoor. The mass was whirling clockwise; it completely filled in the entire rear of the aircraft within seconds."[17] The rest of the crew joined him, and they watched it advance toward the front of the plane. When Pollock placed his hand inside the mist, it vanished from sight. He and the plane's engineer stepped completely inside the unexplainable fog and found it to be blinding, with no light penetrating to allow any vision. The odorless and tasteless substance had no "feel" to it, and it didn't interfere with their breathing. The mass then began to go back the way it had appeared, only in reverse. "When it got back to the place it had first started forming, it whirled counterclockwise and then just disappeared into nothing."[18] One plausible theory is that it was just a super-dense fog created by a combination of humidity, altitude, velocity, and a change of temperature or pressure. Pollock believes it was not something natural.

* * *

Belgian pilot Colonel Remy Van Lierde was a fighter ace who served in the Belgian Army and the British Royal Air Force during the Second World War. One stop during his illustrious career was the Belgian Congo of central Africa in 1959, when he was given command of the large air base at Kamina.[19] During that same year, Van Lierde claims he encountered a giant snake in the jungles of Katanga Province while returning from a mission by helicopter. He turned the bird around and made several passes over the snake to allow another person on board to take a photograph. Van Lierde described the snake as being close to 50 feet (15 meters) in length and colored dark shades of brown and green with a white belly. He estimated the snake's head to be 3 feet long and 2 feet wide, with triangular jaws. The colonel claimed that as he flew lower for a closer look, the giant reptile rose up approximately 10 feet (3 meters), giving the impression that it would have attacked the helicopter if it had been within striking range. The alleged photograph is somewhat blurry and doesn't provide anything to indicate scale, but the respected aviator never faltered in his claim and said the cryptid "could easily have eaten up a man."[20]

Science does have a historical candidate for a snake this size, but it's on the wrong continent. *Titanoboa* is an extinct genus of gigantic snakes that lived in northeastern Colombia, South America. They could grow up to 42 feet (12.8 meters) long and reach a massive weight of 2,500 pounds (1,135 kg). Their fossils date to around 58 to 60 million years ago, indicating the reptile lived during the Middle to Late Paleocene epoch. More likely, the Congo snake could have been an abnormally sized African rock python (*Python sebae*), or perhaps another undiscovered species of giant constrictor. A few documented rock pythons, Africa's largest snake, have approached or exceeded 20 feet (6 meters). Their coloration, triangular head, and habitat range match Van Lierde's description.

* * *

Japanese soldiers defending remote archipelagos in the Ryukyu Island chain reported startling encounters with horror movie–like giant crabs on the beaches and in the coastal forests during World War II.[21] The crustaceans resembled huge spiders, with small bodies and long, spindly legs that had an incredible span of between 6 and 12 feet (1.8–3.7 meters). During the battle for Okinawa, a Japanese unit witnessed a large mass of these huge crabs engaged in a feeding frenzy of dead soldiers on a remote island beach battlefield. Japanese spider crabs (*Macrocheira kaempferi*) would seem to be the likely culprit, as they match the description and can have a leg span up to 12 feet (3.7 meters) and weigh 42 pounds (19 kg), but they can't function well on land and rarely come up from the deep depths of their natural habitat, and never closer than about 160 feet (50 meters) from the surface.

More likely the Japanese soldiers may have witnessed another true monster at work, the coconut crab (*Birgus latro*). The world's largest terrestrial arthropod, they can weigh up to 9 pounds (4.1 kg), average 16 inches (40 cm) long, and have a 3-foot-wide (1-meter) leg span. They possess an acute sense of smell and are instantly attracted to rotting meat, so they will definitely feed on corpses and carrion. Able to climb trees and live up to 60 years, they actually breathe air through a unique branchiostegal lung and will drown if left immersed in water. The problem is, the Japanese are familiar with this creature, calling it the Yashigani, or palm crab. Perhaps the soldiers witnessed an unknown abomination, some hybrid species of spider and coconut crab that remains undiscovered even today.

In the Company of Cryptid Canines

Many people are familiar with the Angels of Mons, entities who are said to have descended from the heavens on August 23, 1914, bows in their hands, fighting to defend the desperate and retreating British Army from the Germans during the battle of the same name in muddy World War I Belgium.[22] Just a month after the battle, Welsh weird fiction writer Arthur Machen published a short story titled "The Bowmen" in London's *Evening News*, inspired by accounts that he had read about the fighting during Mons and entirely created by his imagination. The story described phantom bowmen from the 1415 Battle of Agincourt being summoned by a soldier calling on St. George, who then destroyed the German forces. When published, Machen's story was not labeled as fiction because it was written from a firsthand perspective. The unintended result was that newspaper readers thought it was completely true, to which the author immediately responded that it was completely imaginary, not desiring to create a hoax. It didn't matter, and by the next year the event was so widely believed that any attempt to discredit it was considered almost treasonous. It is theorized that some British officers may have continued to push the story as part of a covert attempt by military intelligence to spread morale-boosting propaganda and disinformation—perhaps the earliest form of PSYOPS being used on their own troops.

Fewer people know about "The Hound of Mons," a terrifying account published in 1919 by Canadian war veteran F. J. Newhouse, which told the story of a gigantic otherworldly canine that mauled British soldiers among the corpses and shell craters of No Man's Land for over two years.[23] No Man's Land, the open space between the trenches of the opposing armies, was described by the poet Wilfred Owen, "like the face of the moon, chaotic, crater-ridden, uninhabitable, awful, the abode of madness."[24] The story ran in the *Ada Weekly News* and the *Daily Oklahoman* newspapers in August 1919, and in other cities, too. It claimed that on November 14, 1914, Captain Yeskes and four mates from the 7th Royal Fusiliers of London had gone on patrol and never returned. When their bodies were found days later, all five had had their throats violently ripped out. A few nights later, a long, paralyzing canine howl stopped the soldiers entering No Man's Land in their tracks. More men disappeared over time—sometimes heard screaming in the wasteland between the trenches—who were later always found dragged down and mutilated by some mysterious animal. The weird, bloodcurdling howls were sometimes detected uncomfortably close to the British and other times at a distance, near the German lines. Several times, sentries glimpsed an enormous gray or black doglike beast moving fast and low to the ground through the barbed wire of No Man's Land, but after two years of terror, the creature was never heard or seen again.

The story further claims that after the war, secret papers were found in the home of a deceased German doctor named Hochmuller. These documents showed that the Hound of Mons was the result of bizarre scientific brain experiments undertaken between a man and a Siberian wolfhound. A less outlandish explanation may be that it was just an abnormally large and aggressive military dog, trained to stalk and kill by the Germans, or perhaps even an escaped feral dog that contracted rabies. By the opening of World War I, Germany had trained thousands of German shepherds and Doberman pinschers along with English dogs they had purchased, such as Airedales, sheep dogs, and collies—though no record of Siberian wolfhounds.

Another howling canine of a different sort was said to inhabit the region around the United States' Hahn Air Force Base in west-central Germany for over 40 years. Once supported by more than 13,000 people and three squadrons of F-16 fighters of the 50th Tactical Fighter Wing, Hahn was turned over to the German government after the end of the Cold War in 1993. Many of the base's personnel lived in Morbach and other neighboring villages, and within the nearby village of Wenigerath was the Air Force's non-nuclear Munitions Storage Area (MSA). Also in the village of Wenigerath was a small shrine where a single candle was always kept burning.

A German deserter fleeing from the suffering of Napoleon's Grande Armée in Moscow, Thomas Johannes Baptist Schwytzer, was passing through the Wenigerath area in 1812.[25] He had joined up with a group of Russians also escaping west, and together they scavenged and stole their way across the countryside. While ransacking a lonely farmstead outside of town, the fugitives were surprised by the owner and his sons. Thomas murdered them all, and when the derelicts were confronted by the wailing wife and mother, she promptly and forcefully placed a curse on Schwytzer, screaming, "By all the powers my grief can summon, I curse you to walk the earth as a beast by the next full moon, so the world can see you as the monster you have become!" The killer responded by crushing her skull with a boot heel and the group moved on.

Over the next month, the German slowly began to change, becoming more brutal and cruel, robbing, raping, and killing more and more victims without any pause or remorse. He became so unpredictable and reckless that the Russians decided to sneak away from him one night. Schwytzer fell in with a new band of brigands, but his sadism and lack of morality was even too much for these hardened outlaws. When they attempted to exile him from the gang, he killed them all and fled into the forest to live alone, preying on random travelers. By the time the next full moon cycled, the deserter had finally morphed into an upright-walking canine hybrid—basically a werewolf. Livestock and children started to go missing from the nearby villages, and locals feared being outside after dark. After a brutal rape of the beautiful daughter of a prominent family from Morbach, the town's villagers decided to go on the offensive. They tracked down and cornered what was once Thomas, mercilessly killing the monster and burying it at a crossroads. A shrine was erected on the spot and a single candle was lit, supposedly as a barrier against the feral beast's return. Nine months later, the victimized daughter gave birth to a normal, healthy child, whose descendants still live in the same area, with none ever reported to have inherited the curse. The legend of the "Morbach Monster" was born.

In 1997, Professor D. L. Ashliman at the University of Pittsburgh started collecting werewolf legends from Germany as part of his ongoing folklore research.[26] Two bizarre reports from military personnel who had been stationed at Hahn Air Base at the same time seemed to corroborate an incident that occurred in 1988. A group of security police (SP) were on their way to their post at Wenigerath when they noticed the candle was out at the shrine, which incited plenty of jokes about the monster they had all heard the legend of. They weren't laughing later that night when an automatic sensor on the fence line went off. While investigating, one of the SPs saw a huge, doglike animal stand up on its hind legs, look at him, and then take three leaping steps before jumping over the 12-foot (3.7-meter) chain-link fence surrounding the munitions area. It was described by one of the security police eyewitnesses as standing 7 to 8 feet (2.1–2.4 meters) tall. A military dog was brought to the spot, but the agitated canine went berserk and would not track the unknown creature.

Another research study with U.S. servicemen was conducted by Matthias Burgard, a German cultural anthropologist at the University of Mainz.[27] An airman claimed to have been stalked by a hidden, howling creature while walking his dogs one night; an army MP also related a similar tale. While walking to town on a road one moonlit night, three off-duty soldiers heard something large thrashing through the forest, coming straight for them. Thinking it might be a wild boar, the men ran to a nearby tall tree and climbed up high in the branches to let it pass. Obscured by leaf cover and the dark, something stopped below them and started sniffing. The reporting MP described being overcome by a weird feeling of terror for what seemed like an eternity, until the mysterious creature finally walked on. Their fear suddenly increased when the thing crossed the road beside them, clearly walking on two feet that clopped on the pavement like hooves. The men waited another 30 minutes before jumping down and running the remaining three miles into town, numbing their fear with alcohol and promising to never speak of the experience again. The official story often given was that it was just the wild hog population startling servicemen, but at least one of the eyewitnesses told Burgard that he grew up on a farm, and what he heard stalking him in the woods that night was no hog.

Other Hahn Air Base veterans claim there's nothing to the Morbach Monster except a humorous initiation tradition, besides it also being the name of the local American football team. "It was always fun to scare the new guys with stories of the werewolf and then make them do a security check of the perimeter on foot. One of our K-9s was this big, black Bouvier with bloodshot eyes. We would always send that dog's handler to meet the new guys."[28] Local Germans even report that the legend has no origin in their country and that it arrived in the 20th century with the American GIs. The type of shrine actually described in the werewolf legend seems to be a *heiligenhauschen,* small Catholic structures dedicated to different saints and often honored with lit candles. The arched one in Wenigerath is endorsed with the painted phrase, "Ave Maria," or "Hail, Mary," and has a dedication date of 1806.[29]

* * *

Cryptid canines have made their appearance in modern Middle East battle zones, too. A three-vehicle convoy of U.S. Army personnel was traveling from Nasiriyah to the port city of Umm Qasr, Iraq, in July 2003.[30] In the early hours of morning, something unexplainable wandered onto the highway and into the spotlight of their headlight beams. Described as a terrifying hybrid of monkey, dog, and rat, the creature seemed to completely ignore them as they drove past it. Unable to identify it, the soldiers concentrated on the road again, and about an hour later were drawing close to their destination. The vehicles rounded a bend and the men were shocked to see the same type of creature again, this time illuminated clearly by an overhead streetlamp. The convoy stopped to observe it this time and witnessed a hairless, emaciated, gray-skinned beast about the height of an adult collie dog. Its protruding ribs were accompanied by a long, "monkey-like" tail and four thin, straight legs. Lengthy sharp teeth, pointed ears, and oversized, glowing gray eyes made it resemble a rat's face. The baffled Americans watched it for two minutes before it shuffled back into the darkness at the edge of the light. They claimed it was not a mangy, burned, or starved dog, but something none of them had ever seen before.

Soldiers on night guard at a Forward Operating Base (FOB) in Helmand Province, Afghanistan, in 2005 spotted what appeared to be two glowing, red eyes about 100 meters (328 feet) out in front of the wire.[31] They could not locate anything using their night vision. For more than 30 minutes, they observed the odd "eyes" as they moved together up and down or side to side. When they finally fired a flare, a large but emaciated, doglike creature the size of a bear was seen. One of the soldiers fired a round at it, and the thing disappeared back into the night.

Logar Province is south of Kabul, Afghanistan. In 2013, an American force was there on a night operation in support of a disabled vehicle recovery.[32] While scanning the area surrounding the dismounted infantry with Night Vision Goggles (NVGs), a gunner spotted a huge, doglike creature moving along an 8-foot-high (2.4-meter) wall. When two other gunners marked it with their lasers, they realized the thing was registering at 4 feet (1.2 meters) tall. A troop on the ground confirmed the creature was the size of an Afghan cow and built like a wolf before "noping" the hell out of the area. The others continued to watch the animal as it stopped by a hole in the wall and stepped into it, hopping down and disappearing around a corner.

The MQ-9 Reaper is a Remotely Piloted Aircraft (RPA) that employs the Multi-Spectral Targeting System (MTS-B), integrating airborne sensors and sophisticated video imagery equipment to monitor airborne, maritime, and ground objects. One night in 2012, an Air Force MQ-9 sensor operator was bringing the aircraft back to base and looking around the neighboring Afghan valleys.[33] They were near the Pakistani border south of Jalalabad in the mountains of Nangarhar Province. He spotted something moving fast, with catlike mannerisms, but the creature was the size of a tiger and had a large, dog-shaped head. It appeared as a black silhouette on the monitor, so details could not be discerned. Many other MQ-9 crews also reported seeing weird and unexplainable things during their frequent missions over the Afghanistan wilderness.

CREATURES OF THE NIGHT

Tim King was returning from a two-month stint as an embedded combat reporter for an Oregon news station when he had a very disturbing 20-minute conversation with a soldier at Bagram Air Base in Afghanistan.[34] Out of nowhere, a strange young man in uniform walked up to him and asked if he was aware of the vampire problems the local area had been experiencing. He went on to describe how the locals were more terrified of the creatures than even the Taliban. "It's been going on for hundreds of years here; people in other parts of the world don't even know about it, but anyone who has lived around here does," he explained. Not knowing how to respond, King listened and soon wished the soldier would just leave. "They come out at night, [and] sometimes people come up missing, especially kids. They even pull their animals inside when the vampires are out," he went on. He further claimed that Afghan folklore said the vampires lived deep in the desert, were taller than normal, and were usually women. "[Our] guys are scared, you're damn right. You just stick with other people and hope for the best sometimes," is how he said the U.S. troops dealt with it. The unidentified soldier ended the conversation just as suddenly as it had begun, and immediately after he left, King was overcome with nausea and spent the next several minutes violently vomiting in the restroom—something out of character for him and not as a result of something he had eaten.

Two soldiers were standing post in southern Afghanistan, barely awake at 0200 hours. Suddenly, terror and adrenaline jarred them fully awake as they spotted a tall humanoid figure emerge from the darkness about 75 yards (69 meters) away from their position. Observed through their night vision goggles, they watched as the thing turned and looked directly at them. The eyes were so bright they caused the optics to "burn out," and the troopers had to pull them off. "Those eyes were like neon red blood. Blood red and bright as the sun," the reporting witness said.[35] He switched to using the thermal sights on his weapon and saw that the eyes burned hot while the body of the unidentified figure registered cold. Not sure if he should engage the unknown entity as a target, he continued to watch as the thing with the bright eyes moved and turned away, walking off and disappearing into the night again. Both men decided to not mention the event to anyone while they were still there.

* * *

Afghan folklore talks of a hostile feminine entity with floating hair, eyes of milky-white orbs, and glacier-pale skin that inhabits the regions of twilight or where the sun rises so high that you cannot cast a shadow. Villagers and nomads avoid being out in the wilderness during these times of day. This entity seems similar to the *ghul*, or female *ghulah*, monstrous humanoids originating in pre-Islamic Arabian religion and Bedouin folklore as vile tricksters and ravenous flesh eaters. They were said to kidnap victims, murder lustful men by taking the guise of beautiful women, prey on young children, drink blood, steal items, and eat the dead. They most often inhabited abandoned places or wilderness wastelands. The Arabian historian Al-Mas'udi recorded that Caliph Umar Bin al-Khattab, one of Muhammad's companions, slayed a ghul with his sword on the road to Syria in the early 600s.[36]

Soldiers during the Gulf War witnessed thousands of rotting corpses strewn all over the desert and six-lane Highway 80 between Kuwait and Iraq, remembered as the "Highway of Death." The mangled bodies half-buried in the drifting desert sands were the victims of a 10-hour turkey shoot of more than 2,000 retreating Iraqi military vehicles by Coalition forces on the night between February 26 and 27, 1991. American soldiers also reported glimpsing terrifying emaciated humanoids emerging from the dark desert at night, crawling on all fours, just naked skin and bones. They seemed impossibly fast, demonstrating their hidden strength when they would pull the bloated bodies from the highway wreckage to drag them off and feed. The local folklore claimed these creatures defended and lived in old tombs out in the desert, practiced a pre-human religion, and spoke their own language. They preyed on lone travelers at night, considering humans inferior and to be punished for forgetting the old gods.

I DREAM OF DJINN

Djinn or *jinn* are shape-shifting spirits made of fire and air that were worshiped by pagan Arabs long before the introduction of Islam in the seventh century.[37] The word means "demons or spirits" and also "hidden from sight," and the word "genie" shares the same Arabic root. Neither inherently good nor bad, the entities practice free will and can appear as both animals and humans. They were believed to be masters of certain crafts and the muses of inspired soothsayers, philosophers, and poets. Elements of nature that could turn land fertile, they could also be asked to protect loved ones and avenge murders. As spiritual beings, djinn are considered interdimensional—having the ability to live and operate in both the human reality and their own separate realm—and are described in the Quran as being able to interact with people despite being made of a "smokeless fire." They inhabit desolate, dingy, and dark places in our world and are most feared when they remain invisible, attacking without being perceived. Black magicians seek to gain and manipulate the power of djinn by performing blasphemous and impure acts and rituals with the Quran, only acquiring the granting of wishes after winning violent battles with the entities.

One type of djinn named the *ifrit* is said to appear in our reality as black smoke. Veteran Jerry Aberdeen recounts a haunting incident that occurred in 2004 at FOB Diamondback airfield in Mosul, Iraq, while he was attached to 2nd Battalion, 3rd Infantry Regiment, 3rd Stryker Brigade Combat Team (SBCT).[38] When a call went out over the radio announcing that the airfield was under attack, he jumped in the closest vehicle heading in that direction, joining an engineer and a PSYOP soldier in a Humvee. When they arrived, the men spotted some insurgents trying to climb over a wall, so they dismounted, taking up a position in a ditch on the side of the road. They all took aim and fired, one of them dropping a man from the top of the wall. They all watched as a strange stream of black smoke seemed to begin coming out of the fallen fighter, and the engineer commented that he must be wearing a malfunctioning suicide bomber vest. After a few more seconds, the black smoke grew larger and started to morph into a humanlike form. The soldiers all watched in disbelief as the fully materialized smoky figure stood upright, flashing its red, glowing eyes. The weird-looking mouth seemed to smile menacingly before it turned to run, the smoke dissipating completely after it took a few steps. "Very hard to describe how it all happened. All three of us just looked at each other wide-eyed for a second or two. After it was all over, we only spoke about it once, then never again," Aberdeen stated.[39]

A Marine veteran calling himself "Talon" served in 2008 at Camp Korean Village in Anbar Province, Iraq.[40] It was midday as he was walking the narrow alleyways created by the HESCO defensive bar-rier perimeter, and he glanced to his right down another alleyway as he passed it. From about 20 feet away, the Marine observed a robed, bearded man standing horizontally on the side of a wall. The man's face was toward the sky, about 5 to 6 feet off the ground, and his clothing was not "hanging" like gravity should have caused it to do. Talon stopped, backstepped, and leaned back warily to see the man now standing on the ground, arms crossed, head cocked, and staring menacingly right back at him. He was definitely a physical person and also knew that he had been seen. The Marine reported the incident to his officers, who didn't know how to respond, and it badly affected his nerves for over a week.

CHAPTER 5

The Ghosts of War

DURING THE ALLIED INVASION OF ITALY IN WORLD WAR II, THE U.S. 82nd Airborne Division's second combat operation was a night parachute drop onto the Salerno beachhead on September 13, 1943. In order to guide the C-47 transport planes to the small drop zones, oil drums filled with gasoline-soaked sand were ignited every 50 yards when signaled, hence the operation being remembered as "The Oil Drum Drop." Private Emile Williams, a paratrooper from the 504th Parachute Infantry Regiment (PIR), was dropped south of the Sele River and found himself pinned down in an all-night firefight.[1] As he laid back and was reloading his weapon, he suddenly spotted the dark silhouette of a man high above him, the obscure figure caught momentarily in the flickering flames. Terrified it was an enemy soldier, the trooper was frozen until he realized it was a fellow American parachutist, tangled up in the top branches of a tree and dangling helplessly. He assumed the man must be dead but called out to him anyway, and was completely surprised when the entrapped soldier whispered back, "Please help me."

Williams reassured his comrade that he would cut him down and get him on the ground as soon as the gunfire eased and the enemy withdrew, and continued to speak to him throughout the long night. The trapped and obviously in shock soldier's desperate reply would always be the same three simple words: "Please help me." Dawn approached as the resistance was finally fading, and the men of the 82nd started to emerge from positions everywhere, reuniting with their units and getting organized. As the sun broke over the horizon and finally illuminated the landscape, the relieved paratrooper on the ground looked up to finally see his new friend's face. What Emile Williams saw left him disturbed for the rest of his life.

The paratrooper in the tree had clearly been dead for quite a while, his neck limply bent and broken, impossibly squeezed by the tangled parachute cords wrapped around his throat. There was absolutely no way he could have spoken in that condition, let alone survive the many hours of the night through which he had continued to respond to Williams. Horrified, but determined to keep his promise, Williams climbed up into the tree and cut the dead man free. Afraid to be labeled insane, he wouldn't share his chilling story with anyone until decades after the war ended.

* * *

As a worldwide phenomenon that spans all religions, cultures, personal beliefs, and time periods, ghosts pass the litmus test for me as a legitimate part of our reality. Battlefields or places of sudden mass murders have always been labeled hot spots for paranormal experiences, which makes sense when you ponder the amount of unexpected and violent death that accompanies war and killing. There are many theories as to what causes a haunting or what a ghost may actually be. One theory is that a haunting is an energy imprint: a place where so much emotional power was spent that it created a lasting effect on the surrounding environment, like an image negative. The haunting is like seeing glimpses of a film that plays on an eternal loop. The mass death of thousands of young fighting soldiers at places like Gettysburg and Normandy would certainly provide that level of emotional energy. My own bizarre experience in Pennsylvania that I described in the "Welcome to Weird War" introduction to this book could almost only be explained by the presence of the lingering ghosts of war.

In December of 2015, I was in rural central Mississippi on the set of the horror film *Don't Kill It*, starring Dolph Lundgren, at the invitation of the director, Mike Mendez. I had written an unproduced screenplay for Mike years before and we had remained friends. I was there for a few days to enjoy seeing him at work and to film a scene as a featured extra; I played a possessed cop and got to shoot and chain-saw a bunch of people—you know, normal everyday stuff. To house the entire crew, the production company had rented a Christian summer camp, which included several different buildings. One of them was the oldest house on the property, which also sat apart from the more modern facilities over the hill. The set gossip was that the large, two-story plantation house was haunted, and the film's costume designer, Toby Bronson, told a harrowing tale of what he had experienced while moving his stuff in on the first night there.

Alone in the place, Toby was unpacking in one of the upstairs rooms when the light started flickering on and off. Then a door downstairs suddenly and violently slammed shut. He yelled, "Stop!" and the light in his room came back on. He raced outside and claimed that when he glanced back at the house, he witnessed what looked like a human "torso" exit the front door and disappear into the nearby woodline. After Mike heard the story, he looked at me and exclaimed, "Yes! That's where we're staying tonight!" My tepid enthusiasm waned even further when we arrived at the house later and I found the only remaining room for me was, of course, number 13.

Either I was too tired to notice, or no ghosts were active that first night in my presence. The next day we shot scenes on location in an old roadside cinderblock bar from dawn till dusk. When Mike and I returned exhausted to the darkened house that night after dinner, we found several of the film's producers, a couple of the actors, and Dolph Lundgren's longtime stunt double, Tony Messenger, seated in the candle-lit living room around a damn Ouija board. They had found it in one of the downstairs closets and were about to start summoning. I took a hard pass on participating, as I do not have any desire to invite such entities into my spaces, but Mike was excited and jumped right in to take the lead. I sat down on the couch and—I'll be honest—my heart began to race.

Their hands joined on the planchette, Mike called out to the spiritual void of the house, "Is anyone here? Is there something here that wants to communicate with us?" No sooner had he spoken the question than an open door to a bedroom behind me suddenly and violently slammed shut. We all jumped, gasped, and turned in disbelief. Tony leaped up and checked the door over, then opened it, and we all looked around inside the empty room. A few of us checked the entire house for open windows or doors, anything that could have caused a powerful draft of air. Everything was sealed up tight. Mike was thrilled, having always wanted to believe in the supernatural but never having experienced anything himself. He was a skeptic who wanted to be a believer. I was already a believer who really wasn't enjoying the validation!

The group focused their mental energy around the spirit board again, and Mike asked, "Can you show us again that you are here?" We all tensely waited in anticipation, but still jumped and gasped when the door suddenly slammed shut once more. Everyone chattered excitedly, and all of us agreed that this was the kind of in-your-face evidence that would prove an actual haunting. Tony opened and checked the door again. The next time, when the spirit was asked, "Who are you? What is your name?" the door slowly moved to close on its own, noisily creaking shut before our amazed eyes. One of the producers also noticed a change on the fireplace mantle, pointing and directing us to look, and terror ran even colder through our bones. A weird, old-fashioned doll that had been sitting there facing away from us had now inexplicably turned its head and was looking in the direction of us and the Ouija board.

Freaking out, we all decided this had to be the most conclusive evidence of a ghost that any of us had ever witnessed. It was thrilling, terrifying, and impossible. How could this be happening?

Tony Messenger suddenly stood up and spoke loudly, his heavy and distinctive Australian accent silencing the rest of us. "Yeah, how could this be happening? I mean, I'm not sure what spirit's been slamming that door, but it also might be because of the fishing line I attached to it earlier and that I've been pulling on all night!" He yanked on a nearly invisible line hidden under the chair he had been sitting in, and the not-so-demonic door slammed shut again. The stuntman also explained that he had turned the doll's head at some point when we had all been focused on the bedroom door. My laughter contained more than a tinge of relief, as it was comforting to know that it had all just been a damn good practical joke. For Mike Mendez, having been 100 percent convinced it was real, the experience confirmed for him that remaining an open skeptic about the supernatural would be smart.[2] Outside of what was intentionally put on film, none of us experienced anything paranormal in the house during our remaining time there, despite our imagination's best attempts to produce something.

Anytime someone claims to have made contact with a spirit or experienced something unexplained, we should always consider all the options before declaring the report valid. More often than not, seemingly impossible and unexplainable events can be both perfectly possible and fully explained. The problem is, sometimes the ghosts of Weird War refuse to cooperate with logic and the skeptics, and leave us grasping for answers with fear in our eyes.

THEY REMAIN

During World War I, the area surrounding the city of Ypres, Belgium, was the setting for several of the conflict's bloodiest battles. It was a gloomy night there in December 1914, and British Lieutenant William Speight was still mourning the recent loss of a fellow officer from his unit.[3] When a shadow slowly crossed his face in the dimly lit trench dugout he called home, he looked up and was shocked to recognize that very same officer standing in front of him, not saying a word. The dead man pointed to a spot on the wood plank–covered floor and then simply vanished. Thinking he may have dreamed the entire incident, Speight made sure to have another witness with him the following night in case it happened again.

The lieutenant and the other officer witnessed the specter enter the hovel again after midnight, and the ghost repeated his action of pointing at the same spot on the dugout floor before disappearing. Disturbed, Speight had his men immediately start digging a hole there, and just a few feet down they discovered a secret German tunnel packed with explosives. It had been rigged to explode within hours and would have killed them all. The bomb was defused and the tunnel was collapsed. The men were thankful that their dead comrade was still watching over them and had saved many of their lives.

* * *

The World War I German U-boat UB-65 seemed to be darkly cursed from its very inception.[4] During construction in 1916, three crew members died of asphyxiation in the engine room and two others were crushed by a falling girder. When the vessel was tested for seaworthiness, another crew member was swept overboard (or possibly jumped off) and never seen again. During the first test dive, a crack in a ballast tank caused the boat to sink to the bottom of the sea. When the ocean water began seeping in, it reached the batteries and caused them to give off deadly fumes, almost suffocating the entire crew. The submarine was finally retrieved after 12 hours. And before UB-65 finally set out to sea, a defective torpedo exploded and injured several crewmen and killed the second officer, Lieutenant Richter. These incidents convinced the Germans that the ship was cursed, and no one wanted to board or be assigned to the submarine.

Soon after UB-65 left port in January 1918, a starboard lookout in the conning tower reported seeing Lieutenant Richter standing on the deck below him. His excited shouts brought the captain to the tower, and he also witnessed the apparition before it disappeared. While the vessel was back in port later for repairs, a sailor claimed he had seen the dead officer come on board; another seaman had watched the lieutenant seem to float up the gangplank toward the bow. The ghost stood there for a few moments before vanishing. The haunting became so severe that the crew no longer wanted to remain on board. The Imperial Navy finally ordered another captain to investigate and assume command, but he soon reported that he believed the men, too.

Looking for a solution to ease the fears of the crew, a Lutheran pastor was enlisted to board the sub and perform an exorcism on the craft. The ritual must not have worked, as the ghostly officer returned again in May 1918 and was seen entering the torpedo room. Moments later, the crew found the space empty. Not long after, the torpedo gunner kept claiming the phantom would not let him be, and is reported to have gone insane before throwing himself overboard and drowning.

UB-65 and all 37 of the remaining, cursed crew were lost off the coast of Padstow, Cornwall, on July 10, 1918. Official German naval records reported a premature explosion of an onboard torpedo as the cause. American submarine USS L-2 had spotted the craft and was maneuvering to line up a shot when they witnessed the huge explosion, which caused the submarine to rise up on its bow and sink. Several U.S. sailors claimed to have seen a mysterious man standing on the deck, seemingly unfazed by everything, just before UB-65 went down. It was a figure in a German officer's overcoat, standing near the bow with folded arms. "If this can be believed, Lieutenant Richter may have put in a final appearance," wrote researcher Tony Allan in 1997.[5]

* * *

Throughout the Pacific Islands, the rusting remains of World War II lie scattered and half-buried in the sand along beaches and inside the defensive fortifications the Japanese once inhabited. Their cave complex located in Central Java, one of the Greater Sunda Islands in Indonesia (then called the Dutch East Indies), maintains an eerie vibe despite the renovations made to attract tourists. The overnight security guard has worked there for over 15 years and has experienced several hair-raising events.[6] He claims that he has seen a Japanese soldier with bloody, severed legs come crawling out of the subterranean darkness. The wraith cried out in pain and then vanished before the guard's eyes. Another time he was patrolling the beach area and was suddenly and inexplicably assailed by deafening machine-gun fire. He dove prone into the sand and kept his head down, as he sensed the bullets actually whizzing above him, although no muzzle flashes could be observed, and distinctly heard the loud shouting of battle orders in Japanese. The firefight ended as suddenly as it had started, and afterward there was no physical evidence of anything having occurred.

A 1st Marine Division veteran of the brutal 1944 Bloody Nose Ridge battle on Peleliu Island returned to the remote location in the 1990s as part of a reunion tour.[7] He walked into one of the many oceanfront caves and was surprised to easily discover the remnants of a Japanese gas mask and a rifle shell casing. He took the souvenirs home with him, and the artifacts were eventually left to his grandson when he passed away. Almost immediately, the grandson began experiencing bad feelings around the mask, and claimed to hear a mysterious and terrifying voice at night coming from the room it was kept in. He believed the unnatural voice was speaking in very broken English with an Asian accent, say-ing, "I'm looking for help." Richard Kimmel, a paranormal researcher, acquired the mask in order to try to document the phenomenon. Perhaps the gas mask belonged to one of the 27 soldiers and 8 sailors who refused to surrender and held out in the caves of Peleliu until April 22, 1947, only giving up after a Japanese admiral convinced them the war was over.

* * *

Throughout what was once the Pacific Ocean Theater, strange, disem-bodied voices—seemingly from the past—are still heard transmitting wartime messages across radio frequencies picked up by spooked modern boat and airplane crews. A more than 70-year-old vintage radio at a Scottish heritage center, Montrose Air Station, still broadcasts big band music and speeches from the World War II era, despite not being opera-tional or connected to any source of electricity. Montrose was established in 1913 by the Royal Flying Corps as Britain's first operational military airfield. The Pye valve wireless radio set is part of a display kept in a re-creation of a 1940s room in the original headquarters building. The mysterious broadcasts come on at random times and can last for up to half an hour.

Bob Sutherland, a trustee and treasurer for the center, said, "I have heard it playing Glenn Miller and recognized the song as 'At Last.' The volume was very low but the music was quite identifiable."[8] Graham Phillip, another volunteer, has heard what he was sure was Winston Churchill delivering a speech to the nation. Sutherland, an experienced former wireless operator with the Royal Air Force (RAF), and other radio technicians were brought in to examine the device. When the back was removed, they found "nothing but cobwebs and spiders." They also said it would probably explode if someone actually got it to switch on. Volunteer Marie Paton, whose father bought the wireless secondhand in 1962, said, "It's a bit scary. I thought someone was playing a prank on us, but I heard it myself last Saturday. It plays Glenn Miller, and that's what everyone has heard. It is very faint and you have to put your ear to it, but that's what it's playing. All the experts say it should be impossible."[9] The wireless broadcasts join a long list of unexplained mysteries at the air station, where visitors have reported strange "energies" felt around the airfield, invisible footsteps, doors opening and shutting on their own, the sound of aircraft engines, shadowy figures walking in and out of rooms, and the sighting of a pilot in a full flying kit.

* * *

At dusk on September 2, 1942, U.S. Army Air Force pilots assigned to the China Task Force were enjoying a peaceful evening coffee under a low, thin, and overcast sky near Kenow, China.[10] Their relaxation was suddenly rattled by adrenaline when the Chinese Warning Net harshly broke over the radio, reporting an unidentified plane approaching from enemy territory and heading in their direction. Two of the pilots immediately sprinted for their waiting P-40 Tomahawk fighters, taking off in a flurry of noise and motion to intercept, quickly climbing above the cloud cover and making visual contact with the plane.

What they saw was unexplainable. The plane's entire fuselage was pockmarked with bullets, most of the canopy was shot away, and it had no landing gear. Even more eerie, the aircraft was an outdated version of the same planes they were flying, a Curtiss P-40B Tomahawk, and displayed obsolete U.S. Army insignia—a white star surrounded by a blue field and outlined in red—that hadn't been used on American aircraft since the attack on Pearl Harbor the previous year. The pilots agreed that this had to be some kind of Japanese trick, as there was no response to radio calls or flashing recognition signals. One pilot fired a short machine-gun burst into the wing roots, and then they both pulled up alongside the mysterious craft.

The phantom pilot was slumped over, apparently dead. Yet the plane flew onward in a straight line, seemingly coming from out of the past and approaching from an impossible direction. With no landing gear, how had the plane even gotten airborne? There were no known friendly airstrips within the 500- to 700-mile (804–1,127-km) range of that type of aircraft, so where had it taken off from? How was a plane that was no longer in use, let alone in such wretched condition, still flying? Lacking any logical answers, the pilots conjectured that they had just encountered a weird paranormal phenomenon with some type of ghost pilot flying a phantom fighter. The legend of the World War II ghost plane was born.

Thanks to decades of individual research by another World War II Air Corps veteran, Curt Norris, this seemingly supernatural enigma was solved an incredible 43 years after the event.[11] While attending a reunion of Bataan and Corregidor defenders, Norris heard the testimony of former Sergeant Milton McMullen of the 701st Aviation Ordnance Squadron, 19th Bomber Group, regarding his firsthand knowledge of that exact plane.

The 1st American Volunteer Group, later famously remembered as the Flying Tigers, was formed right before the Japanese attacked Pearl Harbor. A small number of these mechanics and pilots en route to China were forced to divert when the war started, ending up on the northern coast of the island of Mindanao in the Philippines. Several naturally camouflaged jungle airstrips were established, and combat missions were flown, but losses in the air, no spare parts for repairs, and overall limited resources due to their extreme isolation quickly diminished their inventory of available aircraft.

In February 1942, the army planned to break through the Japanese blockade of the Philippines with several ships carrying food and ammunition to resupply desperate defenders. One of only three freighters that evaded the enemy, the SS *Anhui*, ran aground in Gingoog Bay, off the shores of Mindanao. In addition to the cargo of essentials, three older, disassembled P-40B Tomahawk fighters were on board. The Americans were overjoyed and immediately put them into use. Just a short time later, Bataan, Corregidor, and the Philippines would fall to the Japanese, with most Allies being forced to surrender and taken prisoner. The flying guerillas of Mindanao, hidden deep within the jungle vegetation, carried on their limited actions and regularly salvaged any nearby crashed and wrecked aircraft, hoping to always keep at least one airplane able to take to the sky. The day finally came when the squadron had to face that reality, retaining only one remaining flying craft—the last of the assembled Tomahawks.

The left landing gear had been sheared away during a take-off run, but the pilot was still able to make an excellent landing, convincing the men it was capable of one last flight. The decision was made to try to reach China, the nearest friendly territory to the island, and plead for the marooned unit's rescue. After several failed and then improved fabrications, the ingenious crew designed a skid to aid in taking off, made from a metal frame and shaped bamboo, which could be detached by the pilot after getting airborne.

The normal cruise speed of a P-40 was 300 mph, with a range of 500 to 700 miles. The mechanics removed all nonessential parts to make the aircraft lighter and then welded on an external gas tank underneath. With the extra fuel and by instructing the pilot to throttle back to 180 mph, the crew believed the range should increase to 1,200 to 1,300 miles (1,931–2,092 km).

The unknown pilot, possibly a Pole with a Boston accent, took off the morning of September 2, 1942, on the very last mission of his life. He apparently almost made it to friendly lines, and likely was killed a short time before the Americans encountered his flying corpse. Sergeant McMullen, captured by the Japanese shortly thereafter, never knew the fate of his last P-40 until he met Curt Norris decades later and heard the tale of the ghost plane. Unfortunately, Norris passed in 2002 at the age of 75, and my attempts to locate any family members proved fruitless. We may never know if he ever discovered the actual name of the ghost pilot, the only true phantom that remains in a story where the truth turned out to be more incredible than the myth.

* * *

The fact that America deployed 20,000 troops to Bosnia in 1995 as NATO peacekeepers is often forgotten, but 1st Armored Division cavalry scout Elmer Kilred won't ever forget.[12] He was part of the first units to move into and secure the Posavina Corridor, a critical east–west geographic route connecting the two halves of the contested territory where Bosnian Muslims and Bosnian Serbs had bitterly killed each other during the three-year conflict in the former Yugoslavia. The Bosnian War led to the deaths of around 100,000 people, with millions more displaced, and was marked by ethnic cleansing. The resulting genocide claimed at least 80 percent of Bosnian Muslims, or Bosniaks.

While encamped in a rural area outside a desolate town that had been ethnically cleansed, the American scouts became aware of a possible soldier or sniper spotted inside one of the abandoned houses. The individual's presence was also indicated by a trail of fresh boot prints in the snow, leading up to the window outside the room in the structure. Three Bradley Fighting Vehicles (BFWs) were positioned on the road to surround the house, and a team of dismounted infantrymen entered cautiously. When the soldiers breached the room where the man had been spotted, there was no one there. The tracks outside ended at the window, and there was no escape route from the home or anywhere to hide inside. Kilred and his unit reported the bizarre event and tried to stifle the growing uneasiness they were all feeling.

A few weeks later, in February 1996, Kilred and another soldier were on overnight guard duty at the front gate of their camp. At around 0300 hours, as they were attempting to stay warm around a blazing fire barrel, the men heard someone slowly approaching through the sucking mud. Looking through the dim light, they observed what appeared to be a Bosnian soldier coming up to the gate. As his partner covered him, Kilred walked over and noticed that the stranger's uniform was very dirty and ragged, like he had been wearing it for an extremely long time. His eyes were chilling, holding the dead glare of utter fatigue—otherwise known as the thousand-yard stare of traumatized combatants. "It's like he looked through me while looking at me," Kilred said.[13] By his gestures, it seemed the man was looking for a cigarette, and the American scout obliged by handing over one of his own. Kilred then leaned closer over the concertina wire to light it, and the man shielded the wind around his mouth until the flame caught. The stranger silently waved a thank you, and both men turned away from the camp gate.

Within a moment, Kilred heard the other American soldier who had been covering him exclaim, "Where the hell did he go?" and immediately turned back to look. Inexplicably, the strange soldier had completely disappeared. The bewildered guards quickly opened the gate and spotted the man's footprints in the mud with their flashlights. Following his retreating steps, they were disturbed to find the trackway completely vanished just three or four feet away. Somewhat terrified, they closed the gate and remained on high alert for the remaining two hours of their guard shift. After much deliberation, both soldiers decided not to report the event to their commanding officers.

HURRICANE HAUNTING

More than 51,000 U.S. Army National Guardsmen responded to the devastation caused by Hurricane Katrina in New Orleans and along the Gulf Coast in August 2005. They assisted in search and rescue, medical treatment, evacuation, and security. Troops from every state and territory flooded into the region, working to distribute food, ice, and water. They also plugged broken levees, prevented looting, and searched through thousands of damaged and destroyed buildings. A California Army National Guard unit moved into an evacuated historic building on Napoleon Avenue in New Orleans: the Sophie B. Wright Middle School.[14]

The sprawling 11,000-square-foot, three-story building was built in 1912 and designed by prolific local architect E. A. Christy in the Collegiate Gothic style. Originally, it was the first public high school for girls in the city. With massive masonry walls as thick as 22 inches in some parts, the U-shaped brick building was hardly damaged during the powerful storm and became the perfect staging site for missions around the battered city. It also served as the living quarters for the Golden State soldiers, who often felt another presence was sharing the space with them. Sergeant Robin Hairston said, "I was in my sleeping bag and I opened my eyes and in the doorway was a little girl. It wasn't my imagination."[15] Specialist Rosales Leanor may have seen the same spirit, reporting, "I was using the restroom and I just saw a little shadow, kind of looming in front of me." A third member of their unit opened a closet looking for cleaning supplies and was shocked to see and hear a young girl giggling inside for a brief moment.

The paranormal activity peaked when a soldier was awakened by an odd noise in the middle of the night and turned on his flashlight. Something had moved his rifle to the other side of the room and emptied the bullets from the magazine; they were now scattered and rolling across the floor. He was alone and the door was closed.

The unit's chaplain finally decided to perform an army version of an exorcism, walking through the school and exclaiming, "In the name of Jesus Christ, I command you, Satan, to leave the dark areas of this building!"[16] The unit moved on before they could really know if the ceremony had worked. I just wonder: Which of the behaviors had convinced the overzealous chaplain that the little girl ghost was so evil?

The school has since been beautifully renovated and now operates as a successful charter high school and middle school, with no recent reports of ghostly activity. It seems the little girl just didn't like the army being in her school.

THE SHINING OF SADDAM

"Abu Ghraib was like the Overlook Hotel. It was haunted. It got dark at night. So dark. Under Saddam, people were dissolved in acid there, women raped by dogs, brains splattered all over the walls. This was worse than the Overlook Hotel because it was real. It was like the building wanted to be back in business. There was a darkness about the place," a former guard told writer Jon Ronson in June 2004.[17]

When Saddam Hussein took formal control of Iraq in 1979, he also took control of a sprawling 280-acre prison complex 20 miles (32 km) west of Baghdad named Abu Ghraib. Originally built to house 4,200 prisoners inside five separate cell blocks—with each individual walled compound containing cramped 13- by 13-foot (4- by 4-meter) cells—it also featured primitive dining and washing facilities, a prayer room, an exercise yard, and numerous imposing guard towers.[18] Under Saddam's totalitarian regime, overcrowding with political prisoners almost immediately became a problem, and those tiny cells inhumanely held up to 40 prisoners each at a time, with the prison maxing out at approximately 15,000 captives by 2001.[19] The place became a representation of Saddam's evil reign, synonymous with torture, suffering, and death.

He also had a special addition to the prison constructed, hidden away deep inside an isolated area and dubbed Saddam's "Death House." The one-and-a-half-story building allowed mass executions to secretly take place away from the world's prying eyes; over 4,000 people were believed to have been killed there during just the year 1984, with more than 30,000 murdered in total.[20] Those awaiting execution were corralled into eight small holding cells until there was no more room. Then they would be escorted two at a time to a crudely designed gallows, where two hangman nooses were tied to the large iron beams in the ceiling. The prisoners would be positioned over the two trapdoors in the floor, which were separated by a long metal switch that opened them. Others could be exterminated in the small gas chamber that lay beneath the floor, reached by a tiny set of descending stairs. A mass execution on December 10, 1999, in Abu Ghraib claimed the lives of 101 people in one day.[21] On March 9, 2000, 58 prisoners were killed.

At Al-Zahedi, on the western outskirts of Baghdad, secret graves near a cemetery contain the remains of nearly 1,000 of the executed prisoners. According to an eyewitness, 10 to 15 bodies arrived at a time from the prison and were buried by local civilians. Saddam was even rumored to have brought his sons Uday and Qusay to the Death House when they were young in order to teach them how to kill and to ensure that they would become sadistic.

According to the stories, at night the thousands of cries and pleas for mercy from the unhinged inmates would congeal into one deafening and unearthly song of misery, another true cacophony from hell. That amount of emotional distress, coupled with the atmosphere of hatred and constant death, had to have been absorbed and embedded forever within the spaces there.

At the start of Operation Iraqi Freedom in 2003, Abu Ghraib prison was occupied and used as a Forward Operating Base (FOB) and a detention facility by both the U.S.-led coalition and the Iraqi government. The unlucky unit selected to perform correctional duties there was an activated U.S. Army Reserve force from Maryland, the 372nd Military Police (MP) Company. Never having been trained for corrections, the 300 unprepared soldiers were tasked with overseeing nearly 6,000 prisoners.[22] Anxious and perpetually terrified of a revolt, the MPs checked their fears and carried out their assigned duties. It wasn't long before changes started to take place in them, as if the dark energy of the prison itself was being absorbed into their bloodstream. "The place was just so dark . . . it felt like it was a haunted place," said Sergeant Kevin Davis, reflecting on his time there.[23] The Americans knew the history of the building, saw the Death House, and witnessed wild dogs outside the walls constantly digging up the decaying corpses of the executed to feed on. The permanent odors of rotting trash, nervous sweat, feces, and urine tainted the scent glands forever. Another MP described the setting as being "like *Apocalypse Now* meets *The Shining*, except that this is real."[24] Sam Provance, a military intelligence contractor at Abu Ghraib from 2003 to 2004, remembered, "At nighttime, there were certain hallways you wouldn't go down by yourself, because you were afraid there might be a ghost, and if there was something there, it was really pissed off."[25]

In April 2004, the U.S. television news show *60 Minutes* exposed a world-level scandal investigated by *The New Yorker* magazine, which described inhumane torture, abuse, and humiliation of Iraqi detainees at Abu Ghraib by the 372nd MP Company and contracted government civilians during 2003. The story included disturbing photographs depicting the physical, psychological, and sexual abuse of prisoners. They were hooded and bound, piled like animals in compromising positions, some with their hands and genitals connected to wires. Charles Graner, Lynndie England, Sabrina Harman, and eight others were investigated and convicted in 2005 for war crimes, with several being sentenced to military prison. It seemed like the cursed place had actually encouraged violence and planted evil in the minds of those who had come there, and the shocking incident came to symbolize the worst of the U.S. occupation of Iraq. In March 2006, the U.S. Army was eager to distance itself from such a black mark on their history and transferred control of Abu Ghraib prison to Iraqi authorities, who renamed it Baghdad Central Prison.

A year before the transfer, Captain David Goodwin of the 35th Engineer Brigade, Missouri Army National Guard, was dispatched to Abu Ghraib for a one-day fact-finding tour to assess the prison's technical design. His guide was a prominent U.S. contractor who had previously been the facility's warden. When Goodwin remarked that the prison seemed to be "immersed in a surreal blanket of despair," the contractor opened up and said that the place definitely had its own "energy," especially felt at night.[26] He related that older parts of the prison "played tricks with your mind," and that it was in the deepest, blackest corners where he and other staff had seen strange shadows and heard disembodied voices.

As they approached the locked gate of the now-empty Death House, Goodwin sensed "the sting of 1,000 unblinking eyes" watching him from the dark entrance of the whitewashed monolith. Major Anderson, another officer hosting the tour, told about an unnerving experience he had once before while inside the courtyard of the slaughterhouse. He had been suddenly overtaken by an irrational feeling that someone or something was going to slam the huge gate locked behind him and the group he was with, even though he held the keys in his hand. The fear was crippling, unlike anything he had ever endured before. This time, when Anderson unlocked the gate, Captain Goodwin passed inside and later described smelling a cloud of cool, damp air tainted by rot and decay. He felt an overwhelming emotion of sadness walking through the prisoner holding area and the gallows.

Having taken photographs throughout the building, Goodwin and others in his group were speechless when they reviewed them later that day. All of the group's pictures looked normal until those taken in or around the Death House, which appeared to contain images of strange mists and orbs of flickering light. Adding to the authenticity of the phenomenon, several weeks later another touring group had the same thing happen to their photos—the same location, two different groups, at two different times, experiencing the same phenomena.

Although Abu Ghraib has been closed and vacant since 2014, local Sunni Arab residents blame the dark effect of the cursed prison for an abundance of social, economic, and emotional issues. School enrollment has dwindled, hundreds of acres of farmland lie unused, and more than 70 percent of the 450 homes adjacent to the facility have simply been abandoned.[27] Gurfan Ala, a housewife in the district, said, "I used to laugh at the housewives in my neighborhood when they complained of their children having nightmares, or they talked about ghosts who knocked on doors and tried to enter their homes . . . but then my eight-year-old son Rafid started to tell me strange things that were happening to him."[28] Because the neighborhood schoolhouse overlooks the prison, teachers have pasted newspapers over the windows or replaced them with tinted glass, and they don't allow the children to go in the recess yard.

A real estate agent, Ibrahim Abbas, reported that the only people choosing to remain in the Abu Ghraib area are internally displaced people or those who have nowhere else to go. "Some people rent one of these houses, but they end up moving after a while because of what they believe is the curse that affects this area around the prison. People talk of ghosts inhabiting these houses and some say they heard screams of torture. They believe that these voices were of detainees who were tortured and then killed in Abu Ghraib prison. The land of Abu Ghraib is cursed."[29] One clueless homebuyer, Waled Hamid, filed an unsuccessful lawsuit against the property seller for not disclosing that the house was haunted. "I didn't know anything about the history of this area. Now we are frightened in the house. At night, everything gets creepy and the dogs and cats act strange. People here are grim and miserable. They don't exchange greetings, as if they are zombies. I really want my money back so I can leave this house and neighborhood for good," he said. A local cleric, Sheikh Abdullah al-Zobaie, offered Waled his simple solution: "Evil spirits can be exorcized by reciting the Quran and praying to God in the house."[30]

Let's hope it all worked out for Waled and his family.

SEND 'EM TO THE CEMETERY

The lines separating life from death blurred and merged together at the world's largest graveyard, Wadi-us-Salaam—the Valley of Peace—located 93 miles (150 km) south of Baghdad in Najaf, Iraq. Containing the remains of over five million Muslims, the cemetery comprises 13 percent of the city and is roughly the size of 900 rugby fields, or 5 square miles (13 sq km).[31] It is also the only graveyard in the world where burials have been continuous for over 1,400 years. Absorbing about 50,000 corpses a year, the grounds have often taken in over 200 bodies on a bad day. The soil is considered sacred by Shia Muslims because of its proximity to the gold-domed Sanctuary of Imam Ali—the revered cousin and son-in-law of the prophet Muhammad—and being buried there is believed to assist in the journey of the soul to heaven. Casualties of the war with Iran, the Gulf War, the Shia uprising against Saddam, and the

Iraq War all lay buried there side by side. The grounds had to expand after the American-led invasion, the rough graves at its edges fading into wild desert. Near the main entrance, talismans that are believed to keep away both ghosts and a special class of cemetery djinn that feasts on human flesh are sold in great quantities. Longtime gravedigger Hani Abu Ghnaim reported, "I saw [the djinn] at night, jumping from grave to grave to feed on freshly buried bodies. If we come across it, I scream at it to go away."[32]

In August 2004, soldiers of the 1st Cavalry Division's 5th Regiment and leathernecks of the 11th Marine Expeditionary Unit (MEU) found themselves engaged in a bizarre 36-hour battle among the endless maze of tombstones and mausoleums in Wadi-us-Salaam. Hundreds of Shiite militia belonging to the Mahdi Army had laid siege to the main Iraqi police station in Najaf and then ambushed the U.S. Marine force sent to reinforce it. The fighters then dispersed and disappeared into the nearby sprawling landscape of tombs, heading for the refuge of the Sanctuary of Imam Ali, which had become a mission staging ground once the insurgents had realized Coalition forces wouldn't risk damaging the sacred shrine there. The cemetery surrounding it was quickly determined to be less sacrosanct, however, and the unsettled Americans followed them inside.

Over the next few days, the up-close battle raged through the treacherous gravesites, a jumbled maze of tombs, mausoleums, and catacombs where the enemy could attack from underground or overhead. The Shiite militia would jump out from behind headstones and tombs, crawl up from out of the earth using an intricate underground tunnel network, and shoot from sniper blinds set up in the top floors of hotels along the borders of the graveyard. Other times, soldiers were surprised not by enemy fighters, but by hordes of bats erupting out of disturbed crypts. Sergeant Hector Guzman of the 1st Cavalry Division described the stressful situation: "Most of the time, it was like jungle warfare, only without the jungle."[33] Fellow Staff Sergeant Thomas Gentry added, "You're on top of the vehicle, you can see forever, but all you're looking at is tombs." One of their officers provided a relatable visual: "It was like New Orleans meets Baghdad."

While armored vehicles and dismounted infantry on the ground probed the cemetery expanse, warplanes, helicopters, and armed drones circled overhead and attacked with Hellfire missiles when requested. "We feel bad that we're destroying, that we're desecrating graves and such," admitted Staff Sergeant Gentry. "That's not what we want to do." One of the most haunting aspects was the many photographs of grave occupants that had been framed and left on fresh burial sites; the images stared back at the soldiers as they stumbled and fell through the graves. "You just know you're destroying that tomb," said Sergeant Guzman. "It doesn't feel right sometimes."

When the battle for the graveyard was over, more than 300 enemy fighters and four Marines would add to its always-hungry and ever-increasing body count.[34] Veterans of the nightmare-like fight say nothing will ever do justice to the weirdness of battling among the surreal landscape of the Valley of Peace, and nothing will ever dispel the terrifying imagery permanently imprinted on their minds.

THE BAGHDAD KILL HOUSE

Veteran Dallas Sanchez provided a blood-chilling account of his unexplainable experience in the Al-Dora neighborhood of Baghdad near the end of 2006.[35] He remembered it was near Christmas when he headed out of the Green Zone on his seventh or eighth mission as part of an eight-man Sniper Kill Team (SKT). Their objective was to set up a HIDE—the position for a sniper to occupy—and pull a 24-hour silent overwatch on a certain sector of the city to observe any unusual activity, such as a Fighting Age Male (FAM) digging a hole in the ground to emplace an IED. They would preselect a house to break into that offered excellent cover and concealment, observation, fields of fire, and a "back door" through which the sniper could escape undetected to another HIDE position.

The team left the FOB around 0100 hours and drove around the city for a couple hours, the many unattended bodies in the streets making the whole metropolis smell like decay and death. When satisfied that they had thrown off any potential surveillance, the soldiers silently dismounted near the target house, wary of the roving death squads that were always on the hunt for Americans. As they approached the selected house to break in, his best friend strangely said, "Something is wrong here. Something bizarre."[36] After forcing their way inside, the soldiers all briefly heard what Dallas described as an unwholesome "congregation of whispers," like hundreds of disembodied voices trying to communicate at the same time through a radio speaker. Disturbed, the men broke off into pairs to clear the house.

Upstairs, Dallas and his friend found the top floor to be a stark, empty concrete room with one wall scarred by bullet holes. Inserting a pencil to gauge the angle of the rounds, the holes were determined to be straight, meaning people had likely been lined up against the wall and shot there. The soldiers felt their blood run cold as they realized they were standing in the kill room of a kill house. Dallas suddenly felt constricted and sensed a presence, making him desperate to leave the space. He knew everyone on the team was just as anxious, but wouldn't admit it or talk about it because of the need to complete the mission, as well as their fear of ridicule.

On the first floor was a storage area sealed off by a heavy wrought-iron gate. It took two men to pick it up and open it. Six of them went inside to check out the room's contents, which were stacked floor to ceiling and allowed little room to maneuver. It smelled old and was pitch black inside, so they used the red filters on their flashlights. Losing his sense of time, Dallas worked his way toward the back of the space and found a box of interesting paintings in a box. Turning to share with the others, he saw nothing but darkness around him and with a shock realized that he was somehow now alone in the room. He felt the fear drop like a lead weight in his gut and wanted to panic, scream, and run so badly, but he forced himself to remain silent and maintain mission security. He quickly moved back to the entrance and was horrified to find the heavy gate closed so tightly it felt sealed. Dallas waited a few minutes for someone to come back, the time stretching for what seemed like an eternity, but he was absolutely alone. He violently threw himself against the iron, desperate to escape, but to no avail. Turning off his flashlight, he peered out and saw the moonlight in the distant courtyard, suddenly becoming afraid to look behind him. He began hyperventilating and sweating profusely, feeling his weapon was useless and sensing that something was there and wanted him gone. He felt so terrified that even mission security wasn't important anymore, and he was about to scream. At that moment, he watched as the immovable gate silently and impossibly began to move on its own, swinging completely open.

In sheer terror, he rushed out and went straight to his best friend, angry and demanding to know why he and the others had left him in there. His friend told him he had no idea what Dallas was talking about, as they had all gone in, checked the room out, and then left together. Confused, Dallas waited out the rest of the team's time in the house and tried to focus solely on his duties. When the Quick Reaction Force (QRF) trucks arrived to extract them a day later, he realized that one of the paintings from the storage room was still in his rucksack.

Back on base, their local interpreter, Sam, told the team that the house they had been in was "unclean" and that many people had died there. He said the locals in the neighborhood would not go in there. Dallas was happy to give the painting away to the unit's medic, who really liked it. Five months later, Dallas Sanchez was hit by a VBED (Vehicle Borne Explosive Device) and said that the possibility of death in that moment was not as scary as when he was in the kill house. "I felt that if you died there, in that presence, death would have a very different set of consequences. Maybe being trapped there forever."[37]

OUTSIDE THE WIRE IRAQ

Saddam's Republican Palace in Baghdad was spared during the "shock and awe" bombing campaign that kicked off the invasion. Elements of the 3rd Infantry and 1st Armored Divisions were the first American troops to occupy the grounds in April 2003. One late night several infantrymen were sitting round the fireplace, and all watched in stunned bewilderment as an Iraqi woman seemed to glide by in the hallway.[38] They yelled for her to stop and jumped up to confront her. When they reached the hall just moments later, she had disappeared. A search of the place turned up nothing, and the guards on the entrances had seen no one enter or leave.

* * *

An M1 Abrams tank crew was at FOB Brassfield-Mora in Samarra, Iraq, in 2003.[39] The base was near the Al-Askari Shrine, a Shia mosque and mausoleum built in 944, also known as the Golden Dome Mosque. The soldiers would use their sophisticated optics to scan the ruins at night, looking for any insurgents. The stones held residual heat and produced a glow in their sights. On various nights, several tank crews witnessed cold spots moving through the ruins and in between the burial sites at the mausoleum. These slow-moving icy shapes would appear clear as day on the powerful main gun sights, darting in front of and behind the stones. Yet when viewed with the naked eye, there would be nothing there.

* * *

From the edge of the wire at Camp Blue Diamond in Ramadi, Iraq, it's nothing but open desert for a couple kilometers until a group of abandoned buildings and a cemetery. Scanning the desert with NVGs one late night while on guard duty, a Marine suddenly spotted a man standing about 300 meters (984 ft) directly in front of him.[40] It didn't make sense as he had seemingly popped up out of nowhere in all that empty space. Another Marine saw him too, and tagged the FAM with his aiming laser. When the Marines switched to using PAS-13 thermal scopes, the mysterious man disappeared, displaying no heat signature. Both Marines could see the figure with their NVGs, but not with their thermals, nor when they lit up the area with powerful lights. A fire team was assembled and sent out to investigate while the others kept their eyes on him with the NVGs. As the patrol came up out of a draw about 50 meters (164 ft) from him, the man vanished. They found a set of stationary footprints, with nothing leading up to or away from them. Eight Marines witnessed this event.

* * *

At an undisclosed FOB in Iraq, soldiers on guard in towers would repeatedly witness an unidentified man walk out from the wire about 200 meters (656 feet) and then disappear.[41] He could clearly be seen with the naked eye, but did not display a heat signature on thermal sights. Trying to solve the mystery, the men eventually dug up the ground around where the figure always vanished and were shocked to discover the site of an old mass grave.

* * *

A soldier working alone at FOB Warhorse near the Baquba Airfield in Iraq had a bizarre experience one night.[42] It began when he heard someone walking on the rocks outside his converted office CONEX (cargo container) and went to greet them. Once outside, the sound stopped and there was no one there. The moon was bright and illuminated the ground, where he saw the shadows of "spiked crescent" shapes zipping by, seemingly from overhead. When he looked up, nothing could be seen in the sky. Later, at around 0400 hours, he was backing up to park at the LSA (Logistical Support Area) when someone unseen started banging hard on his truck. Thinking he may have hit someone, he got out and looked around, but no one was present. He also saw a small light out near the HESCO barriers that seemed to be dancing around, which disappeared when he walked out to the area. Finally, when he was returning to his office right before daybreak, he glimpsed a strange man in a white T-shirt sitting on his heels and leaning up against another container nearby. Suddenly processing the out-of-place image, he turned back to go ask the stranger who he was and what he needed, but the man was gone, nowhere to be found.

* * *

FOB Endurance, near Mosul, included the remains of the Qayyarah Airfield West (aka Key West) that had been taken over from Iraqi forces. One old structure remaining there was a sturdy concrete bunker equipped with metal blast doors. The male soldier reporting this incident had developed a rather close relationship with a female soldier named Sarah (hey, it happens), and they had decided it was the perfect setting for their secret nightly rendezvous.[43] It was secure, with only one way in and out. The second night there together, Sarah woke her boyfriend up because she was hearing something inside the bunker with them. He shrugged it off at first, until he clearly heard footsteps too. When they shined their flashlights around, nothing was there.

The next night the male soldier was awakened by whispering coming from a corner of the bunker, followed by footsteps approaching his side of where the couple laid on the floor. He woke Sarah and turned his flashlight on, expecting to have been busted, but again there was nobody there. The blast door was still secured like they had left it. Finally, on what became their final night in the bunker, Sarah spoke to the unseen entity and declared that they weren't in the mood to be messed with and just needed sleep. Her request was obviously ignored, as they were awakened by whispers in the corner again, but this time in two different voices. Terrified, the two lovers heard footsteps approaching their makeshift bed, which was then shaken violently for a few seconds, followed by a deafening sound like a metal plate being dropped next to them. When they finally found and switched their flashlights on, there was nothing to be seen again. They quickly left and reluctantly returned to their separate bunks, never spending another night in the haunted bunker again.

* * *

Anbar Province is both Iraq's largest and least populated province, and a small outpost located there known as "The Ranch" was basically just a couple of tents surrounded by HESCO barriers with a few observation posts. Marine platoons, known as "Ranch Hands," cycled in and out, providing security for contracted advisers working with Iraqi forces. The rugged terrain of the base was punctuated by a strange mixture of abandoned structures and artifacts from wars gone by that locals took great pains to avoid. A Marine who rotated through The Ranch in 2018 reported that right before morning prayer, in the area in front of some decrepit and abandoned Iraqi barracks, they would often hear the sound of kids laughing and running, although no children were anywhere nearby.[44] He also once heard someone sprinting up steps when no one was there. One night he spotted a motionless figure standing beneath a streetlamp about 984 feet (300 meters) away, appearing more like a translucent outline. When he attempted to view the person with thermals, the fully charged batteries suddenly went dead and the man disappeared.

Another unexplainable incident occurred one night while he was watching over the empty desert expanse in front of The Ranch on guard duty.[45] Spotting a close, low, and glowing light—possibly a headlamp on a person—the Marine took a closer look with his PAS-28 thermals. He spotted a small burning bush and nothing else, with no movement detected. The flames extinguished and a new glow ignited about 820 feet (250 meters) to the right and closer to his position. After getting another guard to confirm what he was seeing, they watched the bizarre process continue for the next few hours. The small grass clumps would spontaneously ignite on their own—one going out and another one immediately starting—hundreds of meters apart in a sparse desert with no winds. The cycle ended with no explanation before morning.

* * *

A squad of soldiers was set up in an Iraqi house as a Sniper Kill Team (SKT), overwatching an intersection that was often rigged with IEDs.[46] At the first light of dawn, they spotted a FAM carrying an artillery round toward the road crossing. Although it was too bright for Night Observation Devices (NODs) and still too dark to see very clearly, the threat was confirmed and the sniper took the shot from about 175 meters (574 feet) away. The reporting witness was watching through a scope and saw the round hit the skinny man in a T-shirt, who collapsed and dropped. They reported the KIA to their Tactical Operations Center (TOC) and called in the QRF to pick them up. As per protocol, the QRF team was responsible for checking the body for intelligence, putting the corpse in a body bag, and dropping it off at the local Iraqi Police station.

The QRF team arrived and spent the following 20 minutes searching for the dead insurgent, scouring the area in concentric circles and finding absolutely no evidence—no body, no blood trail, no artillery round. The entire SKT team had seen it happen and were completely bewildered. Back at the FOB, the guys faced a lot of ridicule, as they had reported the kill over the company frequency and had nothing to show for it.

Years later, the witness ran into a fellow veteran at a bar and discovered that he had been in the unit they had replaced in that location. At one point, the conversation turned to discussing the large amount of IEDs they had both encountered there. The other veteran, unprovoked, proceeded to share a weird story about a squad from another platoon in his company who swore they had killed an IED emplacer but could never locate the body. Several of them had been convinced that they had all shot and killed a man at the same exact intersection. Two separate incidents at two different times with the same exact outcome could only be a coincidence—except in Weird War.

OUTSIDE THE WIRE AFGHANISTAN

An army private on night watch at an Afghanistan COP (Combat Outpost) reported seeing someone out in the wilderness who was just standing there.[47] The individual had just suddenly "popped up," seen at first as only a dark blob vaguely shaped like a person. His sergeant and another squad member confirmed with optics, describing a FAM with average height and build, standing motionless with his back turned toward them. When they put thermals on the figure, there was zero heat signature detected. The disturbing presence remained observed in the same place for the next three hours before randomly and unexplainably disappearing. The squad members spent the next six weeks telling anyone who would listen about the "ghost" they had seen that night.

* * *

It was 0100 hours by the time a force of soldiers on patrol in Afghanistan had settled in for a few hours of sleep, leaving four soldiers awake on guard duty. In front of their position was a huge empty field; to their left was an old cemetery. As the witness blindly stared into the darkness in front of him, he heard a rock suddenly come swishing through the air and land at his feet. The space it had originated from was wide open with no cover or blind spots, yet he could not detect any person or movement near him. As he was looking, another rock came spinning by his head. Using both night vision and thermals, he scanned and confirmed the field was vacant. A third rock would be tossed his way before the bizarre happening stopped. The soldier remembered, "This happened right after my team leader died. So, I was freaked out and [there was] nothing to rule out what threw [those] rocks at me because no one was there."[48]

An eerily similar incident occurred in Helmand Province in 2011.[49] A soldier standing post at 0200 hours on a small OP was trying to stay alert. He was in a small plywood structure protected by bulletproof glass and sandbags. Suddenly, a loud "bang" resonated inside the four walls and the trooper instinctively ducked, believing it was an incoming enemy round. He quickly realized it had been a rock. Scanning the area with thermals produced no heat signatures. Whoever or whatever had thrown the projectile quite a distance—at least 200 feet (61 meters)—outside the cleared buffer that lay beyond double-stacked razor wire. The anxious soldier radioed the Combat Operations Center (COC), and they scanned the landscape with a large thermal camera, but found nothing. Finally starting to calm down after about 15 minutes, his adrenaline surged again when a second rock struck one of the walls even harder. The trooper scanned the area again, looking at every possible hiding spot, but could find nothing. He spent the rest of his shift with his rifle ready and his heart pounding.

* * *

A soldier on guard around midnight in early 2012 heard gravel crunching under someone's feet just below his post, in a blind spot.[50] The Helmand Province patrol base used the pebbles to attempt to keep the never-ending dust down. The Americans called the powdery, flour-like substance "moon dust." Knowing that the only other person awake was another guard, a radio operator in the COC, he called out, "Who's that?" There was no reply, but the gravel crunching stopped. The trooper called the radio watch to ask if he was outside, and when he answered "negative," he directed the soldier to assist him in checking the disturbance out. As he watched the man exit the COC, the noises below him started up again, this time sounding like an individual running. Believing someone unidentified was in the wire, the guard yelled, "Stop, or I'll shoot!" in Pashto. The sound stopped just as the radio watch reached the area below him and went around the corner prepared to shoot. No one was there. The aggravated soldier accused the guard of being paranoid or overly tired.

About an hour later, the same exact sound was heard again. Beyond nervous, the soldier woke up his friend, and they stood post together for the last hour of his shift. Nothing else was experienced.

* * *

The FOB Delhi massacre occurred on August 10, 2012, when an Afghan teenager entered an on-base gym and used an AK-47 to kill three Marines and wound another.[51] The base in the Garmsir District of southern Afghanistan was also the site where a Marine had repeatedly reported seeing a mysterious man down at the HESCO barrier wall along the Helmand River.[52] He was described as being dressed in local traditional robes, but possessed unnaturally black eyes and a gaping mouth. A camera on the same wall that was remotely controlled from the COC would often glitch at night, moving on its own to focus on the spot along the river where the man was always seen. Some unlucky Marine would be selected to go out and manually reset the camera, but luckily none of them ever encountered anything.

* * *

An EOD (Explosive Ordnance Disposal) team was requested to check out a possible old landmine reported by a local Afghan farmer to have been found in his field. When they arrived, he brought the American soldiers into his home and then informed their interpreter that his dead father was haunting and cursing the house. The farmer pointed to an ornate urn that sat on a prominent shelf and further explained that he had lied about the reported mine. He just wanted to get them there to help him, as he assumed that the United States would have some type of technology to deal with such matters. The EOD sergeant, thinking creatively, asked the man how attached he was to his dad's ashes, who replied, "Get him out of my house!"[53] The soldiers took the urn out into the middle of the field and applied a 40-pound cratering charge to it, exploding the remains into even further dust. This EOD-style exorcism gives a whole new meaning to the term "ghostbusters."

* * *

A Special Forces team inserted into the mountains of Afghanistan was tasked with secretly observing a village suspected of harboring Taliban fighters, and with gathering intelligence for a future raid.[54] Two Green

Berets would sneak in closer to different vantage points while the other six would hang back and maintain an overwatch. They went in undetected and successfully set up operations. Starting on the second day, the team began having trouble maintaining radio contact with both the two forward observers and their distant TOC. The transmissions were distorted by static or just wouldn't be received at all. At dusk, two men were sent to reposition the satellite communication to try to get a better connection. As they were out doing this, one of them spotted a man wearing a white robe who seemed to be flitting and running through the boulders and rocks.

Anxious about being compromised—as a small force with no reinforcements nearby and suddenly unreliable communications—the team reunited and decided to head for their predesignated extraction point. While on the move, the reporting witness was bringing up the rear, and on one of his glances back he glimpsed something white moving in the darkening distance. He also suddenly felt very odd, sensing the smell of freshly baked bread in the air and being blanketed with a feeling of peace and relaxation, which he knew was emanating from the direction they were leaving. It was so powerful that he actually slowed down, entertaining thoughts about sprinting back to this comfortable place that was pulling on him so hard. He concentrated and dispelled the feeling, telling the others that they were possibly being trailed. Their officer commented that he had seen something white moving behind them, too. A third man chilled them all when he said, "That's strange . . . thought I saw some dude in white on the ridge in front of us."[55]

The atmosphere around them suddenly felt strange, going silent and making their body hairs stand on end. The air felt heavy and smelled sort of sweet. By this time they were wearing their Night Observation Devices (NODs), but no movement was detected and no forms were outlined in the green-filtered haze. A loud, low buzzing was then heard, which slowly increased in pitch until it was similar to the roar of a huge airplane taking off, forcing the team to yell over comms to hear each other. The reporting witness described next seeing what looked like glowing eyes everywhere, appearing in the dark until he would focus directly on them, which seemed to make them disappear. Everyone was holding their weapons at the high ready, expecting an ambush of some kind at any moment—when just as suddenly it all stopped.

The night was silent and dark again. The team dug in and performed SLLS (Stop Look Listen Smell) for the next 10 minutes. Afterward, confused and just a bit frightened, the soldiers resumed their march on heightened alert. The witness would see the ethereal figure once again, on a parallel hillside, where it seemed to be slowly and steadily moving toward them in the moonlight. He could clearly see it was a man, dressed in light-colored robes, who appeared to be gliding and passing through any big rocks or obstacles in an unnatural way. Zooming in with the NOD, he was terrified to see the man stop and look directly back at him—something that should have been impossible to do at that distance without using night optics of his own. The figure seemed to pick up one of his limbs and hold it in the air, like he was waving at the soldier. Then the arm melted back into the form, like it wasn't an arm at all. As the witness briefly looked away to ask the others if they could see the bizarre sight too, it apparently vanished. The last strange thing witnessed were lights flickering in the distance far back near the village.

The Special Forces team was extracted successfully without further incident. After reporting the strange events during their debriefing, they were told the experience was likely just an effect of weariness, panic, and adrenaline. Days later, the raid on the village was conducted by some other operators and the mission deemed a success, even though the place was found to be recently abandoned.

THE SPECTER OF FOB SALERNO

FOB Salerno was located in the southeastern province of Khost, Afghanistan. Its location in a hostile region ensured it stayed kinetic, with many violent attacks made there through the years. But, even after engaging the enemy in 22 firefights during deployment there in 2005, it wasn't the Taliban that scared the leathernecks of the 3rd Battalion, 3rd Marine Regiment—it was a little three-foot-tall girl who just wanted to play.

On the outskirts of the sprawling compound was an old Afghan graveyard overlooked by two high guard towers. Two Marines on duty one late night spotted a young Afghan girl with their night vision optics, who, curiously, was just walking along the dark road that led up to their watch tower, Number Six. When they removed their NODs, they couldn't see her anymore. Placing them back on, the troopers were startled and terrified when they suddenly saw her standing right in front of them on the balcony. They both "noped" the hell out of there and ran down the stairs, refusing to return to their assigned posts even after being threatened with punishment.[56]

In April and May of 2005, 82nd Airborne soldiers from the 2nd Battalion, 504th Parachute Infantry Regiment, began a Relief in Place, taking over regional operations from the Marines at FOB Salerno. The paratroopers laughed at the Marines' ghost stories and accepted them as just another form of military hazing. The joking stopped for Specialists Drew Painter and Jeremiah Jackson two weeks into the deployment.[57]

On duty one quiet night in the same "haunted" tower Number Six, the two soldiers jumped out of their boots when they heard a painfully shrill laugh break radio silence. It was unmistakably a little girl's laughter, impossible for a grown man to imitate. When it stopped, they immediately contacted all the other posts to see if they had also heard it, but none of them claimed any transmission had been received. Painter and Jackson figured the others were playing a practical joke on them, and they were determined not to bite.

The next night, when the two reported back to the tower for their shift, they admitted they were a little anxious and jumpy. A few hours later, some strange events began. They both reported feeling like "something" was moving behind them, and every once in a while they could detect what sounded like someone walking over the trapdoor that led down to the middle level of the structure. They would continually ask each other if either one had made the noises or were moving around. When they both noticed a sudden temperature drop in the space, the troopers instinctively moved together to the corner housing the radio. The radio squelched and the nearest tower reported, "We're detecting a three-foot-tall form walking around the base of your tower that looks like it's waving."

Terrified, Specialist Jackson went to investigate. "I walked around the whole balcony and didn't see anything," he reported later.[58] The other tower didn't see the figure anymore either. Now fully spooked, he and Painter counted down the time remaining on their shift. With less than an hour to go, they were told that their relief was going to be late, possibly by as much as two hours. They cursed and complained, but were put more at ease when the sun dawned without further incident. Painter commented, "That night, you could just feel it," and Jackson added, "There were no jokes that night."[59]

A third related incident happened to two unnamed female aviation soldiers while they were stationed at FOB Salerno.[60] There were basically two compounds that made up the base: the main one with all the facilities where most personnel stayed, and a separate one for all the aviation troops. The two women had decided to walk over from their distant compound to visit a friend on the main side who was pulling tower guard duty one moonless night. The long trip over was uneventful, and after a good visit they realized that they needed to start back. The two women got turned around in the dark and confusion of the mazelike base, and ended up outside the compound and lost. They returned the way they had come, and their friend got them reoriented back at the guard tower.

Starting out again, the soldiers clearly heard someone walking behind them and turned to see who it was. There was no one there and no movement detected. Freaked out a little, they walked on at a faster pace, and both heard something coming up behind them once again. A visual scan revealed nothing, making both wish that they had night optics at hand. The troopers reached the intersection where they had previously made the wrong turn and nervously jogged the rest of the way back to their compound, deciding not to ever make the trek by foot again.

Months after the deployment, their infantry friend who had been on guard duty that night would tell them something that would freeze the blood in their hearts. He said that he had been watching them walk away with his NOD to make sure they went in the right direction. When they reached the intersection to go back to their compound, he had suddenly spotted a small figure walking just behind them. He radioed the other tower to confirm what he was seeing, and they reported they didn't see anything except the two women. Knowing he still had months to serve in the watchtowers of FOB Salerno and not wanting to be forever spooked, the soldier decided to deny what his eyes had seen and convince himself that it was just a trick of the light. He didn't want to tell them then either, because it would mean he'd have to believe it had actually happened.

THE PHENOMENON OF OP ROCK

A singular exposed mound of earth, rising 65 feet (20 meters) from the surrounding landscape like a dirty brown blister, overlooks the low poppy fields in the Garmsir District of Helmand Province, Afghanistan. A natural observation point and defensive position since the time of Alexander the Great, ancient arrow slits and the remnants of fortified turrets on its eastern flank hint that it was once a larger mud fort, not just an exposed giant pile of hardened dirt. The U.S. Marines assigned to this lonely and spartan outpost would also come to recognize it as a place of convergence for unexplainable events and unadulterated horror—earning its rank as one of the most haunted places on earth.

Observation Point Rock sat about 1,969 feet (600 meters) southeast of Patrol Base Hassan Abad near the village of Amir Agha and was manned by rotating squads who stood guard watching for the enemy. Amir Agha is also the home to an important Muslim shrine dedicated to the man of the same name, a revered descendent of Muhammad, making the entire area spiritually sacred. Surrounded by cases of ammunition and rockets, the Marines at the outpost were the first line of defense for the main base, and were expected to engage any incoming bad guys and to call in air support if needed. According to a local scholar in Garmsir, the original foundation of OP Rock was indeed a fort, built in some ancient time by forgotten invaders or defenders.[61] Another bump in the desert, visible in the far distance south of the mound, shows that there was once a line of these primitive forts. When Ahmad Shah Durrani was appointed as the king of Afghanistan in 1747, he sent Pashtun settlers to occupy and farm the area. The tribesmen regarded the mysterious elevated structures as spiritual sites and began using them as burial tombs.

When this practice ended is unclear, but events beginning with the Soviet invasion of Afghanistan would add stacks of fresh corpses to the ground under OP Rock. Local Mujahideen fighters surrounded and captured 40 policemen working for the Communist Afghan government in

1980.[62] These men were taken to the top of the Rock to be mass-executed and buried there in shallow pits. Family members came and disinterred some of the dead, but many were just left forgotten in the ground. In 1982, the Soviets made an offensive push into Garmsir, softening up the Amir Agha resistance with over 50 dropped bombs.[63] One of these missiles actually struck the village shrine dead center, yet miraculously was deflected harmlessly into the sand. This event was considered divine intervention by the locals. When a force of 10 Soviet Armored Personnel Carriers (APCs) and a couple tanks made their approach to attack, they came under heavy fire from insurgents on OP Rock and became bogged down in the mud. The Soviet infantry had to dismount, and they took heavy casualties out in the open. A longtime resident, Abdul Ghani, remembered, "Several tanks went into the earth and disappeared."[64] Two of the marooned APCs' rusted skeletons still remain east of the OP and north of the shrine even today, symbols of the costly Mujahideen victory. The many dead Red Army soldiers were collected and buried together on the Rock, unceremoniously heaped on top of the previously massacred policemen. Ghani warned that the area around Amir Agha and the OP Rock was still considered "heavy and fearful" because "the area is full of dead bodies and haunted."

In early 1995, the Taliban conquered Garmsir, along with the rest of Helmand Province. After the United States invaded in 2001, the Taliban occupied and fortified the elevated structure as its own outpost, possibly adding a tunnel and cave complex underneath it. The Taliban never had a chance to defend the position though, as a 2,000-pound (907 kg) American bomb was dropped on the western side of it, collapsing the structure inward on itself.[65] The occupants were engulfed in flame and entombed inside; their lungs likely collapsed and their organs turned into jelly. When the 1st Battalion, 6th Marine Regiment, occupied the area in 2008, the dominant height of the surviving hardened dirt pile still offered the best position to watch for the enemy. Not knowing anything about its dark history, they chose to ignore the advice of village elders who told them not to stay up there because it was "cursed by the stranded souls of invaders." One of the Marines first assigned to the outpost, Corporal Andrew Rouser, is credited with naming it the "Rock."[66]

Lance Corporal Brendan Kelly discovered the remnants of small tunnels at the base of the mound, all leading to a single central chamber thought to be the main old tomb, not part of the Taliban renovations. "It was creepy," he said.[67] The Marines decided to collapse the tunnels with demolition charges before handing the fortification over to the British troops rotating in to relieve them. This seems to be when the disturbing phenomena began.

The Brits were back on old battlegrounds, having waged a series of three fairly disastrous conflicts called the Anglo-Afghan Wars (1839–1842, 1878–1880, and 1919) in which Great Britain, from its base in India, had sought to extend its control over neighboring Afghanistan and to oppose Russian influence. In "The Lost Legion," an 1892 fictional story eerily presaging the events at OP Rock, English writer Rudyard Kipling tells of a squadron of British cavalry riding out on a night mission in 1887 to arrest some troublesome Afghan tribesmen whose village is in a well-defended position high in the mountains.[68] In the darkness the riders hear the sounds of what they think is another mounted force surrounding them, and find themselves stumbling over little piles of stones, as seen in an old graveyard. The troops make their way up to the village and surprisingly capture the fighters without resistance; the tribesmen claim that they had just been terrified by spirits. The British realize that they had just ridden through the scene of a massacre 30 years before (the Great Mutiny of 1857) when a native Indian regiment, deserting from the British Army into the hills, had been slaughtered by these very same tribesmen. In Kipling's story, the murdered Indian soldiers had returned as ghosts to scare the Afghan fighters, so that the new British soldiers would not be killed—thus, the native Indian troops fulfilled the oath they had violated to the Crown by fleeing and finally were able to rest in peace.

The British unit stationed at OP Rock, believed to be elements from the 2nd Battalion, Princess of Wales's Royal Regiment, apparently had some otherworldly encounters too. There were whispers of unexplainable dancing lights, moving shadows, and hazy forms outside the wire—briefly glimpsed and observable with night vision goggles, but not on thermals. There were tales of weird noises and unidentified voices often heard when no one was there, including bloodcurdling shrieks and screams coming from the empty darkness.[69] These reported events were noted to peak between midnight and 0400. At first, the officers dismissed the talk among the troops as a possible result of round-the-clock guard shifts, hallucinations from months of staring out from sandbagged trenches, and sheer boredom. By the time a new company of U.S. Marines arrived in June 2009 for the next rotation at Patrol Base Hassan Abad, their opinion had severely changed.

When the eight-man squad from the 2nd Battalion, 8th Marine Regiment, first rolled up for duty at OP Rock, they all thought it looked like nothing more than a looming giant anthill standing out in the open, but several of them felt a strange vibe right away—especially Lance Corporal Damian Zolik.[70] The British had literally everything packed up and seemed more than ready to go. They also looked extremely haggard and drained. None of them talked much beyond conducting a rushed orientation, but their commander made a bizarre final point to tell the Marines not to disturb anything buried, and to make sure they put it back if they did. The Americans laughed it off, figuring it was the British way of trying to screw with the new guys.

The squad checked out what would be their new home for the next two months and began to move in. The living area on top of the mound was empty, just bare dirt. The Brits had left only one thing behind, a good-natured mutt they had named Ugly Betty, which they claimed was an excellent sentry. The squad's second-in-command, Corporal Jacob Lima (spelled "Lena" in several secondary sources), immediately decided to become her new caretaker. Later that night, as he watched the dark horizon for any sign of the Taliban on his first shift, the sleeping dog at his feet was awakened by static coming over the observation post's radio. Weird crackling and gurgling sounds faded in and out, unintelligible but seemingly non-English. Corporal Lima radioed the main base to ask if they had transmitted something, but they replied, "Negative, over." Later that night, when his squad leader, Sergeant Green, came by and tapped him twice on the shoulder, he almost jumped out of his boots. He told him about the radio interference, and his sergeant suggested trying new batteries.

After conducting an assessment of the outpost's overall defensive capabilities the next day, the first thing determined was, of course, the need to dig in deeper. Any infantryman knows that when you go static at a location, you dig. Whether it's foxholes, trenches, or filling up HESCO barriers with dirt, you dig. And the British hadn't dug their trenches deep or wide enough, allowing exposure to sniper fire. The Taliban was known to attack OP Rock with small-arms fire and Rocket-Propelled Grenades (RPGs), usually on Sunday mornings, and the men of "America's Battalion" understood the high price of carelessness. By that summer of 2009, 40 Marines had been killed and over 160 wounded in Helmand Province, most by roadside IEDs. The 2nd Battalion, 8th Marines, would lose more than a dozen more during their seven-month deployment there between May and December 2009. The squad got to work.

Almost immediately, one of the Marines hit something metal and recovered what appeared to be an engineering stake. Brushing it off, the men weren't that surprised to see Russian lettering on it, knowing the history of the area. As Lance Corporal Adam Wilson dug into the rock, part of the outcrop collapsed under his shovel, revealing a small hole filled with ancient pottery shards. Another lance corporal named Smith investigated further and pulled out a long, dry bone, easily identified as a human femur. Smith was told to put it back immediately and rebury it. Suddenly, it seemed like every shovelful of dirt was revealing another random piece of human remains, and eventually whole skeletons and dried out, desiccated corpses were found—one still even wearing glasses. The horrific realization that they were basically on top of a multi-layered tomb was confirmed to the squad of troubled Marines. They reburied the bones and tried their best to forget the remains were right there, under the earth they were living on. "Stick a shovel in anywhere and you'll find bones and bits of pottery," remembered Lance Corporal Ausin Hoyt. "This place should be in *National Geographic*."[71]

About two weeks later, Hoyt was on watch—and feeling watched. Out of nowhere, a bloodcurdling scream broke the silence of the night. Assuming someone may have gotten caught in the razor-sharp concertina wire that surrounded the OP, Hoyt was confused when a slow scan beyond his sandbagged position revealed nothing and no movement.

Having also heard the shriek, both Corporal Lima and Lance Corporal Wilson joined him with their weapons ready. Using thermals, Lima could only detect Ugly Betty trotting out in the distance to investigate the sound herself. The next morning, a perimeter check found no footprints or other evidence of an intruder.

The daytime temperatures at OP Rock sometimes rose over 100 degrees F (38°C), and the heat was getting to Lance Corporal Zolik one night on duty. That was, until an unnatural, freezing chill suddenly came over him, and he swore he felt a breath on his face as something whispered in his ear—in Russian. Realizing no one was there, he rationalized that it was just fatigue getting to him. When he heard the unmistakable sound of footsteps in the firing position above him, Zolik figured it was another Marine playing a prank on him, but he found no one there either. He nervously scanned the area around the post with night vision and spotted what looked like a FAM standing out in the desert with balled fists. The Marine prepared to engage, but first had to positively identify the individual as the enemy. When he looked again, the figure had vanished. Corporal Lima remembered, "He [Zolik] was yelling and begging me to go up to the firing point he was guarding. He begged me to stay in there with him till he was relieved from guard duty. After that he really didn't like standing post up there."[72]

Zolik changed after his experience that night, becoming withdrawn and frustrated when no one would believe him that the OP was haunted. He was so unhinged that he soon put in for a transfer, which was immediately granted. The other members of the squad were left feeling abandoned by Zolik, believing that he had been searching for any way out of the punishing assignment.

A night not long after Zolik had left, Lima was on duty and, at around 0130, was alerted by Ugly Betty wildly barking. The corporal raised his night vision goggles and felt his blood freeze when he spotted a figure in the distance. The possible enemy fighter seemed aware of being watched, as it looked like he was staring directly back at the Marine. Wanting to confirm before engaging, Lima switched to thermals, but suddenly couldn't locate the target. He switched back to the NVGs and felt an adrenaline surge when he found the person again, now somehow about 328 feet (100 meters) closer to his firing position. The thermal optics would not register any heat signatures, yet he could clearly find the figure in the fuzzy green world of night vision. Ugly Betty continued to sound off, confirming to Lima that she was sensing something there too, even after he completely lost track of it. When he suddenly felt Sergeant Green's distinctive double tap on his shoulder, Lima drew a deep breath and turned around . . . to find no one was there.

Now understanding and feeling empathy for Lance Corporal Zolik's experience, Lima was worried that his other squad members might think he was going crazy. The situation was making the loneliness and isolation of the deployment more intense and unbearable, and he didn't know how to process it all. He wouldn't have to wait long before realizing the rest of the men were feeling the same way.

Around the sixth week of their rotation at OP Rock, Lance Corporal Hoyt was standing post and heard footsteps approaching behind him. When he turned, expecting Sergeant Green on his rounds, no one was there. Ugly Betty arrived at the scene, growling at something unseen. Hoyt anxiously returned to scanning the landscape and heard the crunching of gravel behind him again. He suddenly felt ice cold and swore he felt something breathe on him. A feeling of dread became overwhelming, and he knew some presence was there. The following night, Lance Corporal Wilson was on the machine gun post when the same kind of cold chill hit him and he heard bizarre whispering. The voices grew progressively louder and more distinctly Russian, until he actually felt something touch his ear. Later, Wilson learned that the phrase he believed he heard, *bros svoye oruzhiye*, translates to "drop your weapon" in Russian.[73]

Every member of the squad eventually experienced similar situations. Even considering the acute anxiety produced by combat, they could find no logical explanation for the multitude of high strangeness they were witnessing, and had to consider supernatural influences. Although they had no exact knowledge of the history of OP Rock, they knew something dark involving the Soviets must have happened there. The men mostly agreed that what was happening to them might have something to do with having disturbed the graves.

The Marines felt like it was all their birthdays mixed with Christmas when the two-month assignment at OP Rock was finally due to terminate. Emotionally and physically drained from constant paranoia and anxiety, they were counting down the hours on their final night before another squad was due to rotate in and take over. Something felt more off than usual and they were all on high alert, which intensified even more when the radio batteries started to abnormally drain power. Within 30 minutes they had exhausted all their available batteries and realized direct communication with the main base was now severed. The sound of machine gun fire suddenly erupted, loud and close.

Corporal Lima sprinted to where Lance Corporal Wilson manned the outpost's machine gun nest, believing it to have been him shooting. Wilson told him he hadn't fired, and then both of them heard the unmistakable sound of an incoming RPG—which never hit. The whole squad ran to man their battle stations, expecting a full-blown Troops In Contact (TIC), but nobody could find any targets to engage. The supernatural firefight ended as suddenly as it had started. The night was empty and silent again, yet they had all heard the attack.

Tom Coghlan, a former journalist for the *London Times*, was the first to interview Corporal Lima and other members of the squad for a newspaper piece on OP Rock as their deployment there was ending in 2009. "It first seemed like stress-induced hokum," he said in an interview, but he soon came to realize "there were some things they just couldn't explain."[74]

The last morning, much like the Brits before them, the Marines waited on the relieving squad with equipment packed and ready. Few words were spoken, but warnings were given about not digging in the ground and being prepared for some strange things happening during their stay. Much like the 8th Marine Regiment had, the incoming troops laughed it off and started unloading. They had no idea yet that they too would be adding another chapter to a legend quickly spreading among the Marines in Helmand Province.

A member of the replacing squad, Corporal Dutch Perkins, remembered, "No one believed them."[75] His own terrifying experience happened one night in the machine gun position, when a detached voice speaking in Russian began whispering around midnight. "Just thinking about it makes my hair stand up on my arm," he said. "It was real faint at first but eventually sounded like someone was standing post with me." Sergeant Josh Brown added, "The local people say that this is a cursed place. You will definitely see weird-ass lights up here at night."[76]

One Marine described the light phenomenon in detail. He said that they would spot what looked like the muzzle flashes of incoming small-arms fire and take cover, but then not hear any gunfire, nor the distinctive snap of any rounds going past in close proximity. The lights would pop up all over the place, disappear, then show up again a few minutes later. Some appeared in the sky, significantly brighter, and seemed to float to the ground like a very dim flare. It seemed like the whole OP was being lit up, but when the Marines would take off their NVGs it would be completely dark again. "As abruptly as it started it ended, and I was back to looking at the land through a fuzzy green lens," he reported.[77]

"The smells were like something was dying. It was really bad at night. And it was like it came in whiffs or gusts," said Corporal Jose Herrera, another veteran of OP Rock.[78] He claims he saw mysterious lights, heard strange noises on the radio, and had the constant creepy feeling of being watched by someone or something. "It was a conduit."

The abandoned outpost will remain, as it always has, surviving centuries of invading armies and eroding winds. It stands as a unique convergence of historical, spiritual, and paranormal significance that will be remembered as a classic ghost story in both Afghan and American cultures. It also stands as a sad reminder of the lonesome deaths of far-sent soldiers, who may have to wander the battlefields of their deaths for a looping eternity.

CHAPTER 6

Domestic Disturbances

HAVING COMPLETED THE NONCOMMISSIONED OFFICER ACADEMY (PLDC) and busted my ass to acquire promotion points in every available way, I was preparing for the final step to become a sergeant by standing before a promotion board. The intimidating panel would be made up of high-ranking personnel who would be asking randomly selected questions intended to test me on a massive amount of required knowledge. I decided the best strategy was to just attempt to memorize it all and be confident in facing any question. Looking back, it was a smart tactic, as I otherwise may have skipped over a piece of information that ended up being the last question I was asked. A question that is the perfect example of how military myth, lore, or legend can often become accepted fact.

The sergeant major on the promotion board I was standing in front of looked me over and simply inquired, "What's inside the truck?" I immediately knew the answer, confidently replying, "A razor, a match, and a bullet. If the base is overrun by the enemy, the last soldier will use the razor to cut the flag down from the pole. The match will be used to properly retire the flag by burning it, as per Flag Code Title 4, Section 8k. The bullet is used to prevent the soldier from falling into enemy hands, by sacrificing their own life." Although my face remained stern and serious, on the inside I was smiling because I knew I was about to be promoted to sergeant.

You see, "truck" is the military term used for the gold ball, or finial, found on top of any base headquarters' flagpole. The real reason a ball is used on most flagpoles is because it won't catch and tear the flag if the standard blows up and over the pole, and it also keeps rainwater out of hollow poles. Although gold eagle finials were used in the past and provided a more traditional approach, flags became hopelessly entangled on them during high winds.[1] The bizarre legend about the contents hidden inside started at some point after the military switched to round trucks, although no one really knows the source. It has become a sort of allegory for the bravery and sense of duty expected from America's warriors when defending our territory.

The U.S. military maintains a presence in at least 70 countries and territories overseas, and in 2022, American servicemen were deployed worldwide to over 150 countries. Most of the time the majority of the nearly 2 million active-duty troops can be found stateside at one of the more than 450 domestic military bases. All 50 states have at least one, but others have multitudes, including California (123), Texas (59), Florida (56), and Virginia (51).[2] Much has definitely changed since the establishment of America's first military installation in 1776—Carlisle Barracks Army Base in Pennsylvania—but one thing that hasn't changed is the chilling reports of weird and unexplainable events and encounters happening at bases across the country.

Most structures on America's military bases, from troop barracks to unit headquarters buildings, were built decades ago and have witnessed multitudes of events as well as the experiences and emotions of countless people. Legends and myths grow around these places, with stories being exaggerated and passed on to new arrivals, and before too long base lore becomes impossible to separate as fact or fiction. It seems that every military facility in existence has its own collection of ghost stories and cautionary horror tales, which servicemen whisper to each other in the early morning hours before dawn while on duty in the field, or during late-night socializing and drinking in the troop barracks.

In addition, the majority of domestic and foreign military bases and installations include massive amounts of undeveloped and uninhabited land, used for training purposes or live fire ranges. Much like protected wilderness areas, the species that live in these spaces enjoy easy access and migration to shelter and food sources and are pretty much left alone to reproduce and flourish. Occasionally, hunting or fishing may be permitted on base, but outside of the random run-in with a service member or outdoorsman, the critters that live in these forests, swamps, deserts, and plains are fairly undisturbed. It would seem that military bases provide the perfect habitat for something that wants to remain undiscovered and hidden, allowed to thrive and multiply in peace.

I was trained or stationed at several places stateside: Fort Dix, New Jersey; Fort Huachuca, Arizona; Fort Irwin, California; Fort Hood, Texas; and Fort Benning, Georgia. I spent the majority of my army time in central Louisiana with the 5th Infantry Division (Mechanized) at Fort Polk, a base that provides a perfect case study example. First established in 1941, it was the training place for thousands of soldiers during World War II, remembered as the Louisiana Maneuvers. In 1962, it became an advanced infantry training center for Vietnam-style jungle combat, immortalized as the legendary Tigerland. The last stop before being sent to the war zone, Tigerland was brutal and as close to real combat as training was allowed to get. It was established at Fort Polk in order to closely mimic the heat and humidity of South Vietnam, which should tell you how wonderful it was to be stationed there, doing physical training every morning and spending a lot of time in the field. The summer heat in Louisiana creates its own unique green inferno and can simply be indescribable.

Beginning in 1974, the reactivated 5th Infantry Division made Fort Polk its home, staying for almost two decades until the Red Devils were deactivated in 1992. In 1993, Fort Polk became the still-operating Joint Readiness Training Center (JRTC), which provides the army's premier pre-deployment light infantry combat training by using highly realistic situations and scenarios, including urban environments with civilian threats and non-threats. The JRTC Opposing Force (OPFOR), a military unit tasked with representing the enemy, are the Geronimos, or G-Men, of the 1st Battalion, 509th Parachute Infantry Regiment.

Fort Polk encompasses approximately 198,000 acres of land, with about half being owned by the U.S. Army and the other half by the U.S. Forest Service, mostly inside the Kisatchie National Forest. Kisatchie consists of more than 600,000 total acres across seven parishes east of the fort. An additional area covering over 100,000 more acres within the post has been designated a wildlife management area.³ The massive amount of space is used for large JRTC maneuvers and live fire operations in a training area I know far too well, named Peason Ridge, also known as "The Box." The land also includes a few archaeological sites, historic houses, and structures within its boundaries. The size of the base, the incorporation of designated wilderness areas around it, and the presence of older cultural remains are all typical of military bases across America—plenty of settings and space for all kinds of weird happenings and encounters.

I spent a lot of time in the wilderness training areas of Fort Polk, especially while serving as the battalion-level intelligence sergeant for 4th Battalion, 35th Armor Regiment. Between my time with M1 Abrams tankers and 4/6 Infantry, preparing for and completing two rotations through the National Training Center within less than a year, it seemed that I permanently lived in the field at Peason Ridge or California's Mojave Desert. Yet, in all those hours spent moving through remote areas and stumbling around in the dark woods or desert, I never experienced anything weird or more terrifying than a spider bite. There's no doubt that sometimes in the woods or in an old building you get that eerie feeling of being watched, or a sudden sense of dread overcomes you when passing through a particular area or room, but actually seeing something like a possible ghost in the barracks or a cryptid behind a tree would have to be absolutely blood-chilling.

Although I didn't witness anything personally, a current active-duty soldier serving at Fort Polk, Nick Orton, has documented many cases of recently reported weirdness going on there through his Instagram page, *Tales From the Gridsquare.* The term "Box Witch" has come to be the name given to anything unexplainable or bizarre that happens out in the training areas. These have included floating orbs, blocks of ice falling from clear skies, dogmen, and black shadows moving through the pine trees. Soldiers have experienced common Sasquatch-like interactions, hearing unearthly vocalizations, and having rocks and pinecones thrown at them from the forest.⁴

The following collected accounts from military bases all over the country constitute just a small sample of the overall amount gathered for research, and are fairly overwhelming when taken together. Even without considering the number of events that have likely never been reported because of fear of ridicule or professional career fallout, it would seem there is a large enough body of convincing eyewitness testimony for even the coldest skeptics to pause and reconsider. Something unknown is occupying both the remote, backwater training spaces and the old, historic base structures of our nation's military installations, proving that a soldier doesn't have to be in combat to become a veteran of this Weird War.

FORT LEWIS/JOINT BASE LEWIS-MCCHORD, WASHINGTON

The Ghillie Dhu, or Gille Dubh, is a solitary male nature faerie from Scottish folklore that is dark-haired and always clothed in leaves and green moss.[5] The unusual figure is also the source for the name given to a particular type of camouflage clothing used by the military, especially snipers. A "ghillie suit" is a net or cloth garment covered in loose strips of material, often made to look like leaves and twigs, in colors that will match the surrounding foliage. The highly effective camouflage gives the soldier's outline a three-dimensional breakup, rather than just a linear one. The Lovat Scouts, a Scottish Highland regiment formed during the Second Boer War, was the first known force to use ghillie suits. They would later become the British Army's first sniper unit in 1916. Similarly, the Australian Army call their ghillie suits "Yowie suits," named for their resemblance to Australian Yowies, the hairy, giant hominins reported to be inhabiting remote areas of the Outback. With literal decades of reported Sasquatch sightings experienced by soldiers at Fort Lewis, Washington, maybe the U.S. Army should start calling their ghillie suits by another name, too.

The Pacific Northwest has long been known as the favorite abode of North America's own mysterious bipedal and hairy hominin. Giant-size and more apelike than human, the Sasquatch species is probably the most recognized cryptid on the planet, thanks to popular culture and the sizable amount of multimedia material dedicated to the subject. Based on extensive Native American history, regional folklore, and a plethora of old newspaper accounts, it seems the creatures were all over the continent long before the contemporary obsession with proving their existence began.

My own theory is that if these creatures do exist, they are actually thriving and growing in population rather than fading out, due to the fact that they are more protected and undisturbed than ever. When President Ulysses S. Grant signed the Yellowstone National Park Protection Act into law in 1872, it was the beginning of a wilderness preservation movement to save America's best landscapes forever. The National Park Service (NPS) was established in 1916 and is the agency within the U.S. Department of the Interior that today manages over 84 million acres of mostly undeveloped and uninhabited land.[6] States also began designating wildlife management areas, adding millions more acres of protected wilderness habitat. It's no accident that most reported Sasquatch encounters happen to hunters and campers in these very same areas. A disturbing thought I've entertained is that perhaps the current uptick in reported sightings nationwide indicates these things are becoming less intimidated by humans, with their genetic prehistoric memory of being relentlessly hunted by our species having finally faded away. The large numbers of people mysteriously disappearing from national parks and wilderness areas without any explanation has been explored extensively by former police officer David Paulides in his "Missing 411" series of case studies and films. Celebrated horror author Max Brooks took the inference even further in his terrifying 2020 fictional novel, *Devolution: A Firsthand Account of the Rainier Sasquatch Massacre.*

Fort Lewis, located 52 miles (84 km) northwest of looming Mount Rainier, was a U.S. Army post from 1917 until 2010, the year it was merged with McChord Air Force Base to become Joint Base Lewis-McChord (JBLM). The property is 647 square miles, with over 300,000 acres making up the Yakima Training Center. Hosting a large and varying number of units from both branches, including the 7th Infantry Division, 1st Special Forces Group, 16th Combat Aviation Brigade, and the 62nd Airlift Wing, it is also the home of the army's 2nd Battalion, 75th Ranger Regiment. The unit hosts and conducts a lot of specialized training, and bizarre rumors have floated around for years claiming that the cadre at JBLM will often warn students who are about to go out on field exercises about something big and dangerous that they might encounter there.

A Navy SEAL team member named "Foster" claims that before heading out on a weeklong night land navigation course at JBLM, army Special Forces cadre told them there would be no weapons allowed and warned them about possibly running into Sasquatch on the base. Thinking it was just another psychological warfare tactic, their attitude changed after several unseen creatures walking on two feet, moving faster than humans could have, stalked and followed them in the dark, seemingly communicating through "catcalls" that sounded like high-pitched primate screams.[7] During a 2021 episode of the television show *Expedition Bigfoot*, an Air Force captain randomly approached show host Bryce Johnson at a gas station in Kentucky and related his 1990 experience while attending elective military training in Washington. He claimed their Ranger instructor told the class that he didn't care if they believed it or not: Bigfoot was real, in the area, and, if encountered, should not be engaged. The instructor claimed things had not ended well for one training team that had done so in the past. The captain went on to say that he believed the government knows these creatures exist and are also aware of and monitoring human disappearances nationwide.[8]

There are various hypothetical reasons as to why the government would choose to not verify the existence of a relict species of giant, hairy hominins in America's wilderness. Following the trail of money, imagine the financial impact on the forest, fracking, and the oil industry from having to regulate habitat protections for yet another endangered species, and then imagine the crushing blow all outdoor-based activities such as camping and hiking would endure from a newly terrified population of wilderness enthusiasts suddenly afraid to go back out in the woods. But, this is all just conjecture until their existence is physically proven without any doubt. Perhaps it will be a soldier at Joint Base Lewis-McChord who finally provides a warm specimen and solves the mystery so many have been attempting to explain.

The earliest report found for Fort Lewis, told by veteran Ron Tribble to researcher Bobbie Short, dates to February 27, 1966. Miss Bobbie Short, who passed away in 2013, collected a wealth of information regarding encounters on military installations for her incomplete book, "The De Facto Sasquatch." Tribble and four other soldiers were conducting survival training in the Nisqually River basin. The 81-mile-long Nisqually River drains part of the Cascade Range southeast of Tacoma, including the southern slope of Mount Rainier, and empties into the southern end of Puget Sound. As they were approaching the river that afternoon, the group of soldiers observed some type of creature kneeling by the water. Moving closer, they watched it stand up on two legs and look at them. "We could see it very clearly; it stood 8 to 9 feet (2.4–2.7 meters) tall and had kind of a reddish brown hair covering most of its body, except for its hands and face," Tribble stated.[9] The cryptid turned, walked into the river on two legs, and easily swam to the other side. Once there, the creature continued watching them for about 10 minutes before disappearing into the forest. Its head was man-shaped but appeared to lack a neck, with protruding lips surrounding a large mouth below a flat, wide nose. The soldiers never felt there was any sign of aggression, just curiosity, and they returned to their camp "more amazed than fearful."[10]

A soldier on guard duty outside his basic training barracks at Fort Lewis in March of 1971 spotted movement on the tree line across a large open field about 100 yards (91 meters) away.[11] The full moon reflecting off a carpet of fresh snow illuminated a black figure moving with a disturbing, swaying gait. Frozen in fear, he watched as the shadow would move forward in increments, stopping and holding deathly still, blending in so well with the landscape that it would have been easily passed over as a tree stump. It appeared taller and thicker than a human, especially the unnaturally broad shoulders. When the shape moved even closer, swaying back and forth, the terrified private turned away and went inside the barracks. He was only armed with an entrenching tool, and the size of whatever or whoever was out there did not make him confident enough to face it. He didn't tell anyone initially due to the fear of being told to go back outside and investigate.

An instructor at the Fort Lewis NCO Academy was observing and grading students as they conducted a nighttime field exercise in October of 1977.[12] He was set up in an observation post along a trail, in a remote training area outside the back gate of the base. The dense, old-growth-timber forest was full of meandering creeks and ponds, wild berries, ferns, and holly, providing the perfect habitat for multitudes of species. At some point during the early morning hours, the soldier began to smell a terribly foul odor, resembling rotten eggs or spoiled garbage. Suddenly, the brush about 70 to 100 feet (25–30 meters) in front of him started rustling, with sticks and branches loudly snapping and popping. His heart dropped when he recognized that there was a pair of glowing orange, teardrop-shaped eyes looking directly at him. Crouched down and frozen in place, he watched as the creature to which the eyes belonged moved from the left to the right in front of him in unnaturally long strides, with the placement of its eyes suggesting it was an incredible 8 to 10 feet (2.4–3 meters) tall. The thing continued on, moving away from his position, taking the foul smell with it. Once the sun rose, the instructor searched for tracks or any other evidence of the encounter, but could find nothing in the wet, marshy ground. He said he would never forget that smell.[13]

Specialist Edwin Godoy was ranked as the U.S. Army's third-best marksman in 1978, the same year his eagle-eye vision may have put a live round in the chest of a Fort Lewis Sasquatch.[14] Returning from a training one evening, the deuce and a half truck he was driving suddenly sputtered to a stop and couldn't be restarted. Because Godoy had signed the vehicle out from the motorpool, he was responsible for staying with it overnight until a tow could be arranged in the morning. Just after midnight, hours after the rest of his platoon had marched back to base, he spotted a massive silhouette near a stand of trees 984 feet (300 meters) away from the vehicle. Focusing on the manlike figure, he realized it was completely covered in long, dark gray hair and was strongly built with a broad chest. It stood next to a pine tree, swinging its body from side to side while looking directly back at him with red, self-luminous eyes. Godoy reported, "The thing started running toward me, so I shouted a halt three times, asking that thing to stop and identify itself. As it wouldn't reply, I made a first shot to the air and then I shot at him, or 'it.' I don't know how to call it. The hairy thing grabbed its chest and emitted a loud moan, stopped and then ran to his right, disappearing into the forest."[15]

The shaking and terrified soldier locked himself in the two-and-a-half-ton truck, but still didn't feel protected enough if the beast decided to come back. He clutched his weapon and didn't dare fall asleep, remaining awake until the tow truck arrived at 0600 hours. After relating the event to the arriving relief team, the skeptical mechanics were amazed to find footprints pressed into the ground and blood in the area where Godoy claimed the thing had been skulking. After a detailed interview conducted by a mysterious Air Force colonel (not army), Godoy was told to never mention the event to anyone ever again.[16]

Researcher Bobbie Short collected the account of Military Police (MP) Sergeant Michael T. Coppola, who was called in to investigate a reported disturbance involving repeated bizarre cries coming from the forest near the post stockade around 0330 hours in May 1984.[17] With a plan to sweep the area, he and a captain went one direction while a K-9 unit went another, agreeing to meet at an old railroad spur located not too far inside the tree line. A few minutes later, Coppola reported to Short, "I heard five distinct pistol shots, at which point I heard a deep, guttural growl building into an extremely high-pitched howling (I'd never heard anything like that) and the sounds of something large crashing through the thick brush and foliage in the area."[18] Coppola continued onward and met the captain at the rendezvous point, not knowing that the K-9 unit, both human and dog, had just hightailed it out of the woods. Detecting movement along the tree line to their left, they could plainly see a large, dark shape walking in the forest on the edge of a meadow toward the southeast direction of distant Mount Rainier.

The nervous MP leveled his 12-gauge shotgun at what he first believed was a bear, until the figure walked out into the open meadow less than 100 feet (30 meters) away on two legs, standing 7.5 to 8 feet (2.3–2.4 meters) tall. Coppola remembered:

All I can figure is the wind must have shifted, for the creature stopped and turned its head and looked directly at me. It turned its whole body and just stood there looking at us, arms by its sides. The creature was not threatening us at all, so I lowered my weapon and did not open fire. I remember the head moving slightly from side to side; it did not move closer and neither did we. We stared at each other for less than 2–3 minutes. Ultimately, it resumed its original direction and walked away, looking back once but kept going, disappearing into the opposite tree line.[19]

Coppola returned to the site the next day and made plaster casts of footprints he found and took photographs, but the three MPs that were involved decided not to reveal anything about the creature in their report, concerned about the future impact it may have on their army careers. He also stated that the Rangers used to have problems with something "nasty" across the Nisqually River, in the South Rainier Ranger Training Area near Fiander Lake, a "creepy" place of overgrown and rugged wilderness about 35 miles (56 km) from the main post.[20]

Two other Fort Lewis MPs were driving on the north side of the post via Flora Road, heading back toward their barracks one evening in the fall of 1986.[21] They both watched in stunned amazement as a large, hair-covered, 8-foot-tall (2.4-meter) creature crossed the road in front of them in four long, unhurried steps. Excited about seeing what they at first thought was a large bear, the soldiers came to a stop and flipped on their high beams to illuminate the animal better. Instead, they saw something inhuman and definitely *not* a bruin standing on the right side of the road at the edge of the tree line. A large head appeared gorilla-like, with a sagittal crest but a more prominent brow, and shaggy and matted dark brown hair covered its entire body. Long arms with fingers dangled to just above its knees. The thing looked at them and then stepped into the forest.

The two soldiers got out of the vehicle and walked to the spot where the parted tree limbs were still shaking; they could still hear the creature walking about 30 yards (27 meters) inside the woodline until it stopped. Using their flashlights, the curious MPs entered the forest and moved in deeper until a large tree limb cracked just ahead of them. Suddenly, a scream unlike anything they had ever heard blasted the air. They both sprinted back to the truck, with the wailing continuing as they drove off in complete fear, immediately agreeing that they had encountered a Bigfoot.

The veteran also claimed that other MP friends had seen similar things, especially in the more remote training areas and roads, near Solo Point at Puget Sound and Sequalitchew Lake on north Fort Lewis.[22]

A November 1989 field exercise found the 864th Engineer Battalion building a three-rope bridge for a Ranger river crossing and then marching about a mile away from the Nisqually River to make camp. Sitting in a foxhole around 0400 hours on a brightly moonlit night, a combat engineer named "Murf" was startled when his fellow soldier exclaimed, "What the hell is that?"[23] Directly to the front of them about 25 yards (23 meters) away was a humanlike form walking past with slightly stooped shoulders, making a low grunting sound. He also smelled a slight musty odor in the air, like a dirty, wet dog. Murf told researcher Bobbie Short that after informing their squad leader and first sergeant, they were both laughed at and nicknamed the "Bigfoot Hunters."

An Oregon National Guardsman with the 1249th Engineer Battalion, Sergeant Todd M. Neiss was in the field conducting demolitions training on April 3, 1993. After hearing a loud, crescending "whooping" vocalization at their second blast site earlier in the day, the combat engineers were driving past the same rock quarry again an hour later. As the convoy descended the hillside opposite the area, Neiss spotted three jet-black, bipedal creatures standing out in the open, shoulder to shoulder, and staring at the procession. Because it was sunny and they were standing in front of a lighter-colored stone cliff, his observation was crystal clear for nearly 25 seconds. "In the middle stood, I assumed [it] to be, the alpha male of the group, as it towered a full head above the two creatures that flanked it. I would estimate it to have stood approximately nine feet high, with the flanking creatures approaching seven feet in height. Their silhouette was unique in that their heads sat directly on their shoulders with no visible neck . . . they were exhibiting a swaying motion (rocking side to side) as the larger creature stood as still as a statue," the eyewitness told researcher Bobbie Short.[24] Back at the staging area, a fellow soldier riding in the convoy, Sergeant Jeff Martin, verified that he had seen the same exact creatures.

A unit of Marines stationed at the Puget Sound Naval Shipyard on the USS *Carl Vinson* was at Fort Lewis on June 24, 1997, conducting a night land navigation course.[25] Off course and lost in a section of dense brush, the Marine on point suddenly sensed a presence and realized there was a very tall, humanlike figure standing only about 10 feet (3 meters) in front of him. He was startled so badly that he pulled the trigger on the M249 Squad Automatic Weapon (SAW), even though it was only loaded with blanks. The loud burst had its desired effect, with the shadow taking off and running downhill through the thick brush on two legs so fast it seemed impossible. The Marine could see that the head appeared to blend right into the shoulders, with no neck visible. Two or three Marines behind him got a look at it too.

It was early summer 2000 and Sergeant Jeffrey Fullerton was a grader for a land navigation course preparing soldiers for their Expert Infantryman Badge test. During the night phase, a missing soldier who had never returned to base was finally found the next day after nearly three hours of searching. He was distraught, sweating, and had scratches all over his face and a contusion under one eye. He had also lost his weapon and helmet, which forced an all-night search until daybreak, when the rifle was finally found. The traumatized soldier told Sergeant Fullerton a harrowing tale of making contact with a large animal he had heard coming his way, breaking branches and suddenly appearing as a tall shape in front of him. It was standing on two legs and swinging its arms as the infantryman turned and rushed away, immediately plowing his face into the side of a tree and knocking his helmet off. The thing was breathing heavily and growled as it kept coming toward him, and the terrified soldier ran off again, losing his weapon in the process and becoming disoriented in the dark. The creature followed him for a long distance, slowing and stopping when he did, and making unearthly whooping and whistling sounds. This continued until the soldier finally stumbled out onto a road and was picked up. The official submitted report stated the creature had been a bear.[26]

In a similarly bizarre incident in November of the same year, two scouts from Sergeant Fullerton's company had apples thrown at them all night while occupying an observation post on a field training exercise. They also reported hearing strange animal-like noises that terrified them so much they kept breaking radio silence. Headquarters verified no other units were in the area, and provided no explanation as to what kind of animal could throw things.[27]

Also in 2000, a Kansas Army Reservist befriended a new member of the unit who was a former 2nd Battalion Ranger at Fort Lewis. As a sniper, he was often alone and static in the woods there for several days at a time. In one particular location that the marksman often used, he reported feeling watched and hearing something very large moving around the forest at night. On occasion, he spotted man-shaped figures with his NVGs, sneaking around his HIDE site but never coming in too close. When agitated, they would make grunting or whistling sounds, and he would respond by talking calmly to them. It seemed this would cause them to move away and leave him alone.[28]

Another Ranger training area around Cat Lake is supposedly notorious for having been the lair of a particular Sasquatch for several years. In 2002, a Ranger from California reported that his squad encountered one there, and that the size of the thing is what frightened them the most. They watched it through night vision scopes as it came within 50 yards (46 meters) of their position. He described it as being 8 feet (2.4 meters) tall, covered in black hair, and making pig-like grunting sounds, but deeper and longer lasting. After calling it in, the Commanding Officer (CO) on duty ordered them to pick up and move immediately.[29]

MARINE CORPS AIR GROUND COMBAT CENTER, TWENTYNINE PALMS, CALIFORNIA

Moving down the Pacific coast to California, about 140 miles (225 km) west of Los Angeles is the Marine Corps Air Ground Combat Center (MCAGCC), also known as Twentynine Palms. Home to the 7th Marine Regiment and one of the largest military training areas in the nation, the base covers a total area of nearly 600,000 acres (931.7 square miles) and is characterized by steeply sloped mountains and flat desert valleys, with elevations ranging from 1,800 to 4,500 feet (550–1,370 meters). Surrounded by Joshua Tree National Park to the south, the Sheephole Valley Wilderness to the east, and the Cleghorn Lakes Wilderness to the north, the base is also dotted with many dangerous and abandoned mines.

Local indigenous tribes have legends about hominin "hairy devils" that were pushed out of the San Bernardino Mountains by human settlement and moved east into the deserts around Joshua Tree. They were considered dangerous supernatural entities to avoid. The Tongva people called them Takwis, pronounced the same as Tahquitz, the Cahuilla tribes' name for them.[30] Tahquitz Canyon and waterfall, at the base of 10,000-foot (3,048-meter) Mount San Jacinto near Palm Springs, was so labeled because it was known as the favorite haunt of these creatures.

Historically reported as long as people have been living there, these eight-foot-tall things have been encountered so many times around Twentynine Palms by both civilians and Marines that they have earned a host of nicknames: Sierra Highway Devil, The Mojave Sandman, Morongo Valley Monster, and Yucca Man.[31] A pattern has emerged through the years that seems to indicate that these bipedal creatures travel a south–north corridor between Joshua Tree National Park directly through the Marine base to Mojave National Preserve, which nearly abuts the army's National Training Center at Fort Irwin. Most reported sightings of Yucca Man walking through the area occur between 0200 hours and dawn. They seem impervious to the harsh temperatures and weather of the region, even seen once walking unhindered through a blistering sandstorm by a Marine NCO in 1991. When he reported the base breach by the creature, he was reportedly ordered not to engage.[32]

The most commonly retold incident, often used to properly spook new arrivals on base before they set out for remote night maneuvers or late-night duty, tells of a young Marine alone on guard at a lonely base gate in 1971. He began to hear strange sounds in the dark, growls and heavy breathing, as something circled the small shack he was in. His challenge unanswered, the Marine stepped out with his rifle raised, encountering a staggeringly foul smell and an eight-foot-tall hairy humanoid with red-glowing eyes. One version of the story claims the leatherneck was then knocked unconscious by the beast and found hours later by the next shift, while the other reports he woke up from the assault to find his weapon bent in half. The wife of a Marine who was on guard duty that night at another location stated the latter was true, and that her husband said it happened to the overnight watchman at a rifle range, not at a base gate.[33]

That same night, people living in the Twentynine Palms neighborhood near the junction of Valle Vista and Utah Trail heard their dogs incessantly barking and reported observing two Yucca Men. One was described as being quite a bit larger than the other. The pair were spotted farther down the road, upsetting horses in a corral, and then even later by some employees at Joshua Tree National Park, many miles south.

EDWARDS AIR FORCE BASE, CALIFORNIA

Edwards Air Force Base (AFB) is just over 150 miles (241 km) northwest of Twentynine Palms, and is home for much of the military's secret flight testing and aerospace research through the 412th Test Wing. The largest chunk of the 470-square-mile (1,200-sq-km) base is the Rogers and Rosamond Dry Lakes. Located at the northwest corner of Rogers Dry Lake, the North Base is the site of the Air Force's top-secret test programs at Edwards.

During the 2009 reunion of the 6510th Air Police Squadron, known as the Desert Rats, 32 veteran officers from the Edwards AFB security force between 1973 and 1979 enjoyed three days of restored camaraderie.[34] Some of the memories excitedly discussed were about the bizarre experiences several of them had while patrolling the expansive base back then. Remembering run-ins with an unknown cryptid known as "Blue Eyes" or "Marvin of the Mojave," there was still the presence of real fear hidden behind the smiles and laughter.

In spring of 1974, Sergeant Michael House was in his vehicle patrolling an area known as "Mars Station," the location of powerful communications technology.[35] He suddenly became aware of what appeared to be two huge blue eyes moving parallel to his direction, about 250 yards to the left. He stopped the truck and observed them moving closer at a right angle, impossibly fast and gliding, like they were running on a wire instead of naturally bobbing up and down. Now 100 yards closer, House estimated the eyes were four inches apart and hovered about seven feet off the ground. At 50 yards, the unknown entity began circling the vehicle, abruptly accompanied by a vile, rank smell. Never seeing anything besides the blue orbs, the sergeant was more than happy to quickly drive off when dispatch called him to return to headquarters. The ridicule he endured after filing an official report of the experience played a hand in preventing future unexplainable events from being recorded by other security officers.

Increasingly bizarre activity began happening around Mars Station, with unidentifiable nighttime vocalizations and dark forms seen walking past the buildings through eight-foot-high windows. Whatever passed outside was so heavy it pulverized a glass soda bottle with its foot.

Air Police Sergeant Barton was on patrol near the end of 1974 outside the Jet Propulsion Laboratory on the far east side of Edwards.[36] He spotted two blue lights in the distance, thought to possibly be headlights of a trespassing vehicle. The source of the lights had vanished when he pulled into the area where he had seen them last, and his truck became stuck in the soft sand there. He exited and started walking back toward the road to meet another patrol, who also arranged a tow. When they all returned to the bogged-down truck a short time later, they saw insane-looking bipedal footprints that circled it and then headed into the dark desert. They were 14 inches long and three-toed, with what appeared to be a clawed digit at the heel.

Three weeks later, Sergeant Jones was parked near the same site and witnessed the outline of an immense dark form moving across a nearby hill's skyline.[37] He called for backup as two green-blue, orb-like eyes moved down toward him, in the same weird gliding way Sergeant House had described. Jones was surprised at how fast his backup arrived, until realizing that they were not responding to his request. Someone else had reported strange lights in the hills. They got out to investigate, but the creature and mysterious orbs had disappeared. Sergeant Barton confirmed that footprints found there later were similar to the ones around his truck. These prints were everywhere though, coming or going from no discernable direction.

Researcher Doug Trapp conducted years of fieldwork and eyewitness interviews about the possible existence of a desert Sasquatch. An Air Force lieutenant opened up to him about his experiences supervising on-base security surveillance at Edwards between 1972 and 1975. When unauthorized trespassers were discovered, it was his responsibility to observe and report the situation to higher command. One night a guard reported a perimeter breach by a "very tall man, but not really a man."[38] The lieutenant drove out to the location and observed the perpetrator himself through a tripod-mounted starlight scope. A very tall, hair-covered, apelike humanoid was walking through the desert, appearing to be searching for something on the ground. Both men watched it clearly as it wandered around almost aimlessly 500 yards distant. He reported it up the chain of command and was told to keep watching it. About five minutes later, a helicopter fast approached from the east and spooked the creature, which looked at the craft and ran "like a deer" around a rock pile and out of sight. The next day the lieutenant was told these creatures were sporadically sighted around base, and to continue to monitor and report on them, but not to engage or disturb the things until command could determine what they were. Over the next few years, they were seen several more times, and he claimed encounters were captured on video surveillance, which immediately became classified. By the time he left Edwards, he claimed they had learned very little about the unknown species.

An enlisted member of the security team also claimed seeing them through his night vision starlight scope several times.[39] He described witnessing at least two creatures over 10 feet tall, several womanly shaped females—including one with a juvenile—and a group of five walking together that ranged from 6 to 8 feet tall. They were all fully hair-covered except the palms of their hands, the base of their feet, and their faces. Personal cameras were not allowed on base, and he felt privileged to have seen these creatures with such clarity. He believed they were not as rare as people assumed and, based on behavior, seemed nocturnal and very shy. All base personnel had been strictly ordered not to harm or engage with the creatures, and he felt that this is why they gravitated to the area, as if they knew they were safe there.

Trapp also interviewed a major who was at the base between 1970 and 1978 and claimed that the creatures were also known to use the extensive subterranean infrastructure used to house secret aircraft at the base.[40] The miles of classified tunnels are said to fan out under the installation, and security cameras aimed at sensitive areas repeatedly captured images of Sasquatch moving through them at night. The hairy monsters seemed to appear and disappear at will, frustrating base police sent chasing after the phantoms. The major also provided an intriguing reason why the military won't confirm the existence of these creatures on our nationwide military installations. He believed the public would lose confidence in the armed forces' ability to keep our bases and secrets secure, and in turn would encourage even more human trespassing, especially by newly motivated Bigfoot hunters.

MARINE CORPS BASE CAMP PENDLETON, CALIFORNIA

Situated on the California coast between Los Angeles and San Diego, Camp Pendleton's diverse geography spans over 125,000 acres, playing host to year-round training for sea soldiers from many units, including the 1st Marine Division and the 1st Marine Special Operations Battalion. The base's 17 miles (27 km) of beachfront remains the last major undeveloped portion of the California coastline south of Santa Barbara. Built on a wide swath of coastal land that once supported an estuary at the mouth of the Santa Margarita River, the base abuts the 460,000-acre Cleveland National Forest and three different mountain ranges. If you follow the meandering Santa Margarita River back into the mountains you will eventually reach its canyon headwaters, at the confluence of Temecula and Murrieta Creeks in southwestern Riverside County. This site was named Takwis, mentioned earlier as the southern California Tongva tribe's name for Sasquatch-like beings.[41]

While in infantry training at Pendleton, a group of Marines were in the small mountains above the San Onofre area, armed with blank rounds and dug in for an expected OPFOR nighttime assault.[42] The reporting witness had another Marine with him, and to their right, 30 yards (27 meters) away, were two more devil dogs in a foxhole. They were in a steep, rock-strewn area with heavy brush and trees. The men could hear something large coming up the hillside, causing rocks to dislodge and roll. They watched in shock as directly in front of them a huge creature clambered up over the steep rock edge and stood up straight, towering over their foxhole. His partner shouted, "Halt!" and the thing stood motionless for around 15 seconds, allowing a good look. The out-lined silhouette stood 7 feet (2.1 meters) tall and an estimated 3.5 feet (1 meter) wide, with long arms and a pointed head. The eyewitness was terrified at the time, trying not to breathe and his hair standing on end. The cryptid walked around them to the right, passing between the two fighting positions. All four Marines turned and watched it go down the reverse slope behind them, and then disappear up and over a small hill. Once it was gone, the men confirmed with each other what they had seen and agreed to not report it to anyone.

* * *

Temporarily assigned to a staff of Marines supervising a mini–boot camp youth program conducted at Camp Pendleton, a veteran Marine was the last one awake besides the half-asleep radio watch on a night in May 1982.[43] All 300 boys were finally settled and asleep, having bivouacked in a large, open meadow shelf above the School of Infantry and the 52 Area north of Basilone Road. Looking west toward the perimeter of the camp, he suddenly focused in on a tall, dark, bulky figure standing about 50 feet (15 meters) beyond the last shelter-halves. "We seemed to be staring at each other . . . I had a strong gut feeling that it was checking me out real good since I was the only thing moving around. I could feel my heart begin to pound and my entire body felt like it wanted to anchor to the ground. There was no doubt someone or something very odd and dangerous was standing there looking at me," the Marine said. The massive silhouette was easily eight feet tall, with broad shoulders, little or no neck, and a powerful physique. It gently swayed its upper body left and right, as though surveying the space. Deciding to retreat up the knoll to retrieve a flashlight from his parked vehicle, the witness moved backward, keeping an eye on the creature as it remained in the same spot. He eventually lost sight of it in the dark as he moved farther away. When he returned moments later, his scan of the area with the flashlight turned up nothing. It was gone.

Instead of waking everyone up and causing an unwanted panic from the teenage boys, the Marine stayed awake and waited to see if anything else would happen. Unarmed, he was nervous the rest of the night that the thing would pop up behind him. After nothing else occurred, at daybreak he immediately ran out to the spot and searched in vain for any evidence left behind. The main thing he did notice was that there was nothing present at the location where he had seen the mystery figure—no bush, tree, rock, or pole—that could have been misinterpreted as the distinct shape he knew he saw.

Fort Carson, Colorado

Leaving the coast and moving east past the Rockies, just south of Colorado Springs, is Fort Carson. The home of the 4th Infantry Division and the 10th Special Forces Group, it was also the pre–Fort Polk home of the 5th Infantry Division during the Vietnam era. A smaller base with an area of only 28 square miles (73 sq km) covering nearly 18,000 acres, there are vast wilderness areas surrounding Cheyenne Mountain and Pikes Peak beginning just steps west of Fort Carson.

A Marine Recon unit, acting as OPFOR, was conducting a nighttime simulated attack on another unit around 0300 hours in July 1986, off-base near the vicinity of Sugarloaf Mountain and the Gray Back Trailhead.[44] Separated from his squad during the withdrawal, the reporting Marine cut through a densely wooded area to intercept them, using the ambient light of a full moon. Reaching the trail, he thought he saw a squad member approaching through the brush, but quickly realized it wasn't even human. The figure stepped out on the trail directly in front of the frozen leatherneck, looking in the opposite direction. It stood around 6.5 feet (1.9 meters) tall with a muscular body and thin waist, was covered in light brown hair, and had long arms that dangled below the hips. "It turned and saw me, at which it exhibited a startle reflex, then immediately crouched down and slowly moved sideways off the trail, watching me the entire time. It knelt behind a bush, at which point it became very hard to see. I realized that I was encountering something few people have the opportunity to see, at only a distance of about ten feet," the witness stated. He further described the head as being slightly conical and sloped from front to back, with large, visible ears that were pointed and foxlike. The large, black eyes were globe-shaped, its nose was flat with large nostrils, and the hair was shorter around the face.

189

FORT LEAVENWORTH, KANSAS

Old Fort Lewis may take the prize as America's most "squatchy" military base, but Fort Leavenworth in Kansas must easily be the most ghostly, claiming upward of 36 haunted buildings.[45] Built in 1827, it is the second-oldest active U.S. Army post and the oldest permanent settlement in Kansas. Having been a cornerstone in American history, the base is now the home of the Army National Guard's 35th Infantry Division, the Combined Arms Center (CAC), the Command and General Staff College, a national cemetery, and the United States Disciplinary Barracks (USDB)—the famous military prison—and is known simply as Leavenworth.

The Department of Defense's only maximum-security lockup, the USDB confines both enlisted and commissioned servicemen convicted by court-martial for violations of the Uniform Code of Military Justice (UCMJ) resulting in sentences over 10 years, including the death penalty. The largest buildings of the original 1874 facility, known as The Castle, were torn down in 2004, but the walls and 10 of the original buildings remain. A new state-of-the-art disciplinary barracks became operational in 2002, built about a mile north.

The Castle has 12 towers along the wall. Tower Eight had never been renovated and wasn't manned during the later years that the old prison was open. It was closed off, and the only way you could get into it was to walk along the wall from an adjacent guardhouse. Guards would often see something moving inside anyway, rumored to be the ghost of a soldier who had committed suicide in the tower with his service shotgun. When the old prison was still open, the main control tower would often get phone calls from Tower Eight, even though there was no phone located there, and when answered there would be no response except static. Guards would also report hearing the sounds of someone walking up the stairs and knocking on the trapdoor entrance to the other towers when clearly no one was there.[46]

Prisoners who die while in custody and are unclaimed by any family members are buried just north of the original prison. There are 300 graves in the Military Prison Cemetery, dating from approximately 1894, 56 of which are unmarked and 14 that belong to German prisoners of war executed for the murder of fellow POWs in 1945. In the U.S. military's last mass execution, the Nazis were hung on a specially built gallows in three groups: five on July 10, two on July 14, and seven on August 25.[47]

Having run out of room on the gallows for the last, largest group, the executioners are said to have improvised and used the elevator shaft in the prison hospital. Today, the unused elevator shaft in Building 65 is often reported to be the source of bloodcurdling, shrill screams despite no one being seen there. Nazi ghosts in Kansas? That's weird, even for this book.

* * *

Before it was the 190-acre Trails West Golf Course beginning in 1920, some of the ground beneath the greens is believed to have been part of the old base graveyard, and the entire western side of the property abuts the National Cemetery. On occasion, a phantom wearing an old calico dress and black shawl is still seen searching for her lost children along the fairways and between the hedgerows. Sometimes carrying a lantern, her desperate voice calls out their names from the darkness, "Ethan! Mary! Are you there?"[48]

The sad story of Catherine Sutter (or possibly "Rich") begins with her arrival at the fort in the fall of 1880, with her husband Hiram and their two children, as they were heading west.[49] When the children were sent down to the Missouri River bottoms to collect firewood and didn't return, she became frantic and was relentless in her search for them. As their bodies were never found, it was assumed they had somehow drowned in the river, but Catherine continued combing the area throughout the winter and became a familiar sight to fort personnel. All that time in the elements must have taken its toll, as she contracted pneumonia and died in the spring of 1881. Hiram returned to Indiana alone, a broken man. Imagine his joy when he received word a few weeks later that his children were alive, returned to the fort by a friendly band of Meskwaki Fox. The tribe, who migrated between spending winters in Oklahoma and summers in the Dakotas, had plucked the drowning kids from the river the previous fall on their way south and had taken care of them until they could return.[50]

Shortly after the kids left for Indiana, soldiers began seeing Catherine's ghost wandering near the base graveyard and down by the river, and sometimes heard her calling out the children's names. Never knowing the true fate of her brood, it seems she is cursed to wander the area forever, searching in vain. It is still reported that on crisp autumn nights, as the sun sets over the hills and manicured greens of Trails West, the soft flickering glow of a swinging lantern can be seen, and the desperately whispered names of Catherine's children hauntingly float on the breeze.

* * *

The Parade Field has existed since the fort was first opened and has been the site of several paranormal encounters. A strange mist often clings to the sunken center of the field, and the sounds of gathering troops can sometimes be heard, accentuated with muffled commands, but nothing can actually be seen. Galloping phantom horses and riders have also been reported.[51]

For years, soldiers walking past the historic house at 1 Scott Avenue have seen a pacing specter on the porch, likely the lingering presence of Captain David Hillhouse Buel, who lived there with his family in 1870. The 30-year-old officer also died there, shot and murdered by a disgruntled private named James Malone. The soldier was angry over being made to chop firewood as punishment for some infraction.[52] The captain is likely not the only presence in the space, as it turns out that 1 Scott Avenue was built on the site of the original Enlisted Soldier's Cemetery. The burial ground was established at the founding of the fort in 1827, with the 70 or so graves later relocated to the post National Cemetery in 1859. It seems they forgot at least one, as the wife of an officer unfortunately discovered in 1966 while gardening. Thinking she was digging out an oddly shaped stone in the backyard, the woman was horrified to realize she was holding a human skull in her hands when it finally broke free. The rest of the disturbed skeleton's bones were recovered and respectfully reinterred.

* * *

Far from the battlefields of Gettysburg and Little Bighorn, another Leavenworth legend claims that the spirit of Lieutenant Colonel George Armstrong Custer and his beautiful wife, Elizabeth (Libbie), linger at the residence of 4 Sumner, known as the Syracuse House. Their legendary love was so strong that Custer risked his entire career and left his troops in the field just to spend one night of fevered passion in Libbie's arms. Custer was subsequently arrested and kept at Fort Leavenworth, Kansas, with his court-martial trial lasting from September 15 to October 11, 1867. He was suspended from rank and command for one year and forfeited pay for the same time period. The Syracuse House at 4 Sumner is where the hearings were held and where he and Libbie stayed during the proceedings. Custer was reinstated as commander of the 7th Cavalry Regiment the following year, where he served until his death at the Battle of Little Bighorn on June 25, 1876. His brother and two-time Civil War Medal of Honor recipient Captain Thomas W. Custer died fighting beside him and is actually buried in the National Cemetery at Fort Leavenworth. Perhaps the time spent there in the house with his beloved wife and the fact that his brother's remains are present keep him coming back.

People spending time in the residence have claimed to witness the ghost of Colonel Custer roaming the first floor, walking from room to room. During the early 2000s, a mover who was packing up a departing family's belongings in an upstairs room suddenly saw an attractive lady dressed in an old-fashioned, long black dress and bonnet pass through the room and enter an adjoining room. Having believed he was alone in the house, he called out and followed her, but the room she had just entered was empty. There was no way that the woman could have moved past him downstairs. Discussing the event with the lady of the house who was vacating—and who also happened to be a board member of the post's Frontier Army Museum—the mover was shown a collection of antique photos that had been collected for a Historic Homes Tour. The man immediately exclaimed, "That's her!" when viewing a photograph of Libbie Custer. The disturbed mover told the woman he needed to leave, claiming that he felt ill, and he never returned to finish the job.[53]

Another haunted house, built in 1878, is located at 16–18 Sumner Place. Although the name given to the resident spirit seen there sounds evil, the Lady in Black actually seems like a benevolent nanny and housekeeper. She might do the dishes, make the beds, or even read to the toddlers at bedtime if there are any in the home. After one officer's young son told the family about the "nice" lady who read to him every night, they found a mysterious book in his room that none of them had ever seen before. The phantom doesn't seem to like anyone else minding the children though, creating an oppressive atmosphere for babysitters and grandmothers, and sometimes giving them a rude push or undoing work that they have completed.[54]

Considered the most haunted house in all of Kansas, the residence next door at 12–14 Sumner Place, known as The Rookery, is also the oldest, having been erected as the bachelor officers' quarters when the fort first opened in 1827. The Lady in White is reported to be one terrifying resident apparition that chases visitors, screaming and flying through the house with unwashed, matted hair and long fingernails on silent, moonless nights. Legends say the woman in a white gown is the wife of a young officer from the 19th century who was brutally murdered along with her children by a local tribe while the soldiers were off-post. Other spirits include a young girl who whistles and throws tantrums, an old woman who chatters in the corners, and the ghost of Major Edmund Ogden, a former post quartermaster who died in 1855 and is still seen walking in his spurred boots.[55]

The family of a lieutenant colonel revealed the insane amount of paranormal activity they were experiencing while living at The Rookery to the *Fort Leavenworth Lamp* newspaper in 2009.[56] The wife, Anne, and her four boys started to notice how things would disappear and then mysteriously show up in places already searched, often grouped together. The weird occurrences progressed to hearing locked doors open and close on their own at night, footsteps ascending the stairs, and furniture being moved around in upstairs rooms. One night Anne noticed the basement light had been left on and sent one of the boys down to turn it off. As he returned to the top of the stairs, the light came on again. The family cats were treated with disdain, being let outside when no one was home and leading to loud banging when they tried to sleep on the beds. One night Anne saw one of her felines seemingly unable to move, like something was holding it down. When Anne moved nearer, she noticed the cat's hair was standing on end except for one spot on her back about the size of a human hand.

One day Anne opened the door that led downstairs to the furnace room to grab some cleaning supplies. A man's face appeared at the bottom of the staircase in the doorway that led to the furnace room. Thinking he was part of a previously expected maintenance crew, Anne said, "Oh, hey," grabbed what she needed, and shut the door. The mustached man with salt-and-pepper hair smiled at her. The next day, when the real maintenance crew showed up, they said they didn't know anyone matching the description of the person she had seen. Some time later, she was looking at a book about Fort Leavenworth history and immediately recognized a photograph of Major Edmund Ogden as the mysterious visitor.

The old quartermaster, or possibly another presence in the home, liked to punish the boys when they gave their mother a hard time, making important personal belongings disappear at inconvenient moments. After a disagreement the night before, one of the boy's new track shoes went missing the morning of his meet, lost for days until found in a corner of the basement furnace room. When another one of her sons argued with her, the next morning he couldn't find his boots anywhere. They had been seen on the living room floor and then inexplicably went missing just moments later. The boy apologized to the ghost, saying he would be late for church if he didn't find them. He walked through the house again and easily spotted the boots sitting underneath the dining room table.

* * *

Not looking to be left out of the high strangeness going on at Fort Leavenworth, Sasquatch makes an appearance in a report from a soldier with the 205th Military Police Battalion in 1976.[57] The post had a history of sightings down near the Missouri River, where the area was dense flooded timber and lowlands, with little or no human activity. On base, MPs had previously reported unexplained banging on building doors and the opening and slamming of the tops on trash dumpsters. One soldier had heard a low, gurgling growl while on walking patrol one night—a sound so frightening it made him run inside to the duty desk.

An MP officer had seen a big, hairy thing along the Missouri River bank a few days before the reporting witness and a few other military policemen had been sent into the woods searching for a possible runaway teenage dependent. The officer had made the mistake of filing a formal report about what he had seen, which reportedly negatively affected his future military career. During the search, the dispatched MPs were already spooked when they discovered abnormally large humanlike footprints in the heavy snow down by the riverbank. After agreeing that none of them were willing to go on record, they decided to not report the evidence. It later turned out that the officer's missing daughter had just gone to Kansas City with her boyfriend.

FORT LEONARD WOOD, MISSOURI

Another Midwestern base, Fort Leonard Wood (aka Lost-in-the-Woods), is remotely located in the beautiful south-central Missouri Ozarks, covering more than 61,000 acres. A major Basic Combat Training (BCT) installation for the United States, it also houses the U.S. Army's Military Police, Engineer, and Chemical, Biological, Radiological, and Nuclear Schools. The 1.5 million acres of Mark Twain National Forest begin just a few miles east of the installation.

The fort is also the setting for a story that marks it forever as cursed land, powered by the hatred of an entire village. Once located near the current center of the installation, Bloodland was a long-established town of more than 40 buildings and approximately 100 people, mostly of German descent.[58] On Halloween night of 1940, the hapless residents had all gathered for the annual fall community celebration. During the festival, it was unceremoniously announced that the town, including all their buildings and land, were being taken over by the federal government through the power of eminent domain in order to establish a new military base. The citizens of Bloodland were rightfully outraged. It was later reported by a local newspaper that, after a day of heavy drinking, a small riot against the government broke out in the town. The people also reportedly turned to old Germanic pagan witchcraft to curse the land— and the outsiders using it—forever.

The site of the former town is now an area of small-arms firing ranges located south of the main base. The original Bloodland Cemetery is located between Range #10 and #11, and Bloodland Lake is also nearby. The tiny burial ground predates the creation of the fort and is the only remaining physical evidence that the little town ever existed. Leonard Wood's command and control building for the various ranges on the post is named Bloodland Range Control in the town's honor. The curse has come to be the scapegoat for any kind of misfortune occurring to soldiers and their families on the post.

* * *

A basic training recruit at Leonard Wood in February 2014 experienced a harrowing haunting in her barracks building.[59] The three-floor structure was fairly dilapidated, reflected by the fact that her cycle was going to be the last to live there before major remodeling was slated to start. Platoon gossip related an event that had allegedly happened there four years previously. A distraught female basic trainee, who had decided the army was not for her, was trying to go AWOL and escape the base. She had attempted to climb down the old laundry chute from the third floor and fell to her sudden death. Some versions said she did it on purpose, having wanted to commit suicide.

The reporting witness would hear strange things, including a girl's laughter, when it was her turn for guard shifts at night. Other trainees had experienced unexplained events like closed and locked windows in their rooms being found wide open in the middle of the night, or waking up to briefly glimpse a girl with long dark hair standing next to their bed, just staring out the window. Platoon-mates reported the ghost was most active on the first floor of the building, where she was also seen staring out the barrack windows. On a night right before graduation, the witness was walking down the barrack's long hallway, checking the bed counts. She reached the end of the hallway and turned to come back, walking slowly. "I noticed something out of the corner of my right eye. Turned my head and definitely saw a formed black shadow of what looked like a girl, in the corner of the empty room," she remembered. The last claimed sighting was by another trainee, who had seen an unknown female soldier standing outside the drill sergeant's office door with her head down. When she called out a greeting, the mysterious phantom looked in her direction, laughed a little, and then ran off, seemingly disappearing without explanation.

* * *

Bigfoot sightings already had a long history at Fort "Lost-in-the-Woods" before a group of soldiers stationed there had their own disturbing experience on the morning of October 1, 2014.[60] On the northeast corner of the base is the Engineer Trail, a 2.6-mile loop through the dense woods. Inside the perimeter of the track is about 10 acres used for land navigation exercises, and at the far corner of the loop the trail meanders through the edges of the great forest outside Leonard Wood, with the Big Piney River behind it. A group of 15 soldiers conducting their morning physical training set out as a group to run the trail around 0600 hours. They quickly became spread out, as everyone found their comfortable pace.

About midway, they came across a 3- to 4-foot-diameter (1.2-meter) tree that had been laid across the trail. It was in good shape, not rotted, and there had been no recent storms. Thinking nothing of it at the time, they ran on. Not far ahead, they observed another knocked-down tree of the same size, but this one looked like it had been dragged off to the side of the trail. As the fastest runner, the reporting soldier found himself alone by the time he had reached the remote corner where the path entered the big forest. He began to notice a musky, sewage-like smell that was different from anything else in the area. From about 200 feet (61 meters) away, he began hearing the first of several animal-like "whoops," and he stopped running to listen more closely. He distinctly heard five separate calls coming from different directions: three from inside the circling track and two or more from the densely forested off-base side. Shaken and feeling stalked, the soldier sprinted to get out of that section of the trail and finish the loop.

Back at the starting point, he waited for the others to arrive, not planning to say anything due to fear of ridicule. That quickly changed as the returning soldiers all began excitedly talking about the sounds and the idea that it could have been a group of Sasquatch communicating with each other. They had all heard the same noises around them at that spot on the run: calls, whoops, wood-knocks, and snapping branches. To a man, the 15 soldiers agreed that they had felt surrounded, tracked, and monitored by a group of something not human there on the Engineer Trail.

FORT DRUM, NEW YORK

Leaving the Midwest and heading toward the East Coast, our next stop is on New York's northern border with Canada along Lake Ontario and the St. Lawrence River. Home of the 10th Mountain Division, Fort Drum and its training areas sprawl more than 25 square miles and include over 107,000 acres (434 sq km) of wilderness land.

With the outbreak of World War II in Europe, the military installation then known as Pine Camp was selected by the U.S. Army for a major expansion. Enforcing the largest use of eminent domain in New York history, the government acquired 75,000 acres, displacing 525 local families. Much like what happened at Fort Leonard Wood, five entire villages were eliminated, and 3,000 buildings, including 24 schools, six churches, and a post office, had to be abandoned.[61] Not much evidence of these once-thriving communities remains besides old stone foundations and limestone basements scattered throughout the training areas, and the buried skeletons under the ground at 13 historic cemeteries.[62] Imagine how terrifying it would be to find yourself out in the field alone on night maneuvers or land navigation, accidentally stumbling into a mist-shrouded and gothic old graveyard in the middle of the dense woods.

Woods Mills Cemetery beside the Indian River is one of the most remote, a burial place that was accidentally desecrated once during a training exercise, resulting in 20 headstones being leveled.[63] Signs posted on the trees in these lost areas of the base decree "Historic Area—Training Permitted—No Digging" for a good reason, as there may be forgotten bones buried anywhere under the earth on Fort Drum. (Refer to "The Phenomenon of OP Rock" chapter if you don't remember what happens when you dig where you've been told not to.) Dr. Laurie Rush, an archaeologist and cultural resources coordinator for the U.S. Army, oversees the discovery of buried human remains at the base. Referring to Woods Mills, Dr. Rush said, "We used radar to explore the ground. I think there are six others buried in the woods over there."[64]

Sterlingville was a community founded in 1837 by James Sterling, a true "giant" of a man. The "Iron King of the North Country," James was said to have weighed 40 pounds at 10 months of age, 200 pounds by age 14, and eventually reached nearly 400 pounds as an adult man.[65] His tall monument of a headstone is in the ghost town's Gates Cemetery off Plank Road, which has been the scene of several incidents involving weird, floating orbs and flitting figures moving between and behind the trees and 19th-century stones. The ruins of the Sterlingville Hotel can be found nearby, hidden in a wooded intersection of the Antwerp Tank Trail.

During World War II, the post also served as a POW camp for hundreds of captured Italian and German troops. If a prisoner died and was not claimed by their family, they were buried in Sheepfold Cemetery. This was the depressing case for one Italian and six Germans who perished in captivity. People have often claimed to see a soldier waving for help from the old cemetery, only to vanish as mysteriously and quickly as he appears.[66]

LeRaysville, named for wealthy landowner Count James LeRay de Chaumont, once stood where Fort Drum's Remington Park now exists. A recreation area for soldiers near the center of the base, it offers a small lake to relax and swim in. An overgrown trail nearby is all that's left of Main Street, and a stone-lined cellar hole is the last evidence of the village's hotel. The count's father had been a friend of Benjamin Franklin and a key financial supporter of the American Revolution. James had purchased 600,000 acres of northern New York to sell in parcels to immigrants and rebuild the family fortune. He also built the impressive LeRay Mansion between 1826 and 1827, which became the "social and intellectual center of the North Country for many years"[67] and was the centerpiece of a community of exiled French aristocrats during the French Revolution. Five of the original structures remain standing: the mansion, servant's quarters, farm manager's house, land office, and icehouse.

Throughout the years, the Classical Revival–style mansion has served as a post commander's quarters, a residence for visiting dignitaries, and an event center for formal military receptions. The structure is also the epicenter for base hauntings. LeRay's granddaughter, 15-month-old Clotilde, died in the home and is buried on the property, near the formal pond, across a field in the forest. Her tombstone stands alone in the woods.[68] Clotilde is reported to haunt the upstairs bedrooms, where guests have heard her crying from beyond the grave. The little girl's mother, Therese de Gouvello, has also been spotted in the house, wearing a white nightgown. Ghost children have been seen playing on the stairs, and old family slaves are glimpsed eating in the kitchen. Security guards patrolling the grounds have seen mysterious figures moving through the house on nights when they know the place is locked up and empty of living guests. Footsteps are often heard inside the home, and furniture is found inexplicably moved around overnight.

Brittany Brown, during her time as an intern at the mansion, remembered, "I was actually counting the china and doing inventory in the cabinets. I looked over and saw a black shadow kind of duck down and hide underneath the cabinet."[69]

With all the abandoned cemeteries, old house foundations, and carved-out limestone basements, it's probably not that surprising that Fort Drum has attracted a lot of bizarre trespassing through the years. Evidence of satanic or black magic rituals have been found in these desolate places, and squatters living on the "Back 40" have also reportedly been a problem. Building crude huts or using caves, these derelicts have been seen moving through the forests or on the back corner tank trails. There's even an unsubstantiated report about a "return-to-the-earth"–type cult that had been living on the base for months before they were discovered.[70] They were rounded up and arrested after they tried to start blocking off training roads and violently engaging with soldiers.

* * *

And, as you might be expecting, Bigfoot is found in the Empire State as well. During just the year 2020, New Yorkers reported 113 Sasquatch sightings in their state.[71] However, around Fort Drum there are more likely to be sightings in the wilderness of a bizarre ghost named "Huck-leberry Charlie." Reported to be the phantom of a wanderer who used to pick and sell huckleberries from the area north of the Black River then known as Pine Plains, the eccentric spirit is often noticed because of his brightly colored and odd clothing.[72] Soldiers have reported encountering this enigma in the most remote training areas, disturbingly out of place. He is sometimes heard loudly singing a rhyme. The man was known in all the old communities that are now ghost towns, and he was still alive in 1908 when the area was acquired by the military. It seems Huckleberry Charlie is still searching for his long-lost customers.

FORT A.P. HILL, VIRGINIA

Fort A.P. Hill is a drilling and maneuver center that provides realistic joint and combined arms training about 60 miles south of Washing-ton, D.C. All branches of the armed forces and foreign allies train on the 76,000 acres of diverse terrain there, which includes a modern 28,000-acre live-fire range complex. The post is also the home of the Explosive Ordnance Disposal School and the Night Vision and Elec-tronic Sensors Directorate—an important provider of the technology used to witness many of the forces fighting in Weird War.

Three Marines training on those ranges in 2008 will never forget the thing they saw moving in the trees above them with their own naked eyes.[73] After being dropped off by helicopter and patrolling into the bush, their unit had set up bivouac for the night. Three Marines were pulling guard duty, separated and without contact with one another. At some point between 0200 and 0400 hours, the reporting witness said the woods became eerily silent; when he looked up from his seated position on the ground, he saw a large, humanlike shape standing in the tree above him. The heavily built figure stood out clearly against the starlit sky, about 30 feet (9 meters) away, holding onto the tree with long, outstretched arms. Its height was estimated between 7 and 8 feet (2.1–2.4 meters) tall, but the Marine couldn't see exactly where the creature's feet ended. As he watched in frozen terror, the thing silently moved from one large tree to the next until vanishing from sight.

The next morning, one of the other men who had been on watch asked the unit if anyone else had seen something in the trees during the night. Another guard responded "affirmative" and described the man-like figure he had also watched silently moving above his position. The reporting witness came forward, too, and all three Marines confirmed they had seen the same bizarre thing. It apparently had encircled the encampment, using the towering old-growth trees above them in a way no human being could have.

This incident illustrates a possible behavior of Sasquatch in which they use trees to travel and stay hidden, something gorillas are known to do. The best place to hide—even in plain view—is up, as human beings have a tendency to ignore that direction when searching for or observing something. It could also explain why witnesses so often claim these creatures seemingly disappear right before their eyes or why footprint trackways suddenly end with no explanation. If Sasquatch are real and they are primate, it could be a natural ability and behavior to make use of the trees.

Fort Bragg, North Carolina

The military's largest base in overall population and size, Fort Bragg consists of 251 square miles (160,700 acres) outside Fayetteville, North Carolina. Among the many units there, it is the home of the All Americans of the 82nd Airborne Division, 3rd Special Forces Group, and the Special Operations Command.

Traveling west from Reilly Road, one encounters the secluded wilderness and swamplands of the off-limits Manchester Impact Area. Beginning in the 1960s, there have been so many sightings of a hairy, eight- to nine-foot-tall giant lurking near the ammunition storage facility there that it has given it a name. The "Manchester Monster" has even been featured in newspapers such as the *Fayetteville Observer* and the *Paraglide News*.[74]

A soldier attending the 82nd Airborne Division's Recondo School in July 1974 shared his experience in the swamps around Manchester Road.[75] The intense training was described as a "baby" Ranger school, condensing months' worth of instruction into just three weeks. After having heard something hidden pacing their squad in the underbrush all day, a group of soldiers had gathered with their platoon to be briefed and given operations orders for their next mission. As they all settled in to listen, the men suddenly heard the unmistakable sound of heavy footsteps walking behind the dense woodline. The grader for the platoon, known as a Black Hat, sent two men out to investigate. They returned with no answers about 20 minutes later, but the platoon continued to be followed by the sound of the mysterious footsteps. The men started to take it more seriously when they realized how anxious the grader, a tabbed Ranger, was becoming. Two more men were sent out, just as the sun was going down and the light was getting dim.

Moving slowly through the area the sound was coming from, the soldiers noticed what looked like a large shrub of some kind ahead. As they were stepping around it, the thing suddenly stood up on two legs and raised its arms over its head, towering above them both. The men screamed and turned back toward the platoon, so frightened that they ran right by their group and had to be called back. Nothing more was heard the rest of the night.

Months later, after learning more about the history of the Manchester Monster, the reporting soldier ran into the Black Hat on post. Reluctant to talk about the incident at first, the Ranger finally admitted that he believed there was something out there in the woods, but wouldn't speculate as to what exactly it could be.

MARINE CORPS BASE CAMP LEJEUNE, NORTH CAROLINA

Located 120 miles southeast from Fort Bragg to the Atlantic Coast, Camp Lejeune is a 246-square-mile (640-sq-km) Marine training facility in Jacksonville, North Carolina. Its 14 miles (23 km) of beaches make the base a major area for amphibious assault training, and it's the home of several major forces, including the 2nd Marine Division and three of the seven Marine Expeditionary Units. The base is literally surrounded by wildlands, with the 75,000-acre Holly Shelter Game Land abutting to the south and the 25,000-acre Angola Bay Game Land to the west. Much of the land is so remote and inaccessible that a U.S. Army observation plane that crashed there in 1943 wasn't rediscovered until 1978.[76]

Four Marines and their squad leader were manning dug-in hilltop fighting positions during a training exercise in February 2005 at Camp Lejeune.[77] Turning around to see the source of a loud noise, they viewed what at first appeared to be a bear only 10 yards (9 meters) behind them in a clearing, until realizing that the creature was "taking a knee." It rose up to stand on two legs, reaching a height of at least 7 feet (2.1 meters) tall, and began casually walking toward them down the hill under the light of the full moon "like he owned the place." The cryptid kept its eyes on the two Marines sharing the closest foxhole as it walked between them and the others, who were in a position 15 feet (4.5 meters) away. The thing looked directly down at the reporting eyewitness, who described it as being muscular and covered in very thick dark brown and black hair. Once past, the creature turned back to look at them one last time, its whole upper body twisting around instead of just its head and neck. An unusual and strong smell followed it. The Marines and their staff sergeant gathered and compared notes on what they had all witnessed, but none of them would go on record and say what it was.

FORT STEWART, GEORGIA

Located in the northeast corner of Georgia near Savannah, Fort Stewart is the largest U.S. Army base east of the Mississippi River and home to the 3rd Infantry Division. The post's 280,000 acres (1,100 sq km) amount to a space 39 miles (63 km) across and 19 miles (31 km) running north to south. The Canoochee River runs along the northern boundary; the wild Altamaha River is a few miles southeast of the fort and is the legendary abode of a giant aquatic, snakelike cryptid known as Altamaha-ha or "Altie."

It was on a remote tank trail back in the overgrown, swampy areas on that north side of base that a gunner on a Bradley Fighting Vehicle (BFV) encountered something unknown in November 1998.[78] Tactically driving blacked out with no lights on around 0200, he was searching the night for any simulated enemy through his thermal sight system. After turning right at a tight intersection, about 50 yards (46 meters) ahead, the gunner observed a bipedal creature come out of the thick vegetation from the right side of the dirt road. It crossed the 15- to 20-foot (4.6- to

6-meter) span to the other side in a casual stride and disappeared into the high vegetation again. Through the thermal sight, the thing appeared as one color, indicating it had no clothes on. Clothes or equipment on humans will show noticeable variations in surface temperature, appearing cooler or darker, while exposed skin stands out brightly. Based on the background surroundings as scale, the monster stood approximately 8 feet (2.4 meters) tall. "I announced to the vehicle commander over the internal comm system that something just walked across the road and it wasn't a man or an animal. He got spooked and told the driver to punch it," the soldier stated.

A squad of nine soldiers on field maneuvers were patrolling through the wilderness of Fort Stewart in 2004.[79] They began hearing "a low, feel-it type of growl," which grew into a high-pitched scream. They came out of a woodline and saw what they believed was an OPFOR trooper about 250 feet (76 meters) to their south, and started to move in on him. The bewildered soldiers heard the growl again, and the figure suddenly stood up, obviously not human and covered in matted, reddish hair. Compared to nearby trees, it stood 7 to 8 feet (2.1–2.4 meters) tall and had arms that were longer than a human's. The reporting witness claimed it threw rocks at them as they retreated, then moved off in a relaxed but incredibly fast pace by taking "twice the normal step a man would take." The cryptid vanished into the forest within seconds.

Back at their nearby camp that night, the men heard the disturbing noises of what seemed like multiple creatures in the woods surrounding them. The sounds of breaking sticks, wood-knocks, something splashing in water nearby, and crunching footsteps were heard on all sides of the perimeter throughout the sleepless night. The terrified soldiers didn't know how to process the encounter, but truly believed a man could not have been as tall or moved as quickly as what they had witnessed.

FORT WAINWRIGHT, ALASKA

Concluding our continental tour, we leave the Lower 48 behind and head to our nation's northernmost border on the last frontier. Located between the Alaska Range to the south and the Brooks Range in the north, Fort Wainwright sits in the interior of the state beside the city of

Fairbanks. Home to the 25th Infantry Division, the post manages over 1.6 million acres of training and recreational land on both sides of the Chena River, including 8,825 acres of ranges and nearly 900,000 acres of military maneuver areas. Also of note, there are some 650 prehistoric archaeological sites within the confines of the fort.

Perhaps somebody should be digging around the on-base enlisted housing neighborhood of Bear Paw, discovering why so many hauntings seem to be taking place there. Various families living in apartments along 599th Street have been the victims of several unexplainable phenomena, including feelings of being watched, family pets aggressively reacting to something unseen, sudden cold spots in rooms, and children and babies being unnaturally frightened and upset. When one young daughter of a soldier took a picture of her baby sister on a tablet, the image of an unknown little girl who was not there showed up in the background.[80]

The wife of another soldier experienced a haunting in their family housing that became progressively worse. "I started having nightmares, which I don't usually have, and would wake up in the middle of the night feeling like something was standing over me. My cat would stare at random spots on the walls and ceiling. My dog would bark and growl for no reason. Sometimes I would be alone and feel like I was being watched," she said.[81] Random items like remote controls and toothbrushes started disappearing with no explanation, mysteriously turning up days later in places that were obvious and out in the open. When her husband deployed for Iraq, the feelings of something unseen constantly watching her became overwhelming and made the home an uncomfortable place to be. She finally had another witness to the phenomena when a friend stayed over one night to keep her company shortly before she finally was able to move. "I went to my room and almost as soon as I laid down, I heard her door slam shut. I jumped up to see what was wrong. I opened the door and she was terrified. She said that she watched the door slowly close, and then as it got closer to being shut, it just slammed."

Hopefully, she checked for strings.

* * *

A Special Forces captain and 11 seasoned operators on his A-Team were conducting a strategic reconnaissance training mission in March of 1988 out of Fort Wainwright.[82] The team had been flown by helicopter in a southeast direction and then dropped off in the wilderness for a several-day mission. The highly trained professionals had marched through the deep snow on cross-country skis, changing to snowshoes when the woods in one area became too thick. About 200 meters (656 feet) inside this woodline, a set of bizarre tracks were discovered. Something on two legs was walking in gigantic strides in a course perpendicular to the team. The distance impossibly amounted to over 5 feet (1.5 meters) between steps. The Green Berets studied the tracks and tried to form rational explanations. Collectively, they had over 150 years of Special Operations experience all over the world and had tracked everything known to man with two or four legs. Defying logic, the group consensus was that the stride and depth of the tracks indicated a being around 9 feet (2.7 meters) tall that weighed between 500 and 600 pounds (227–272 kg)!

Overcome by curiosity and being the type of men who were never afraid of danger, the team decided to follow the trail. "Whatever was making the tracks was moving through the woods exactly as one of us would have if we were conducting an escape and evasion. Whatever it was knew the land (as it maneuvered to bypass clearings well before they came into view) and was making a concentrated effort to remain unseen," the captain reported. They followed the footprints, which traversed the military crest of ridgelines, crossing only in saddles and staying low as much as possible, for over an hour.

Suddenly, from some unknown distance ahead of them, the team heard the most horrific sound any of them had ever witnessed. Sounding like an angry hybrid of a roar and a howl, the guttural, growling scream froze the warriors in their tracks. Unnerved and taking it as a warning, the soldiers decided that they really didn't want to meet the source of the noise anyway and agreed to resume the training mission. They felt that even their combined martial talents might still be no match for whatever the hell was walking in front of them. These Green Berets were honestly afraid of what they had seen and heard. They also agreed to keep the incident to themselves.

Like so many other events in this collection, the unknown stayed just out of reach over the next dark horizon, ensuring that the ultimate mysteries remain unsolved for the armed forces members training and fighting in this strange, surreal reality, found somewhere between fact and fiction, that we call Weird War.

After Action Review

Looks like the sun is coming up and we survived the long, dark night of our dangerous reconnaissance patrol, soldiers. Clear your weapons and hit the rack; you've all earned the right to some real rest and relaxation as new veterans of this Weird War. I hope your dreams are better than the nightmares we encountered together on this menacing watch. Know to be prepared tomorrow for more action, because I need all of you to stay on high alert for any signs of future troops in contact with the unexplained, paranormal, and bizarre.

If you have your own Weird War military story to report, please email the author at weirdwarsitrep@gmail.com.

ACKNOWLEDGMENTS

One of my best friends from my time in the U.S. Army was killed in action (KIA) in Afghanistan while commanding B Troop, 1st Squadron, 91st Cavalry Regiment (Airborne) at Combat Outpost (COP) Keating on July 27, 2007. Major Thomas G. Bostick Jr., from Llano, Texas, was awarded the Distinguished Service Cross (the second-highest medal for extraordinary heroism in combat) for his sacrifice during the Battle of Saret Koleh. Forward Operating Base (FOB) Naray, in the Kunar Province of Afghanistan, was renamed FOB Bostick in July of 2008, and the paratroopers of 1/91 Cavalry have honored his legacy since 2018 with the Bostick Cup. Long before he became a national hero, he was just a lowly enlisted private enduring Basic Combat Training (BCT) and Advanced Individual Training (AIT) with me for nearly a year. We became very close friends during that time, and now, as I grow older, I treasure the letters, photographs, and golden memories of our youth even more. He also was a veteran of Operation Just Cause in Panama with the 75th Ranger Regiment in 1989 and Operation Iraqi Freedom as a platoon leader with the 3rd Ranger Battalion in 2003. A real Captain America, Tom embodied everything a professional soldier is expected to be. I wear a metal remembrance bracelet with his photo and KIA date every day—to the point where it has become a serious superstition and protection charm. When I wear it, I still feel like Tommy has my six. He was the absolute greatest. This book is dedicated to his sacrifice and memory.

* * *

My original assignment within 5th Infantry was in G2, the division-level military intelligence staff, during some lively times at Fort Polk,

Louisiana. In May of 1989, we deployed the Roadrunners of 1st Battalion, 61st Infantry Regiment, in support of Operation Nimrod Dancer to protect American interests in Panama. In September, the Regulars of 4th Battalion, 6th Infantry Regiment, from our 2nd Brigade, rotated in-country and replaced them. They would see all-out combat as part of Operation Just Cause on December 20, 1989, helping overthrow Panamanian dictator Manuel Noriega by storming the Panama Defense Force (PDF) headquarters, La Comandancia, in their M113 Armored Personnel Carriers (APCs). Although rarely documented, I also know our 5th ID soldiers (from B Company of 4/6 INF) completed the emergency extraction of five injured Delta Force operators and their rescued hostage when their MH-6 Little Bird helicopter was brought down in the street by PDF small-arms fire. The first successful hostage rescue ever made by Delta Force, known as Operation Acid Gambit, was executed by 23 Delta operators to rescue a CIA asset, Kurt Muse, codenamed "Precious Cargo," from Modelo Prison, located across the street from La Comandancia during the battle.

The violence of Operation Just Cause resulted in 32 soldiers wounded and 2 killed in action from the 5th Infantry Division—Corporal Ivan D. Perez from B Company and Private Kenneth D. Scott of A Company—who I strive to ensure are always acknowledged and remembered. In 1991, I would be attached for several months to 4th Battalion, 6th Infantry, as their lone S2 intelligence sergeant for an NTC deployment. It was a privilege to serve with the Regulars who had carried out their mission in Panama so successfully and honorably. They were the last unit from 5th ID to ever earn the right to wear the distinguished Red Diamond as a combat patch on the right sleeve.

Notes

Welcome to Weird War

1. Miller, W. (n.d.). *The Cavalry Battle Near Gettysburg*. Archival files of the Gettysburg National Military Park Library.

2. Wert, J. (1996). *Custer: The Controversial Life of George Armstrong Custer*. New York: Touchstone.

3. Holbrook, T. (April 17, 2016). "Men of Action: The Unsung Heroes of East Cavalry Field." Retrieved April 5, 2021, from http://npshistory.com/series/symposia/gettysburg _seminars/5/essay5.htm.

Chapter 1

1. Germer, W. (December 21, 2014). Sasquatch Chronicles Radio // SC 66: "Giants in America." Retrieved March 2, 2021, from https://sasquatchchronicles.com/sc-ep66 -giants-in-america/.

2. Shackley, M. (1986). *Still Living? Yeti, Sasquatch and the Neanderthal Enigma*. New York: W.W. Norton & Co Inc., 118.

3. Colyer, D., Mayes, M., and Wells, J. (November 2008). "Case 01080124 (Class 3a): Woman Reports Early Morning Visual Encounter on Rural Property Near Navarro Mills Lake." Retrieved September 2, 2021, from https://reports.woodape.org/data/ ?action=details&case=01080124#CaseNum; Colyer, D. (February 2006). "Case 01060005 (Class 1d): Husband and Wife Report Close Road Encounter Near Navarro Mills Lake." Retrieved September 2, 2021, from https://reports.woodape.org/data/?action=details &case=01060005#CaseNum.

4. Blackburn, L. (2017). *Beyond Boggy Creek: In Search of the Southern Sasquatch*. San Antonio, TX: Anomalist Books.

5. Blaxland, B. (February 10, 2020). "Hominid and Hominin—What's the Difference?" Retrieved April 15, 2021, from https://australian.museum/learn/science/human -evolution/hominid-and-hominin-whats-the-difference/.

6. Plackett, B. (January 24, 2021). "How Many Early Human Species Existed on Earth?" Retrieved April 15, 2021, from https://www.livescience.com/how-many-human -species.html.

7. Barras, C. (May 3, 2017). "Ancient Humans: What We Know and Still Don't Know About Them." Retrieved April 18, 2021, from https://www.newscientist.com/article/2129775-ancient-humans-what-we-know-and-still-dont-know-about-them/.

8. Cirotteau, T. (director). (2017). *Who Killed the Neanderthal?* (documentary). France: Bonne Pioche Television.

9. Olson, A. (December 1, 2021). "Mysterious Footprints in Tanzania Made by Early Humans, Not Bears." Retrieved February 12, 2022, from https://home.dartmouth.edu/news/2021/12/mysterious-footprints-tanzania-made-early-humans-not-bears.

10. Olson, "Mysterious Footprints in Tanzania."

11. Barras, "Ancient Humans."

12. Barras, "Ancient Humans."

13. Liqiang, H. (December 28, 2021). "Dragon Man Skull Prompts Rethinking of Evolution." Retrieved March 10, 2022, from https://global.chinadaily.com.cn/a/202112/28/WS61ca4bc0a310cdd39bc7dbf9.html.

14. Longrich, N. (November 2, 2020). "War in the Time of Neanderthals: How Our Species Battled for Supremacy for Over 100,000 Years." Retrieved March 15, 2021, from https://theconversation.com/war-in-the-time-of-neanderthals-how-our-species-battled-for-supremacy-for-over-100-000-years-148205.

15. Longrich, "War in the Time of Neanderthals."

16. Vendramini, D. (2009). *Them and Us: How Neanderthal Predation Created Modern Humans*. Armidale, Australia: Kardoorair Press.

17. Scoop Independent News. (September 18, 2009). "Neanderthals Hunted, Raped and Ate Humans." Retrieved April 22, 2021, from https://www.scoop.co.nz/stories/WO0909/S00246/neanderthals-hunted-raped-and-ate-humans.htm.

18. Longrich, N. (November 21, 2019). "Were Other Humans the First Victims of the Sixth Mass Extinction?" Retrieved April 20, 2021, from https://theconversation.com/were-other-humans-the-first-victims-of-the-sixth-mass-extinction-126638.

19. Alex, B. (January 14, 2020). "In Russia's Far North, A Lone Group of Neanderthals May Have Been the Last of Their Kind." Retrieved April 22, 2021, from https://www.discovermagazine.com/planet-earth/in-russias-far-north-a-lone-group-of-neanderthals-may-have-been-the-last-of.

20. Roach, J. (May 15, 2011). "Neanderthals Made a Last Stand at Subarctic Outpost?" Retrieved April 22, 2021, from https://www.nationalgeographic.com/history/article/110513-neanderthals-last-stand-science-tool-kit-russia-slimak-tools.

21. Wenzel, N. (2009). "The Legend of the Almas: A Comparative and Critical Analysis." Retrieved August 25, 2021, from https://digitalcollections.sit.edu/isp_collection/801.

22. Porshnev, B. (July 1968). "The Struggle for Troglodytes." *Prostor Magazine*, 113–16.

23. Shackley, *Still Living?*

24. Germer, "Giants in America."

25. Neumann, K., Schiltberger, J. and Telfer, J. (1879). *The Bondage and Travels of Johann Schiltberger, a Native of Bavaria, in Europe, Asia, and Africa, 1396–1427*. London: T. Richards Printer. Retrieved April 23, 2021, from https://www.gutenberg.org/files/52569/52569-h/52569-h.htm#Page_22.

26. Krystek, L. (1996). "The Wild Man of Central Asia." Retrieved March 23, 2021, from http://www.unmuseum.org/alma.htm.

27. Wenzel, "The Legend of the Almas."

28. Rawicz, S. (2016). *The Long Walk: The True Story of a Trek to Freedom*. Guilford, CT: Lyons Press.

29. Occultopedia. (n.d.). "Almas." Retrieved March 20, 2021, from https://www .occultopedia.com/a/almas.htm.

30. Dawn News. (April 19, 2009). "Wildlife: Barmanu-Fact or Fiction." Retrieved May 15, 2021, from https://www.dawn.com/news/882743/wildlife-barmanu-fact-or-fiction.

31. Short, B. (n.d.). "The De Facto Sasquatch." Retrieved August 30, 2021, from https:// static1.squarespace.com/static/596c0bae4c0dbfa1d26e86be/t/5b9bff06562fa7cfcdf1bfc8 /1536950038606/The+de+facto+Sasquatch+premier+installment.pdf?fbclid=IwAR3763 B1leKUEQofPRbPvzAItNH5K-RUVoKU-vOLW_iXvSFkdKSg4o4xBXw.

32. BBC News. (April 30, 2019). "Yeti Footprints: Indian Army Mocked Over Claim." Retrieved March 12, 2021, from https://www.bbc.com/news/world-asia-india-48101717.

33. Tapper, J. (2012). *The Outpost: An Untold Story of American Valor*. New York: Little, Brown & Company.

34. Germer, W. (July 16, 2021). Sasquatch Chronicles Radio // SC 775: "Sasquatch in Afghanistan." Retrieved August 23, 2021, from https://sasquatchchronicles.com/sc -ep775-sasquatch-in-afghanistan/.

35. Germer, "Sasquatch in Afghanistan."

36. Dawn News, "Wildlife: Barmanu-Fact or Fiction."

37. Dawn News, "Wildlife: Barmanu-Fact or Fiction."

38. Germer, W. (July 25, 2021). Sasquatch Chronicles Radio // SC 778: "Military Encounters/What Is a Box Witch?" Retrieved August 15, 2021, from https:// sasquatchchronicles.com/sc-ep778-military-encounters-what-is-a-box-witch/.

39. Martin, B. (March 31, 2013). Report #40652 (Class B): "U.S. Soldier Views Unexplainable Subject Near Bargi Matal." Retrieved August 30, 2021, from https://www.bfro .net/GDB/show_report.asp?id=40652.

40. Germer, "Military Encounters/What Is a Box Witch?"

41. Strickler, L. (2016). *Phantoms & Monsters: Mysterious Encounters*. Self-published: CreateSpace Independent Publishing Platform.

42. Swancer, B. (February 7, 2017). "Bizarre Encounters with the Weird in the Middle East Wars." Retrieved May 6, 2021, from https://mysteriousuniverse.org/2017/02/bizarre -encounters-with-the-weird-in-the-middle-east-wars/.

43. Reedy, K. (March 26, 2013). "Most Afghans Are Certain the Demons of Myth Actually Roam the Earth." Retrieved April 20, 2021, from https://www.businessinsider .com/afghan-mythology-is-home-to-monsters-2013-3.

44. BBC News. (April 15, 2017). "MOAB Strike: 90 IS Fighters Killed in Afghanistan." Retrieved May 15, 2021, from https://www.bbc.com/news/world-asia-39607213.

45. Merkel, L. (November 28, 2018). "Legends of the Giant." Retrieved April 30, 2021, from https://www.theconfessionalspodcast.com/the-blog/are-old-legend-giants-living -in-the-modern-day-world?rq=giants.

46. BBC News. (April 29, 2003). "Gilgamesh Tomb Believed Found." Retrieved July 25, 2021, from http://news.bbc.co.uk/2/hi/science/nature/2982891.stm.

47. ABC News. (May 6, 2003). "Experts Search for Grave of Legendary Gilgamesh." Retrieved July 25, 2021, from https://www.abc.net.au/news/2003-05-06/experts-search-for-grave-of-legendary-gilgamesh/1849534.

48. ABC News. "Experts Search for Grave."

49. UFOmania [screen name]. (October 11, 2020). "From the Hillary Clinton Email . . . Location of Buried Nephilim???" Retrieved August 29, 2021, from https://www.youtube.com/watch?v=HHXuDWHj8gk.

50. Ryan-Byrne, K. (n.d.). "Ali Air Base: An Abandoned Military Base in Iraq." Retrieved February 12, 2022, from https://www.worldabandoned.com/ali-air-base.

51. Feeney, N. (2003). "The Secret of Nimrud: 265 Photographs." Iraq Museum International. Retrieved March 30, 2021, from http://www.baghdadmuseum.org/secret_s/index.htm.

52. Luhnow, D. (June 6, 2003). "Treasure of Nimrud Is Found in Iraq, and It's Spectacular." Retrieved May 10, 2021, from https://www.wsj.com/articles/SB105485037080424400.

53. Fisher, M. (January 19, 2006). "Tomb Raiders." Retrieved May 10, 2021, from https://www.theguardian.com/artanddesign/2006/jan/19/heritage.iraq.

54. Department of State. (2018). "Department of State Freedom of Information Act: FOIA Log 2018." Retrieved March 25, 2021, from https://foia.state.gov/Search/Results.aspx?searchText=gilgamesh&beginDate=&endDate=&publishedBeginDate=&publishedEndDate=&caseNumber=.

55. Hemmings, J. (April 5, 2019). "Rock Apes: The Cryptids That Supposedly Once Plagued GI's." Retrieved March 25, 2021, from https://www.warhistoryonline.com/vietnam-war/rock-apes-not-a-70s-rock-band.html?chrome=1.

56. Stilwell, B. (April 16, 2021). "This is the Story of US Troops Who Think They Saw Bigfoot in Vietnam." Retrieved May 15, 2021, from https://www.wearethemighty.com/mighty-history/us-troops-saw-bigfoot-vietnam/.

57. Felton, M. (May 23, 2020). "Vietnam War Rock Apes—Bigfoot or Big Fraud?" Retrieved March 29, 2021, from https://www.youtube.com/watch?v=BpNxWxSHDoA&t=3s.

58. Felton, "Vietnam War Rock Apes."

59. Hemmings, "Rock Apes."

60. Hegge, M. (November 12, 2021). Personal interview with author.

61. Hegge, personal interview.

62. Personal interview with author. (October 8, 2021).

63. Felton, "Vietnam War Rock Apes."

64. Short, "The De Facto Sasquatch."

65. First Recon Battalion Association. (April 5, 2021). "Dong Den Mountain." Retrieved August 25, 2021, from https://1streconbn.org/dong-den.html.

66. Felton, "Vietnam War Rock Apes."

67. Rowton, L. (July 21, 2017). "Battlefield Horrors: 5 Terrifying Wartime Monster Sightings." Retrieved March 22, 2021, from https://www.paranormalscholar.com/5-terrifying-wartime-monster-sightings/.

68. Delaney, T. (July 3, 2017). "Marine Says Vietnam Was Like No Other Place." Retrieved November 10, 2021, from https://www.mysoutex.com/refugio_county_press/news/features/marine-says-vietnam-was-like-no-other-place/article_3e202d8a-5de4-11e7-9fc8-532d34aeb212.html.

69. Delaney, July 3, 2017.

70. Stilwell, April 16, 2021.

71. CryptoVille. (September 6, 2012). "Vietnam Bigfoot (Forest Man/Batutut): Is It Real?" Retrieved March 15, 2021, from https://visitcryptoville.com/2012/09/06/vietnam-bigfoot-forest-manbatutut-is-it-real/.

72. CryptoVille, September 6, 2012.

73. Short, "The De Facto Sasquatch."

74. Germer, W. (July 7, 2015). "Vietnam Sasquatch." Retrieved March 25, 2021, from https://sasquatchchronicles.com/vietnam-sasquatch/.

75. Baylett, R. (March 30, 2014). Personal conversation with the author.

76. Bello, P. (May 10, 2021). Posted comment. Retrieved August 23, 2021, from https://www.youtube.com/watch?v=BpNxWxSHDoA&lc=UgysV6XHnsTr4kfemxp4AaABAg.

77. Short, "The De Facto Sasquatch."

78. Short, "The De Facto Sasquatch."

79. Hegge, personal interview.

80. Short, "The De Facto Sasquatch."

81. Hai, T., Meldrum, J., and Viet, T. (June 28, 2021). "Research on Wildmen in Vietnam." In *The Relict Hominoid Inquiry* (10), 6–28. Retrieved August 30, 2021, from https://www.isu.edu/media/libraries/rhi/research-papers/Viet-manuscript_final.pdf.

82. Young, E. (September 27, 2017). "Giant Tree-Dwelling Rat Discovered in Solomon Islands." Retrieved March 2, 2022, from https://www.nature.com/articles/nature.2017.22684.

83. Boirayon, M. (2010). *Solomon Islands Mysteries: Accounts of Giants and UFOs in the Solomon Islands*. Kempton, IL: Adventures Unlimited Press.

84. Swancer, B. (April 1, 2014). "Pacific War Mysteries—Part 1 of 2." Retrieved February 15, 2022, from https://mysteriousuniverse.org/2014/03/pacific-war-mysteries-part-1-of-2/.

85. Swancer, B. (April 1, 2014). "Pacific War Mysteries—Part 2 of 2." Retrieved February 15, 2022, from https://mysteriousuniverse.org/2014/04/pacific-war-mysteries-part-2-of-2/.

86. Patterson, G. (2020). *Beyond the Secret Elephants: On Mystery, Elephants, and Discovery*. Gauteng, South Africa: Tracey McDonald Publishers.

CHAPTER 2

1. Felton, M. (May 20, 2019). "The Strange Ambush of Team Rock Mat, Vietnam 1970." Retrieved January 10, 2022, from https://www.youtube.com/watch?v=zpDnlGT3LxY&t=3s.

2. Nyhus, P., and Tilson, R. (eds.). (2010). *Tigers of the World: The Science, Politics, and Conservation of Panthera Tigris.* Burlington, MA: Academic Press.

3. No author. (January 15, 1969). "Marine in Cat's Mouth Saved by His Swift Moving Partner." *Pacific Stars & Stripes* Vol. 25 (14).

4. No author, "Marine in Cat's Mouth."

5. Koons, M. (2020). Comment retrieved May 15, 2021, from https://www.youtube .com/watch?v=zpDnlGT3LxY&lc=UgzT_x2oZi5m4vfonYp4AaABAg.

6. Lagimoniere, B., Leland, R., and Stamper, S. (2006). "Discerning the Tiger!" Retrieved May 20, 2021, from the 1st Battalion (Mech) 50th Infantry, https://www .ichiban1.org/html/stories/story_46_tiger.htm.

7. Lagimoniere et al., "Discerning the Tiger!"

8. Lagimoniere et al., "Discerning the Tiger!"

9. Lagimoniere et al., "Discerning the Tiger!"

10. No author. (n.d.). "Man-Eaters: Tanning the Tiger." Retrieved May 24, 2021, from http://www.lairweb.org.nz/tiger/maneating14.html.

11. Kumar, M. (August 20, 2013). "From Gunpowder to Teeth Whitener: The Science behind Historic Uses of Urine." Retrieved February 18, 2022, from https: //www.smithsonianmag.com/science-nature/from-gunpowder-to-teeth-whitener-the -science-behind-historic-uses-of-urine-442390/#:~:text=Its%20high%20pH%20breaks %20down,softening%20and%20tanning%20animal%20hides.

12. Chong, E. (April 29, 2014). "Death of Man Stung by Bees Ruled Accidental." Retrieved February 16, 2022, from https://www.straitstimes.com/singapore/courts-crime /death-of-man-stung-by-bees-ruled-accidental.

13. Fish, J. (February 22, 2021). 5th Infantry Division Veterans Group. Conversation with the author.

14. Evon, D. (July 4, 2021). "Is This Giant Jungle Centipede Real?" Retrieved February 20, 2022, from https://www.snopes.com/fact-check/giant-jungle-centipede-real/.

15. Fifth Infantry Division Veterans Group. (February 22, 2021). Conversation with the author.

16. Fifth Infantry Division Veterans Group, February 22, 2021.

17. Fifth Infantry Division Veterans Group, February 22, 2021.

18. Fifth Infantry Division Veterans Group, February 22, 2021.

19. Huggins. (n.d.). "Trench Rats." Retrieved January 20, 2022, from https:// schoolhistory.co.uk/modern/trench-rats/.

20. Historynet. (June 19, 2020). "Jungle Fights Back: Crocodiles at Ramree Island." Retrieved May 18, 2021, from https://www.historynet.com/ramree-battle-crocodiles/?f.

21. Historynet. "Jungle Fights Back."

22. Wright, B. S. (1962). *Wildlife Sketches Near and Far.* Fredericton, NB: Brunswick Press.

23. Wright, "Wildlife Sketches Near and Far."

24. Teng, J. (April 26, 2021). "Saltwater Crocodiles Devoured 500 Japanese Soldiers in Burma During World War 2." Retrieved May 5, 2021, from https://historyofyesterday .com/saltwater-crocodiles-devoured-500-japanese-soldiers-in-burma-during-world-war -2-3225172aaffe.

25. Rasmussen, C. (March 18, 2022). "Crocodile Attacks! How Common Are They?" Retrieved February 20, 2022, from https://a-z-animals.com/blog/crocodile-attacks-how-common-are-they/.

26. AP Archive. (March 9, 2002). "Afghanistan Pest Threat." Retrieved January 15, 2022, from http://www.aparchive.com/metadata/youtube/cbd64794b59401645cc6815f31aa8069.

27. iPest Solutions. (December 12, 2018). "American Troops in Afghanistan Are Forced to Contend with Dangerous Scorpions." Retrieved February 15, 2022, from https://wacopest.com/american-troops-in-afghanistan-are-forced-to-contend-with-dangerous-scorpions/.

28. iPest Solutions. "American Troops in Afghanistan."

29. Hsu, J. and Metcalfe, T. (September 26, 2017). "Beasts in Battle: 15 Amazing Animal Recruits in War." Retrieved September 13, 2021, from https://www.livescience.com/60518-animals-used-in-warfare/2.html.

30. Mikkelson, D. (July 10, 2007). "Camel Spiders." Retrieved February 2, 2022, from https://www.snopes.com/fact-check/camel-spiders/.

31. No author. (n.d.) "Solifugae." Retrieved July 10, 2021, from https://en-academic.com/dic.nsf/enwiki/287031.

32. Pappalardo, J. (September 12, 2012). "Beware the Monkeys: Animal Bites Plague Troops in Afghanistan." Retrieved August 23, 2021, from https://www.popularmechanics.com/military/a8047/monkey-bites-plague-troops-in-afghanistan-12636466/.

33. Pappalardo, "Beware the Monkeys."

34. Wolf, M. (April 26, 2017). "Let Slip the Hogs of War: Wild Pigs Thwart ISIS Ambush, Kill 3 Militants." Retrieved February 3, 2022, from https://www.militarytimes.com/news/your-military/2017/04/26/let-slip-the-hogs-of-war-wild-pigs-thwart-isis-ambush-kill-3-militants/.

35. Russell, R. (April 22, 2003). "US Troops Kill Four Escaped Lions of Baghdad Zoo." Retrieved June 23, 2021, from https://www.rediff.com/us/2003/apr/21iraq5.htm.

36. Aljazeera News. (September 20, 2003). "US Soldier Kills Iraqi Tiger." Retrieved February 2, 2022, from https://www.aljazeera.com/news/2003/9/20/us-soldier-kills-iraqi-tiger.

37. Pye, D. (n.d.) "Virtual War Memorial Australia: Paul Harold Denehey." Retrieved April 15, 2021, from https://vwma.org.au/explore/people/617184.

38. Mirror News. (October 17, 2008). "British Soldier Survives Elephant Attack During Bush Mission." Retrieved April 26, 2021, from https://www.mirror.co.uk/news/uk-news/british-soldier-survives-elephant-attack-348619.

39. The Scotsman. (November 25, 2011). "Scots Soldier Is Attacked in His Sleep by Hyena." Retrieved April 26, 2021, from https://www.scotsman.com/news/scots-soldier-attacked-his-sleep-hyena-1653151.

40. Hsu and Metcalfe, "Beasts in Battle."

41. Alexander-Rodriguez, J. (2020). Comment on post. Retrieved April 30, 2021, from https://www.quora.com/Are-military-special-forces-soldiers-ever-attacked-by-wild-animals.

42. Military Wiki. (August 8, 2019). "Animal-Borne Bomb Attacks." Retrieved February 23, 2022, from https://military-history.fandom.com/wiki/Animal-borne_bomb_attacks.

43. Military Wiki, "Animal-Borne Bomb Attacks."

44. Military Wiki. (July 22, 2019). "Anti-Tank Dog." Retrieved February 10, 2022, from https://military-history.fandom.com/wiki/Anti-tank_dog.

45. Military Wiki, "Anti-Tank Dog."

46. Hsu and Metcalfe, "Beasts in Battle."

47. Capshew, J. (1993). "Engineering Behavior: Project Pigeon, World War II, and the Conditioning of B. F. Skinner." *Technology and Culture*, 34(4), 835–57. Retrieved February 12, 2022, from https://www.jstor.org/stable/3106417.

48. Gross, R. (March 28, 2016). "Some Historically Fueled Guesses on What Russia Will Do with Its War Dolphins." Retrieved January 22, 2022, from https://slate.com/technology/2016/03/a-short-history-of-war-dolphins.html.

49. Gross, "What Russia Will Do with Its War Dolphins."

50. Roblin, S. (January 9, 2021). "Secret Is Out: Russia Weaponized and Trained Dolphins and Whales." Retrieved February 3, 2022, from https://nationalinterest.org/blog/reboot/secret-out-russia-weaponized-and-trained-dolphins-and-whales-176151.

51. Roblin, "Secret Is Out."

52. Roblin, "Secret Is Out."

53. Stilwell, B. (January 21, 2020). "Iran May Have a Fleet of Communist Killer Dolphins." Retrieved January 26, 2022, from https://taskandpurpose.com/news/iran-navy-communist-killer-dolphins/.

54. McDonald, G. (December 29, 2017). "The Story of Wojtek: The Soldier Bear Who Was Promoted to Corporal." Retrieved February 5, 2022, from https://inews.co.uk/inews-lifestyle/travel/wojtek-soldier-bear-edinburgh-113664.

55. Crew, B. (August 4, 2014). "The Great Emu War: In Which Some Large, Flightless Birds Unwittingly Foiled the Australian Army." Retrieved March 27, 2021, from https://blogs.scientificamerican.com/running-ponies/the-great-emu-war-in-which-some-large-flightless-birds-unwittingly-foiled-the-australian-army/.

56. Crew, "The Great Emu War."

57. Crew, "The Great Emu War."

58. Crew, "The Great Emu War."

CHAPTER 3

1. Schmidt, H. (2001). *SS Panzergrenadier: A True Story of World War II*. Pensacola, FL: H. Schmidt Publications.

2. Harvin, I. (July 2, 2016). "Himmler's Witches Library Discovered in the Czech Republic." Retrieved April 18, 2021, from https://www.warhistoryonline.com/featured/himmlers-witches-library-discovered-czech_republic.html?chrome=1.

3. Ancient Origins. (January 29, 2021). "Was Heinrich Himmler's 'Nazi Witch Library' Discovered in a Czech Library?" Retrieved April 30, 2021, from https://www.ancient-origins.net/news-general/stash-books-witch-library-nazi-chief-himmler-found-prague-005570.

4. Murray, M. (1921). *The Witch-Cult in Western Europe.* Oxford: Clarendon Press.

5. Murray, M. (1931). *The God of the Witches.* London: Faber & Faber.

6. Crowley, A. (1973). *Magick Without Tears.* Phoenix, AZ: Falcon Press.

7. Lachman, G. (2014). *Aleister Crowley: Magick, Rock and Roll, and the Wickedest Man in the World.* New York: Penguin Group.

8. Lachman, *Aleister Crowley.*

9. Nieuwint, J. (September 14, 2015). "Wewelsburg Castle: The Nazi Temple of Doom." Retrieved August 23, 2021, from https://www.warhistoryonline.com/world-war -ii/wewelsburg-castle-the-nazi-temple-of-doom.html?D3c=1.

10. Heritage Daily. (June 6, 2021). "Wewelsburg: The Real Castle Wolfenstein." Retrieved August 23, 2021, from https://www.heritagedaily.com/2021/06/wewelsburg -the-real-castle-wolfenstein/139389.

11. Black, J. (May 8, 2013). "Ahnenerbe: Nazis and the Search for Relics." Retrieved May 23, 2021, from https://www.ancient-origins.net/myths-legends-europe/ahnenerbe -00424.

12. Military Wiki. (June 6, 2021). "Ahnenerbe." Retrieved February 23, 2022, from https://military-history.fandom.com/wiki/Ahnenerbe.

13. Rennie, D. (September 10, 2019). "Heinrich Himmler Thought Germans Were Descended from Nordic Gods, So He Tried to Prove It." Retrieved January 23, 2022, from https://allthatsinteresting.com/ahnenerbe.

14. Frolov, S. (September 5, 2022). "The Mysterious Skull of the Alien and the Foot-print of the Ahnenerbe." Retrieved November 15, 2021, from https://earth-chronicles.ru /news/2016-11-23-98569.

15. Sinelschikova, Y. (March 10, 2020). "What Hitler's Occultists Were Secretly Searching for in the USSR." Retrieved January 12, 2022, from https://www.rbth.com/ history/331804-hitlers-occultists-search-ussr.

16. Totally Chaos. (November 23, 2016). "Scientists Dug Out a Bizarre Nazi Chest. What They Found Inside Is Unlike Anything Known to Man." Retrieved March 5, 2021, from https://totallychaos.com/scientists-discover-bizarre-nazi-chest/.

17. Sinelschikova, "What Hitler's Occultists Were Secretly Searching For."

18. No author. (n.d.) "Gate to Hell at Houska Castle." Retrieved March 30, 2021, from https://www.mcgeesghosttours.com/gate-to-hell-at-houska-castle/.

19. No author, "Gate to Hell at Houska Castle."

20. Margaritoff, M. (April 7, 2022). "The Eerie History of Houska Castle: The Gothic Fortress Built to Seal a Gateway to Hell." Retrieved April 25, 2022, from https:// allthatsinteresting.com/houska-castle.

21. Margaritoff, "The Eerie History of Houska Castle."

22. Tanaka, Y. (1996). *Hidden Horrors: Japanese War Crimes in World War II.* Boulder, CO: Westview Press.

23. Stockton, R. (May 17, 2021). "Inside Japan's World War II-Era Reign of Terror." Retrieved August 28, 2021, from https://allthatsinteresting.com/japanese-war-crimes/2.

24. Lenoir, A. (November 5, 2020). "Intense Hatred and Intense Hunger: The Grisly Story of Japanese Cannibalism During WWII." Retrieved August 28, 2021, from https: //allthatsinteresting.com/japanese-cannibalism-ww2.

25. Lenoir, "Intense Hatred and Intense Hunger."

26. Lenoir, "Intense Hatred and Intense Hunger."

27. Stockton, "Inside Japan's World War II-Era."

28. Lenoir, "Intense Hatred and Intense Hunger."

29. Kuroski, J. (April 28, 2021). "Inside the Chichijima Incident, George H. W. Bush's Harrowing Escape from Cannibal Enemies During World War II." Retrieved August 29, 2021, from https://allthatsinteresting.com/george-bush-cannibalized-chichijima-incident.

30. Kuroski, "Inside the Chichijima Incident."

31. Kuroski, "Inside the Chichijima Incident."

32. Kuroski, "Inside the Chichijima Incident."

33. Lenoir, "Intense Hatred and Intense Hunger."

34. Stockton, "Inside Japan's World War II-Era."

35. Bradley, J. (2003). *Flyboys: A True Story of Courage*. Boston, MA: Little, Brown and Company.

36. Kuroski, "Inside the Chichijima Incident."

37. Lenoir, "Intense Hatred and Intense Hunger."

38. AP News. (September 6, 1993). "Filipinos Seeking Compensation for Cannibalism by Japanese Troops." Retrieved February 23, 2022, from https://apnews.com/article/61eaf879b3dd907cf2cb48d2fad7455a.

39. Beaman, A. (1920). *The Squadroon*. London: John Lane Company.

40. Deutsch, J. (September 8, 2014). "The Legend of What Actually Lived in the No Man's Land Between World War I's Trenches." Retrieved March 2, 2022, from https://www.smithsonianmag.com/history/legends-what-actually-lived-no-mans-land-between-world-war-i-trenches-180952513/.

41. Deutsch, "Legend of What Actually Lived in the No Man's Land."

42. Orton, N. (September 12, 2021). "Mysticism, Cults, and the Iraq War." Retrieved October 2, 2021, from https://www.instagram.com/p/CTto1J3Lgpp/.

43. Brown, L. (May 31, 2012). "10 Things You Always Wondered about Cannibalism." Retrieved February 4, 2022, from https://www.businessinsider.com/10-things-you-always-wondered-about-cannibalism-2012-5.

44. Brown, "10 Things You Always Wondered about Cannibalism."

45. Lynch, F. (1998). *The Aswang Inquiry*. Manila, Philippines: GCF Books.

46. Ichimura, A., and Severino, A. (October 19, 2019). "How the CIA Used the Aswang to Win a War in the Philippines." Retrieved July 15, 2021, from https://www.esquiremag.ph/long-reads/features/cia-aswang-war-a00304-a2416-20191019-lfrm.

47. Lansdale, E. (1991). *In the Midst of Wars: An American's Mission to Southeast Asia*. New York: Fordham University Press.

48. Friedman, H. (2002). "The Wandering Soul PSYOP Tape of Vietnam." Retrieved March 3, 2022, from https://www.pcf45.com/sealords/cuadai/wanderingsoul.html.

49. Palmlof, O. (January 16, 2016). "Operation Wandering Soul Remastered." Retrieved May 15, 2021, from https://www.youtube.com/watch?v=THMAchwBwgs&list=PLqwaoKK7fYGnjGrj52MjrIja1QmswIBjF&index=6.

50. Nye, L. (February 5, 2021). "That Time US Soldiers Pretended to Be Vampires and Ghosts to Scare the Hell Out of the Enemy." Retrieved April 13, 2021, from https://www.wearethemighty.com/popular/soldiers-vampires-ghosts/.

51. Friedman, "The Wandering Soul PSYOP Tape."

52. Military History Now. (October 30, 2013). "Operation Wandering Soul: Ghost Tape Number 10 and the Haunted Jungles of Vietnam." Retrieved May 20, 2021, from https://militaryhistorynow.com/2013/10/30/trick-or-treat-the-strange-tale-of-ghost-tape-no-10/.

Chapter 4

1. Unknown director. (January 27, 2009). "Cave Demons" [television series episode]. In Animal Planet's *Lost Tapes*. Los Angeles, CA: Go Go Luckey Entertainment.

2. Walters, G. (October 22, 2016). "Mystery of the WWI U-Boat and the Sea Monster Solved." Retrieved July 24, 2021, from https://www.dailymail.co.uk/news/article-3862842/SOLVED-mystery-World-War-U-Boat-condemned-depths-savaged-sea-monster.html.

3. Walters, "Mystery of the WWI U-Boat."

4. Walters, "Mystery of the WWI U-Boat."

5. North Atlantic Blog. (October 20, 2014). "Did the U-28 See a Sea Monster?" Retrieved February 18, 2022, from https://northatlanticblog.wordpress.com/2014/10/20/did-the-u-28-see-a-sea-monster/.

6. Swancer, "Pacific War Mysteries: Part 2 of 2."

7. Beck, M. (January 16, 2020). "Top Mermaid Sightings in the Last Century That Are Hard to Deny." Retrieved February 23, 2022, from https://folklorethursday.com/folktales/top-mermaid-sightings-in-the-last-century-that-are-hard-to-deny/.

8. Beck, "Top Mermaid Sightings."

9. Peck, M. (July 14, 2021). "The Sinking of Soviet Submarine K-219: A Cold War Conspiracy?" Retrieved February 12, 2022, from https://nationalinterest.org/blog/reboot/sinking-soviet-submarine-k-219-cold-war-conspiracy-189608.

10. North Atlantic Blog. (March 14, 2014). "The Elusive Quackers." Retrieved February 12, 2022, from https://northatlanticblog.wordpress.com/2014/03/14/the-elusive-quackers-3/.

11. National Oceanic and Atmospheric Administration. (February 26, 2021). "How Much of the Ocean Have We Explored?" Retrieved April 2, 2022, from https://oceanservice.noaa.gov/facts/exploration.html.

12. Harder, R. (October 15, 2019). "Gremlins: A Pilot's Worst Nightmare." Retrieved February 3, 2022, from https://www.historynet.com/gremlins/.

13. Harder, "Gremlins."

14. Harder, "Gremlins."

15. Swancer, B. (July 2017). "The Real Gremlins of World War II." Retrieved March 23, 2021, from https://mysteriousuniverse.org/2015/07/the-real-gremlins-of-wwii/.

16. Swancer, B. (April 11, 2018). "Military Encounters with Supernatural Entities." Retrieved March 12, 2021, from https://stillnessinthestorm.com/2018/04/military-encounters-with-supernatural-entities/.

17. Estelle. (November 23, 2015). "10 Unbelievable Wartime Monster Sightings." Retrieved May 25, 2021, from https://listverse.com/2015/11/23/10-unbelievable-wartime-monster-sightings/.

18. Estelle, "10 Unbelievable Wartime Monster Sightings."

19. Moncure, B. (April 28, 2019). "The WWII Ace Whose Helicopter Was Attacked by the World's Largest Snake." Retrieved January 21, 2022, from https://www.warhistoryonline.com/war-articles/the-wwii-ace-whos-helicopter-was-attacked-by-the-worlds-largest-snake.html?D5c=1&A5c=1&D_4_6cALL=1&D_4_6_10cALL=1.

20. Estelle, "10 Unbelievable Wartime Monster Sightings."

21. Swancer, "Pacific War Mysteries Part 1 of 2."

22. Brigden, J. (n.d.). "The Angel of Mons and Other Supernatural Stories from WWI." Retrieved January 23, 2022, from https://www.history.co.uk/articles/the-angel-of-mons-and-other-strange-supernatural-stories-from-world-war-i.

23. Estelle, "10 Unbelievable Wartime Monster Sightings."

24. Owen, W. (1965). *The Collected Poems of Wilfred Owen*. New York: New Directions Publishing.

25. Buddy. (September 12, 2010). "Morbach Monster: Werewolf in Wittlich Germany." Retrieved March 30, 2021, from https://ilovewerewolves.com/morbach-monster-real-werewolf-in-wittlich-germany/.

26. Ashliman, D. L. (October 6, 1997). "Werewolf Legends from Germany." Retrieved September 3, 2021, from https://sites.pitt.edu/~dash/werewolf.html.

27. Estelle, "10 Unbelievable Wartime Monster Sightings."

28. Estelle, "10 Unbelievable Wartime Monster Sightings."

29. No author. (2022). "Ortsbezirke Wenigerath: Morbach." Retrieved February 18, 2022, from https://www.morbach.de/leben-arbeiten/unsere-gemeinde/ortsbezirke/ortsbezirk-wenigerath/.

30. Swancer, B. (February 6, 2017). "Bizarre Encounters with the Weird in the Middle East Wars." Retrieved May 12, 2021, from https://mysteriousuniverse.org/2017/02/bizarre-encounters-with-the-weird-in-the-middle-east-wars/.

31. Orton, N. (August 2, 2021). "Weird Stories: Strange Sightings." Retrieved October 2, 2021, from https://www.instagram.com/p/CSFI6YZJPaZ/.

32. Orton, "Weird Stories."

33. Orton, N. (March 1, 2022). "Eye in the Sky." Retrieved March 10, 2022, from https://www.instagram.com/p/CajXtdurmD2/.

34. King, T. (October 29, 2007). "Vampires in Afghanistan? Soldiers Say It's True." Retrieved April 15, 2021, from http://www.salem-news.com/articles/october292007/afghan_vampires_102907.php.

35. Swancer, "Bizarre Encounters with the Weird."

36. Al-Rawi, A. (2009). "The Mythical Ghoul in Arabic Culture." Retrieved March 24, 2022, from https://www.ocf.berkeley.edu/~culturalanalysis/volume8/pdf/ghouls.pdf.

37. Ettachfini, L. (October 31, 2018). "What Are Jinn: The Arab Spirits Who Can Eat, Sleep, Have Sex, and Die." Retrieved February 25, 2022, from https://www.vice.com/en/article/9k7ekv/what-are-jinn-arab-spirits.

38. Swancer, B. (April 29, 2020). "Bizarre Paranormal Encounters in the War in Afghanistan." Retrieved April 30, 2021, from https://www.wearethemighty.com/mighty-trending/war-afghanistan-paranormal-experiences/.

39. Swancer, "Bizarre Paranormal Encounters."

40. Germer, W. (July 27, 2019). Sasquatch Chronicles Radio // SC 566: "Strange Experience in Iraq." Retrieved March 2, 2021, from https://sasquatchchronicles.com/sc-ep566-strange-experience-in-iraq/.

CHAPTER 5

1. Williams, E. (November 20, 2021). Personal interview with author.

2. Lundgren, D., and Mendez, M. (March 20, 2017). "Mike Mendez & Dolph Lundgren Share Nightmares: Don't Kill It Junket." Retrieved April 2, 2022, from https://www.youtube.com/watch?v=L44keniUVQ8.

3. Brigden, "The Angel of Mons and Other Supernatural Stories."

4. Brazil, E. (August 23, 2017). "Meet UB-65, the Haunted Submarine of World War 1." Retrieved September 23, 2021, from https://www.spookyisles.com/haunted-ub-65/.

5. Allan, T. (1997). *Tales of Real Haunting*. Tulsa, OK: E.D.C. Publishing.

6. Anonymous. (November 23, 2021). Personal email sent to author.

7. Belanger, J. (2006). *Ghosts of War: Restless Spirits of Soldiers, Spies, and Saboteurs*. Franklin Lakes, NJ: The Career Press.

8. Carr, K. (June 15, 2010). "Radio Ghost Mystery at Former RAF Station." Retrieved September 17, 2021, from https://katycarr.com/2010/06/15/radio-ghost-mystery-at-former-raf-station-world-war-two-radio-continues-to-pick-up-vintage-broadcasts-despite-not-having-any-power/.

9. Carr, "Radio Ghost Mystery."

10. Lemish, M. (September 1993). "The Ghost Plane from Mindanao." *The American Legion* 135(3), 30–31, 56.

11. Lemish, "Ghost Plane from Mindanao."

12. Belanger, *Ghosts of War*.

13. Belanger, *Ghosts of War*.

14. Unknown (director). (September 2013). "Katrina Cannibal" [television series episode]. In History Channel's *Haunted History*. New York: A&E Television.

15. Yee, J. (September 20, 2005). "Guardsmen Sense Ghostly Presence in New Orleans." Retrieved August 18, 2021, from http://www.southernghosts.com/daily-dose/hurricane-katrina-and-the-ghosts-left-behind.

16. Yee, "Guardsmen Sense Ghostly Presence."

17. Ronson, J. (2004). *The Men Who Stare at Goats*. London: Picador.

18. Goodwin, D. (2005). "Cries in the Dark." Retrieved August 27, 2021, from https://www.militaryghosts.com/prison.html.

19. Goodwin, "Cries in the Dark."

20. Wikipedia. (September 6, 2021). "Abu Ghraib Prison." Retrieved October 1, 2021, from https://en.wikipedia.org/wiki/Abu_Ghraib_prison#:~:text=The%20events%20created%20a%20substantial,24%20detainees%20and%20injuring%2092.

21. Wikipedia, "Abu Ghraib Prison."

22. Kennedy, R. (director). (2007). *The Ghosts of Abu Ghraib* (documentary). United States of America: HBO Documentary Films.

23. Kennedy, *The Ghosts of Abu Ghraib.*

24. Kennedy, *The Ghosts of Abu Ghraib.*

25. Kennedy, *The Ghosts of Abu Ghraib.*

26. Goodwin, "Cries in the Dark."

27. Institute for War and Peace Reporting. (December 17, 2010). Retrieved September 24, 2021, from https://www.refworld.org/docid/4d1047c71e.html.

28. Institute for War and Peace Reporting.

29. Institute for War and Peace Reporting.

30. Institute for War and Peace Reporting.

31. Castelier, S., and Muller, Q. (September 10, 2019). "Gravediggers Claim Ghosts Haunt World's Largest Cemetery in Iraq." Retrieved September 23, 2021, from https://www.aljazeera.com/features/2019/9/10/gravediggers-claim-ghosts-haunt-worlds-largest-cemetery-in-iraq.

32. Castelier and Muller, "Gravediggers Claim Ghosts Haunt."

33. Vick, K. (August 11, 2004). "Cemetery Fight Haunts Some U.S. Troops." Retrieved September 15, 2021, from https://www.washingtonpost.com/archive/politics/2004/08/11/cemetery-fight-haunts-some-us-troops/72fa02bb-0fcd-41ed-98c2-41528502cb10/.

34. Vick, "Cemetery Fight Haunts Some U.S. Troops."

35. NPR Radio. (August 15, 2018). Spooked // Episode 203 "The Iron Gate." Retrieved June 12, 2021, from https://spookedpodcast.org/episode-203-iron-gate.

36. NPR Radio, "The Iron Gate."

37. NPR Radio, "The Iron Gate."

38. Anonymous. (October 18, 2021). Personal email to author.

39. Orton, N. (August 7, 2021). "Iraq Ghosts." Retrieved January 3, 2022, from https://www.instagram.com/p/CSSQgRppynN/.

40. Orton, N. (September 15, 2021). "Ramadi." Retrieved January 3, 2022, from https://www.instagram.com/p/CT1XJGUrz_6/.

41. Anonymous, personal email.

42. Swancer, B. (May 5, 2017). "Strange Military Encounters with the Jinn." Retrieved April 13, 2021, from https://mysteriousuniverse.org/2017/05/strange-military-encounters-with-the-jinn/.

43. Swancer, "Strange Military Encounters with the Jinn."

44. Orton, N. (October 31, 2021). "Ghosts of Al Anbar." Retrieved January 3, 2022, from https://www.instagram.com/p/CVsF6DOriN9/.

45. Orton, N. (November 28, 2021). "Al Anbar Burning Bush." Retrieved January 3, 2022, from https://www.instagram.com/p/CW1uCH_vRIs/.

46. Orton, N. (January 24, 2022). "The Invisible Man." Retrieved February 13, 2022, from https://www.instagram.com/p/CZGsHjFLD7E/.

47. Swancer, B. (April 29, 2020). "Bizarre Paranormal Encounters in the War in Afghanistan." Retrieved March 13, 2021, from https://www.wearethemighty.com/mighty-trending/war-afghanistan-paranormal-experiences/.

48. Swancer, "Bizarre Paranormal Encounters."

49. Strickler, L. (April 1, 2022). "U.S. Soldier Describes Creepy Incidents in Afghanistan." Retrieved April 28, 2022, from https://www.phantomsandmonsters.com/2022/04/us-soldier-describes-creepy-incidents.html.

50. Strickler, "U.S. Soldier Describes Creepy Incidents."

51. Degrandpre, A. (August 18, 2012). "Report: Deadly Attack on Marines at FOB Delhi Was Carried Out by Unvetted Afghan Teen." Retrieved March 1, 2022, from http://battlerattle.marinecorpstimes.com/2012/08/18/report-deadly-attack-on-marines-at-fob-delhi-was-carried-out-by-afghan-teen/.

52. Orton, N. (November 5, 2021). "FOB Delhi." Retrieved January 3, 2022, from https://www.instagram.com/p/CV4ubaXLzFQ/.

53. Orton, N. (June 29, 2021). "Afghanistan." Retrieved January 3, 2022, from https://www.instagram.com/p/CQskdsXLiDG/.

54. Swancer, "Bizarre Paranormal Encounters."

55. Swancer, "Bizarre Paranormal Encounters."

56. Swancer, "Bizarre Paranormal Encounters."

57. Maurer, K. (June 16, 2005). "Eerie Incidents Spook Guards." Retrieved March 23, 2021, from https://forums.spacebattles.com/threads/us-fob-in-afghanistan-is-haunted-by-ghost-of-child.84974/.

58. Maurer, "Eerie Incidents Spook Guards."

59. Maurer, "Eerie Incidents Spook Guards."

60. Miss Airborne [screen name]. (June 23, 2006). "I Did Two Deployments to Afghanistan and Spent Alot of Time at FOB Salerno." Retrieved April 10, 2021, from https://www.unexplained-mysteries.com/forum/topic/43251-ghost-spooks-soldiers-in-afghanistan/.

61. Gibbons-Neff, T., and Shah, T. (November 12, 2020). "An Ancient Hill and Forgotten Dead: Afghanistan's Haunted Outpost." Retrieved April 25, 2021, from https://www.nytimes.com/2020/10/31/world/asia/afghanistan-haunted-outpost.html.

62. Gibbons-Neff and Shah, "An Ancient Hill and Forgotten Dead."

63. Malkasian, C. (2013). *War Comes to Garmser: Thirty Years of Conflict on the Afghan Frontier.* New York: Oxford University Press.

64. Gibbons-Neff and Shah, "An Ancient Hill and Forgotten Dead."

65. Coghlan, T. (December 28, 2009). "Eerie Outpost Unnerves US Marines with Strange Lights and Whispers in the Night." Retrieved April 25, 2021, from https://www.thetimes.co.uk/article/eerie-outpost-unnerves-us-marines-with-strange-lights-and-whispers-in-the-night-km2cq2r7jdk.

66. Gibbons-Neff and Shah, "An Ancient Hill and Forgotten Dead."

67. Gibbons-Neff and Shah, "An Ancient Hill and Forgotten Dead."

68. Havholm, P. (October 26, 2007). "The Lost Legion." Retrieved February 1, 2022, from https://www.kiplingsociety.co.uk/readers-guide/rg_lostlegion1.htm.

69. Swancer, "Bizarre Paranormal Encounters."

70. Smith, S. (director). (November 15, 2015). "Beneath the Rock" [television series episode]. In B. Layton and M. Lewis (producers), *Paranormal Witness.* New York: SyFy Channel.

71. Coghlan, "Eerie Outpost Unnerves US Marines."

72. Coghlan, "Eerie Outpost Unnerves US Marines."

73. Smith, "Beneath the Rock."

74. Smith, "Beneath the Rock."

75. Gibbons-Neff and Shah, "An Ancient Hill and Forgotten Dead."

76. Coghlan, "Eerie Outpost Unnerves US Marines."

77. Anonymous. (December 12, 2021). Correspondence with author.

78. Gibbons-Neff and Shah, "An Ancient Hill and Forgotten Dead."

CHAPTER 6

1. Sicard, S. (July 19, 2021). "What's Really Inside the Gold Ball on Top of Military Flagpoles?" Retrieved August 30, 2021, from https://taskandpurpose.com/community/whats-really-inside-gold-ball-top-military-flagpoles/.

2. Mathieson, M. (September 3, 2021). "How Many Military Bases Are in the US?" Retrieved March 7, 2022, from https://www.omnimilitaryloans.com/military-life/how-many-military-bases-are-in-the-us/.

3. Wallace, J. (2022). "Fort Polk Louisiana." Retrieved March 7, 2022, from https://militarybase.net/fort-polk/.

4. Germer, "Military Encounters/What Is a Box Witch?"

5. Cutchin, J., and Renner, T. (2020). *Where the Footprints End: High Strangeness and the Bigfoot Phenomenon (Volume I: Folklore)*. Independently published.

6. History Editors. (August 21, 2018). National Park Service. Retrieved March 15, 2022, from https://www.history.com/topics/us-government/national-park-service.

7. Germer, W. (October 28, 2018). Sasquatch Chronicles Radio // SC 485: "Navy Seal 1989 Fort Lewis." Retrieved April 22, 2021, from https://sasquatchchronicles.com/sc-ep485-navy-seal-1989-fort-lewis/.

8. Unknown (director). (February 7, 2021). "Bigfoot's Lair?" [television series episode]. In M. Ginsburg and T. Healy (producers), *Expedition Bigfoot*. New York: Railsplitter Pictures.

9. Short, B. (n.d.) "The De Facto Sasquatch." Retrieved August 30, 2021, from https://static1.squarespace.com/static/596c0bae4c0dbfa1d26e86be/t/5b9bff06562fa7cfcdf1bfc8/1536950.

10. Short, "The De Facto Sasquatch."

11. W., K. (June 20, 2005). Report #11930 (Class B): "Soldier Sees Large Figure While on Patrol at Fort Lewis." Retrieved June 12, 2021, from https://www.bfro.net/GDB/show_report.asp?id=11930.

12. Taylor, S. (September 4, 2010). Report #28197 (Class B): "Man Recalls His Possible Nighttime Encounter While Instructing at Ft. Lewis." Retrieved June 12, 2021, from https://www.bfro.net/GDB/show_report.asp?id=28197.

13. Taylor, "Man Recalls His Possible Nighttime Encounter While Instructing at Ft. Lewis."

14. Swancer, B. (June 26, 2018). "Mysterious Encounters with Bigfoot at Military Bases." Retrieved April 10, 2021, from https://mysteriousuniverse.org/2018/06/mysterious-encounters-with-bigfoot-at-military-bases/.

15. Swancer, "Mysterious Encounters with Bigfoot at Military Bases."

16. Swancer, "Mysterious Encounters with Bigfoot at Military Bases."

17. Short, "The De Facto Sasquatch."

18. Short, "The De Facto Sasquatch."

19. Short, "The De Facto Sasquatch."

20. Short, "The De Facto Sasquatch."

21. Taylor, S. (January 30, 2012). Report #32824 (Class A): "Recollection of a Road Crossing at Dusk While Working as an MP on Fort Lewis." Retrieved February 15, 2021, from https://www.bfro.net/GDB/show_report.asp?id=32824.

22. Taylor, "Recollection of a Road Crossing at Dusk While Working as an MP on Fort Lewis."

23. Short, "The De Facto Sasquatch."

24. Short, "The De Facto Sasquatch."

25. Taylor, S. (January 7, 2016). Report #50678 (Class B): "Marines on a Training Mission Have a Possible Night Encounter on Fort Lewis." Retrieved February 7, 2021, from https://www.bfro.net/GDB/show_report.asp?id=50678.

26. Short, "The De Facto Sasquatch."

27. Short, "The De Facto Sasquatch."

28. Smykal, K. (January 11, 2008). Report #22899 (Class B): "Possible Daylight Encounter on Fort Rucker Army Base." Retrieved April 7, 2021, from https://www.bfro .net/GDB/show_report.asp?id=22899.

29. Short, "The De Facto Sasquatch."

30. Layne, K. (Winter 2015). "The Known Unknown: Tales of the Yucca Man." Retrieved March 2, 2021, from https://longreads.com/2018/04/25/the-known-unknown -tales-of-the-yucca-man/.

31. Stilwell, B. (July 22, 2020). "The Yucca Man Is a Beast That Stalks Marines at 29 Palms." Retrieved February 23, 2021, from https://www.wearethemighty.com/popular /yucca-man-stalks-marines-twentynine/.

32. Short, "The De Facto Sasquatch."

33. Short, "The De Facto Sasquatch."

34. Camplin, L. (April 29, 2009). "Desert Rats Reunite 30 Years After Last Patrol." Retrieved October 10, 2021, from https://www.edwards.af.mil/News/Article/395782/ desert-rats-reunite-30-years-after-last-patrol/.

35. Skookum Report. (April 19, 2021). "Bigfoot at Edwards Air Force Base!" Retrieved March 13, 2021, from https://www.youtube.com/watch?v=txiQh_OEWE4.

36. Skookum Report, "Bigfoot at Edwards Air Force Base!"

37. Skookum Report, "Bigfoot at Edwards Air Force Base!"

38. Swancer, "Mysterious Encounters with Bigfoot at Military Bases."

39. Short, "The De Facto Sasquatch."

40. Short, "The De Facto Sasquatch."

41. Layne, "The Known Unknown: Tales of the Yucca Man."

42. Withers, K. (July 27, 2001). Report #2907 (Class A): "Four Camp Pendleton Soldiers Confront Bigfoot During Nighttime Training Exercise." Retrieved February 24, 2021, from https://www.bfro.net/GDB/show_report.asp?id=2907.

43. Bigfoot Field Researchers Organization. (July 27, 1999). Report #2816 (Class A): "Late Night Encounter Near Meadow Above the Infantry Training School." Retrieved February 20, 2021, from https://www.bfro.net/GDB/show_report.asp?id =2816.

44. Hovanec, K. (February 19, 2007). Report #17767 (Class A): "Nighttime Sighting by Marine Training Near Ft. Carson." Retrieved March 8, 2021, from https://www.bfro .net/GDB/show_report.asp?id=17767.

45. Stilwell, B. (January 2, 2020). "11 Scary Ghost Stories, Legends, and Haunted Military Bases." Retrieved March 26, 2021, from https://www.wearethemighty.com/articles/ here-are-the-11-most-haunted-us-military-bases-around-the-world/.

46. Weiser, K. (March 2022). "History and Hauntings of Fort Leavenworth." Retrieved April 22, 2022, from https://www.legendsofamerica.com/ks-fortleavenworth/.

47. Reichley, J. (1995). *The Haunted Houses of Fort Leavenworth*. Fort Leavenworth, KS: Fort Leavenworth Historical Society.

48. Gonsalves, C., and Pioppi, A. (2009). *Haunted Golf: Spirited Tales from the Rough*. Guilford, CT: Rowman & Littlefield.

49. Weiser, "History and Hauntings of Fort Leavenworth."

50. Stilwell, "11 Scary Ghost Stories, Legends, and Haunted Military Bases."

51. Reichley, *The Haunted Houses of Fort Leavenworth*.

52. Reichley, *The Haunted Houses of Fort Leavenworth*.

53. Reichley, *The Haunted Houses of Fort Leavenworth*.

54. Reichley, *The Haunted Houses of Fort Leavenworth*.

55. Stilwell, "11 Scary Ghost Stories, Legends, and Haunted Military Bases."

56. Bower, M. (October 15, 2009). "Family Has Unusual Experiences Living in a Haunted House." Retrieved March 13, 2022, from https://www.army.mil/article/28851/ family_has_unusual_experiences_living_in_a_haunted_house.

57. Courtney, S. (December 14, 2003). Report #7558 (Class B): "Military Police Find Tracks at Fort Leavenworth." Retrieved April 2, 2021, from https://www.bfro.net/GDB /show_report.asp?id=7558.

58. Goodwin, D. (2003). "Camp Leonard Wood: The Riotous Ghosts of Bloodland." Retrieved December 20, 2021, from https://www.militaryghosts.com/l_wood.html.

59. Razrbladesuitcse [screen name]. (September 19, 2014). "Fort Leonard Wood; So I Lived in a Haunted Barracks." Retrieved January 5, 2022, from https://www.reddit.com /r/nosleep/comments/2gx1sb/fort_leonard_wood_so_i_lived_in_a_haunted_barracks/.

60. Buschardt, C. (October 3, 2014). Report #46676 (Class B): "Soldier Reports Possible Vocalizations During a Morning Group Run at Fort Leonard Wood." Retrieved March 15, 2021, from https://www.bfro.net/GDB/show_report.asp?id=46676.

61. Wagner, H. (November 7, 2017). *Fort Drum Lost Villages History Tour*. Fort Drum, NY: Fort Drum Cultural Resources Program. Retrieved March 20, 2022, from https:// api.army.mil/e2/c/downloads/539628.pdf.

62. Case, D. (August 26, 2012). "The Ghosts of Fort Drum: Visiting the Small Communities Wiped Out by Eminent Domain." Retrieved March 20, 2022, from https:// www.syracuse.com/opinion/2012/08/the_ghosts_of_fort_drum_visiti.html.

63. Case, "The Ghosts of Fort Drum."

64. Case, "The Ghosts of Fort Drum."

65. Wagner, *Fort Drum Lost Villages History Tour.*

66. Kleen, M. (September 8, 2020). "Fort Drum Specters Preserve the Past." Retrieved March 20, 2022, from https://michaelkleen.com/2020/09/08/fort-drum-specters-preserve-the-past/.

67. Case, "The Ghosts of Fort Drum."

68. Farnsworth, C. (2009). *The Big Book of New York Ghost Stories.* Lanham, MD: Globe Pequot.

69. Higgins, O. (October 21, 2019). "Your Hometown: LeRay Mansion Hosts Haunted Ghosts from the Past." Retrieved March 22, 2022, from https://spectrumlocalnews.com/nys/watertown/news/2019/10/21/haunted-leray-mansion.

70. Orten, N. (June 25, 2021). "Fort Drum Weirdness." Retrieved August 23, 2021, from https://www.instagram.com/p/CQiBVhDLFGz/?igshid=YmMyMTA2M2Y=.

71. Addison, H. (June 26, 2021). "Is a Bigfoot Roaming the Woods of St. Lawrence County?" Retrieved January 5, 2022, from https://www.nny360.com/news/stlawrencecounty/is-a-bigfoot-roaming-the-woods-of-st-lawrence-county/article_389bdbf2-c773-52a7-b276-74cc1f7b419c.html.

72. Wagner, *Fort Drum Lost Villages History Tour.*

73. K., D. (March 11, 2012). Report #34337 (Class B): "Large Man-Like Figure Seen in the Trees by a Marine Training at Fort A.P. Hill." Retrieved March 10, 2021, from https://www.bfro.net/GDB/show_report.asp?id=34337.

74. Short, "The De Facto Sasquatch."

75. Green, M. (n.d.). "82nd Airborne Div. Soldiers See Bigfoot at Fort Bragg." Retrieved March 11, 2021, from https://www.gcbro.com/NChoke001.html.

76. Short, "The De Facto Sasquatch."

77. Poland, T. (August 2, 2008). Report #24334 (Class A): "While Training a U.S. Marine Witnesses a Large Creature Near Camp Lejeune." Retrieved March 11, 2021, from https://www.bfro.net/GDB/show_report.asp?id=24334.

78. Willis, S. (December 23, 2006). Report #17089 (Class A): "Night Sighting Through Thermal Viewer by Soldier on Fort Stewart." Retrieved March 10, 2021, from https://www.bfro.net/GDB/show_report.asp?id=17089.

79. Johnson, K. (November 19, 2010). Report #28526 (Class A): "Encounter by a Squad on Maneuvers While Training at Fort Stewart." Retrieved March 10, 2021, from https://www.bfro.net/GDB/show_report.asp?id=28526.

80. Jason [screen name]. (September 16, 2013). "I Live in an Apartment on 599th Street." Retrieved August 25, 2021, from https://www.ghostsofamerica.com/9/Alaska_Fort_Wainwright_ghost_sightings9.html.

81. Deetaylor85 [screen name]. (October 17, 2007). "This Wasn't Funny Anymore." Retrieved November 20, 2021 from https://www.yourghoststories.com/real-ghost-story.php?story=2166

82. Fahrenbach, W. (June 13, 2003). Report #6486 (Class B): "Special Forces Team Follows Bipedal Trackway, Gets Screamed At." Retrieved March 10, 2021, from https://www.phantomsandmonsters.com/2014/12/bigfoot-vs-military-reports.html.

Acknowledgments

1. No author. (February 9, 1990). *Operation Just Cause: Honoring Task Force Regulars.* Fort Polk, LA: 5th Infantry Division.

INDEX

Vietnam Traveling Memorial
Wall, 10
Vietnam Veterans Memorial, 10
Vietnam War, 30–31, 47–49, 52;
PSYOPs in, 100
Villarreal, Alfonso, 36
vipers, 58
Volkisch, 79

Wade, Latrel, 103
Wadi-Us-Salaam, 144–45
Warhorse, 150
Washington, D.C., 202
Watchers X, 23
Webb, Brandon, 68
Weightman, William Albert, 56
Weingerath, 118, 119
wild boars, 119
Wildlife Sketches Near and Far
(Wright), 56
Williams, Emile, 127–28
Williams, John "The Mole," 48
Wilson, Adam, 164, 165, 166
Wilson, Larry, 37
The Witch-Cult in Western Europe
(Murray), 79
witch library, 78, 83

Woellhof, Lloyd, 94
Wojtek (bear), 69–70
wood-knocks, 11–12
Wood Mills Cemetery, 199–200
World War I, 64, 96–97, 107–
8, 131
World War II, 18, 40–41, 66, 67,
112–13, 127, 133, 199
Wright, Bruce Stanley, 56

Yakima Training Center, 174
Yehudis, 113
Yellow National Park Protection
Act, 174
Yeren, 16
Yeti, 16; in Afghanistan, 19–21
York, Grady, 94
Yowie, 16, 173
Ypres, 131
Yucca Man, 183

Zagros mountain range, 23
Al-Zahedi, 141
al-Zobaie, Abdullah, 144
Zolik, Damian, 163, 165
zoos, 62–63, 70